AF828816

INTERNATIONAL CRIMINAL TRIBUNALS

In the last two decades there has been a meteoric rise of international criminal tribunals and courts and also a strengthening chorus of critics against them. Today it is hard to find strong defenders of international criminal tribunals and courts. This book attempts such a defense against an array of critics. It offers a nuanced defense, accepting many criticisms but arguing that the idea of international criminal tribunals can be defended as providing the fairest way to deal with mass atrocity crimes in a global arena. Fairness and moral legitimacy will be at the heart of this defense. The authors take up the economic and political arguments that have been powerfully expressed, as well as arguments about sovereignty, punishment, responsibility, and evidence; but in the end they show that these arguments do not defeat the idea of international criminal courts and tribunals.

LARRY MAY is W. Alton Jones Professor of Philosophy, Law and Political Science at Vanderbilt University. He has published extensively in both books and leading journals and twice won the prize for best work on the philosophy of war and peace from the American Philosophical Association.

SHANNON FYFE is currently a Ph.D. candidate in philosophy at Vanderbilt University, where she previously obtained her J.D. in 2010. Her prior work includes an internship with the International Criminal Tribunal for Rwanda's Office of the Prosecutor, the American Society of International Law's Arthur C. Helton Fellowship for international human rights law in Tanzania, and a fellowship with the Syria Justice and Accountability Centre.

International Criminal Tribunals

A NORMATIVE DEFENSE

LARRY MAY
Vanderbilt University

SHANNON FYFE
Vanderbilt University

CAMBRIDGE
UNIVERSITY PRESS

DAMAGED

CAMBRIDGE
UNIVERSITY PRESS

University Printing House, Cambridge CB2 8BS, United Kingdom
One Liberty Plaza, 20th Floor, New York, NY 10006, USA
477 Williamstown Road, Port Melbourne, VIC 3207, Australia
4843/24, 2nd Floor, Ansari Road, Daryaganj, Delhi – 110002, India
79 Anson Road, #06-04/06, Singapore 079906

Cambridge University Press is part of the University of Cambridge.

It furthers the University's mission by disseminating knowledge in the pursuit of education, learning, and research at the highest international levels of excellence.

www.cambridge.org
Information on this title: www.cambridge.org/9781107128200
10.1017/9781316414569

© Larry May and Shannon Fyfe 2017

This publication is in copyright. Subject to statutory exception and to the provisions of relevant collective licensing agreements, no reproduction of any part may take place without the written permission of Cambridge University Press.

First published 2017

A catalogue record for this publication is available from the British Library.

Library of Congress Cataloging-in-Publication Data
Names: May, Larry, author. | Fyfe, Shannon, author.
Title: International criminal tribunals: a normative defense / Larry May, Shannon Fyfe.
Description: Cambridge [UK]; New York: Cambridge University Press, 2017. |
Includes bibliographical references and index.
Identifiers: LCCN 2016041862 | ISBN 9781107128200 (hardback)
Subjects: LCSH: International criminal courts.
Classification: LCC KZ7230 .M39 2016 | DDC 345/.01–dc23
LC record available at https://lccn.loc.gov/2016041862

ISBN 978-1-107-12820-0 Hardback

Cambridge University Press has no responsibility for the persistence or accuracy of URLs for external or third-party internet websites referred to in this publication and does not guarantee that any content on such websites is, or will remain, accurate or appropriate.

Contents

Introduction

In the last two decades there has been a meteoric rise of international criminal tribunals and courts. It should come as no surprise that in the last decade there has also been a strengthening chorus of critics of these institutions. Indeed, today it is hard to find strong defenders of international criminal tribunals and courts. This book attempts such a defense – and against a wide array of critics of international criminal law. Our defense will be a nuanced one, accepting many criticisms but arguing that a core of the idea of international criminal tribunals can be defended as providing the fairest way to deal with mass atrocity crimes in a global arena. Indeed, fairness and moral legitimacy will be at the heart of our defense. In the end we will show that the range of criticisms, often powerfully expressed, do not defeat the idea, or perhaps the promise, of a system of international criminal courts and tribunals.

The questions of the legitimacy and fairness of international criminal tribunals are some of the most important, but they are not the only challenges raised recently. In addition, there are questions about economic feasibility and ideological bias. Some of the strongest critical voices have arisen from those who are concerned about the justification of punishment internationally, given the lack of evidence for either a deterrent effect or a retributive reaction when the crimes have been committed by political and military leaders who claim to be acting in the interest of their people. And even those who defend criminal punishment generally on expressivist grounds have nonetheless found fault with international criminal punishment for failing in this way.

The world's relatively new experiment with holding international criminal trials in the aftermath of mass atrocity is by no means perfect. As this book proceeds we will do our fair share of criticizing the existing practices at the various international criminal courts and discuss particular, and sometimes grievous, instances of failure. But we will argue that it is also not nearly as flawed as the critics have claimed, and we will propose various changes to those practices that will make these courts more defensible. Again, we want to stress that we believe that international criminal tribunals, in some amended form from the way they now exist, can be normatively defended, and defended strongly.

By normative defense we mean a broad array of ways of discussing what institutions should be through the application of various norms (legal, moral, social, economic, etc.) to international tribunals. We will, of course, defend these norms along the way, but in general the norms we will employ are well-established norms of various communities. We will also bring some empirical considerations to bear on the various disputes about international criminal courts. But the empirical considerations we will consider will only be those that have a direct bearing on the normative critique and defense of international criminal tribunals. And while we will also spend time describing the actual practices of these courts and tribunals, again we will do so only as it has bearing on the normative debates. We will not, accordingly, advance conclusions about the actual practices of international courts. Instead, our conclusions will be normative.

These normative conclusions do not rely on one vision of the goals of and justifications for the international criminal courts and tribunals. In each chapter, we address multiple criticisms of the courts. Our defense attempts to respond to each criticism without presenting a specific construction of how we should all see international criminal law and how it can be defended. Rather, our defense embraces the variety of justifications for and benefits of international criminal courts and tribunals. Our objective is to show how the system of international criminal justice can be defended against criticisms from victims and their families, defendants, states, other international institutions, and scholars.

The critics of international criminal tribunals have worked with a wide variety of fields, methods, and approaches. In responding to the critics of international criminal tribunals we will attempt to engage with the critics in their own terms. But we will not dispute largely empirical matters, since our focus is on a normative defense. What this means is that we will sometimes offer suggested changes to the way that international criminal tribunals currently proceed, so as to improve their alignment with the overarching goals of those institutions.

In Chapter 1, we argue that international criminal tribunals can legitimately exercise jurisdiction over international criminals via several different routes, including consent, a recognition of an international legal system, or the demands of justice and equity. In Chapter 2, we address sovereignty concerns and argue that the protection of the complementarity principle prevents the International Criminal Court (ICC) and the international criminal tribunals from usurping the sovereignty of states. We argue in Chapter 3 that all three main theories of punishment, namely, retributivism, deterrence, and expressivism, have a role to play in justifying international criminal justice through international courts. In Chapter 4 we give an account of individual and group responsibility, a "group-based model," that we argue can provide a basis for responding to many criticisms of the international criminal courts and tribunals in their apportionment of legal responsibility. In Chapter 5 we consider the economic criticisms of an international criminal legal system and argue that the motivations of domestic criminals, which can be used to predict behavior and ensure compliance, do not easily translate to international criminals, and that moral considerations do influence states. We argue in Chapter 6 that despite the fact that most international criminal prosecutions have been focused on African leaders, there are signs that this situation is changing, and we also argue that there are not structural political biases within the international criminal legal system. In Chapter 7, we argue that the current barriers to fact-finding in the international criminal courts and tribunals are not determined by their construction, but rather can be mitigated or addressed with the outlay of sufficient resources. Finally, in Chapter 8, we argue that prosecutorial discretion helps ensure fairness, rather than contributing to unfairness in the international criminal justice system.

The ICC and other international tribunals begin operations with a democratic deficit. Unlike domestic prosecutors and criminal courts, international tribunals are not part of a government that has checks and balances, or that regularly must face voters or legislative investigative committees. Because of this democratic deficit, international tribunals and their prosecutors must make sure that they do not appear to be abusing the often-considerable power that they wield. While this is true, it is also true that international tribunals have achieved some small degree of success in bringing a few of the worst international criminals to justice. And the outlook for the future is that there will be other political and military leaders who will face prosecutions for atrocities, either in international tribunals or in domestic courts that are enforcing international criminal law. While there are problems, there is no strong reason to lose faith in the tremendous promise of international criminal tribunals to confront mass atrocities.

We completed the research and writing for this book in May 2016. As we were revising the copyedited manuscript, Burundi and South Africa announced their intentions to leave the ICC.

1

Legitimacy

International tribunals are free-standing courts that prosecute international crimes. The best known international tribunal was the International Military Tribunal (IMT) that sat in Nuremberg and prosecuted some of the political and military leaders of Nazi Germany. In more recent times, there have been ad hoc tribunals established to deal with international crimes committed in the 1990s in Rwanda and the former Yugoslavia, along with more recent atrocities prosecuted in tribunals in Sierra Leone, Kosovo, Timor Leste, and Cambodia, to name only the most prominent. The International Criminal Court (ICC), a permanent court seated in The Hague, was established by treaty to prosecute individuals who have been charged with international crimes committed since July 2002, and whose domestic courts cannot or will not prosecute. A defense of international tribunals, understood in the narrow sense of the ICC and ad hoc tribunals, is similar to but not quite the same as a defense of international criminal courts, or of international criminal law more generally.

In Section I of this chapter, we begin by discussing arguably the first recorded international tribunal, the one organized by Athena to determine the guilt or innocence of Orestes in Aeschylus's play *Eumenides*. In Section II we will characterize some problems of legitimacy of the Nuremberg tribunal. We then discuss two problems of legitimacy for current international criminal tribunals. In Section III we discuss the problem of the lack of a legislature to establish the laws on the basis of which the tribunals prosecute. In Section IV we consider the problem that international tribunals may not be created by those who have the legitimacy to do so. In Section V we argue that despite these two problems, international criminal tribunals can achieve legitimacy by a kind of bootstrapping procedure that, while not without problems, is sufficient for establishing legitimacy.

I THE TRIBUNAL OF ATHENA

In Aeschylus' play *Eumenides*, Orestes, the son of the king Agamemnon, is being pursued by the Furies, who demand revenge as a matter of straight justice[1] for those who have killed by their own hands. Orestes is confronted by the Furies for having killed his mother, Clytemnestra. To evade the death sentence that the Furies seek, Orestes appeals to the goddess Athena. When Athena arrives on the scene, she announces, "From far away I heard a cry summoning me."[2] Indeed, Athena calls both Orestes and the Furies by the term "stranger," apparently indicating that she and they are from different regions of the world. Athena makes it clear that she has intervened because she believes that Orestes is being held responsible for his mother's death and is in jeopardy of "being injured."[3]

Athena describes the ensuing trial as "the first trial for bloodshed."[4] And insofar as the trial is not under the jurisdiction of a municipal judge, but a judge who claims a wider – perhaps even universal – jurisdiction, the case can also be seen as one of the first "international" criminal trials. The court, which is constituted just for this case, is best seen as something very close to an international criminal tribunal administered under universal jurisdiction. We will see as this section of the chapter proceeds that this trial also illustrates the main legitimacy problems that we will address more directly in subsequent sections of this chapter.

The trial of Orestes before the tribunal of Athena is of course a mythical trial, but we can see here on display the rudiments of the rule of law. Of prime consideration is the refusal of Athena to judge merely on the basis of oaths sworn by acquaintances of the parties, as had been the practice in Greece prior to the rise of the Areopagus – the first properly criminal trial court. Instead, Athena insists that the jury that she has picked from "the best of all citizens" will administer a system of justice that "is neither anarchic nor despotic."[5] The jury is "untouched by thought of gain, reverend, [or] quick to anger" and is thus a "sentinel" to protect the innocent.[6] The jury is to judge on the basis of the evidence, not prejudices, and only on the basis of that evidence that is

1 Aeschylus, *Eumenides*, in *Aeschylus' Oresteia*, 310, edited and translated by Alan H. Sommerstein (Cambridge, MA: Harvard University Press/Loeb Classical Library, 2008), p. 395.

2 *Eumenides* 400, p. 405.

3 *Eumenides* 410, p. 407.

4 *Eumenides* 680, p. 441.

5 *Eumenides* 485, p. 417.

6 *Eumenides* 695, p. 443.

strictly relevant. Here, we can see most of the important characteristics of the rule of law.

But the trial of Orestes also manifests some of the legitimacy worries of all tribunals that are not based on the criminal statutes of a municipality. First, Athena arrives to constitute the tribunal seemingly from above as a deus ex machina. In fact, the story of Athena's birth is indicative of how she is regarded – namely, as someone who was born fully formed from the head of Zeus – as someone who did not begin life as a baby. In this context of being a judge at her own tribunal Athena did not go through the normal tribulations of developing by starts and stops, learning from experience along the way. Athena's tribunal arises, as tribunals often do, from a very specific need, and at a time seemingly standing with no history. Most importantly, tribunals like that of Athena are not constituted by those who represent a particular population (i.e., not by a community of the victors, victims, or alleged perpetrators), although it is true that both Orestes and the Furies eventually agree to allow Athena to be the judge of their case.

Second, Athena's tribunal stands completely outside the charges and countercharges of the people who have been affected, namely, the victims. Here there is some evidence for thinking that the Furies hold masks with the likeness of Clytemnestra on them to try to include the victim in the trial. But it is clear that Athena pushes the proceedings forward by focusing on the question of Orestes' guilt. Athena is chiefly concerned with Orestes' possible defenses and excuses and in thus countering the revenge that the Furies claim to demand in Clytemnestra's name. However, it must be noted that Apollo, the god who commanded Orestes to kill his mother in the first place and is seen by the Furies as an accomplice, refers the case to Athena. Apollo sees Athena as a newer deity like himself and may see her as less amenable to the claims of the primitive Furies.[7]

Third, Athena claims to be the convener of this tribunal because there is no one else who stands willing to do so except those, the Furies, who seem likely to administer vigilante justice at best. But Athena's tribunal looks like a plausible dispute resolution mechanism only because the existing alternatives seem worse, not because of the intrinsic value of Athena's tribunal. The justification for Athena's tribunal is thus a kind of lesser evil justification, not the kind of justification that would afford this tribunal proper legitimacy in the normatively rich sense of this term. In the sections of the chapter that follow, we will attempt to provide a stronger grounding for the legitimacy of international criminal tribunals, but in the end, at least for some tribunals, it may be that the best we can hope for will be lesser evil justifications.

7 *Eumenides* 222, p. 385.

Fourth, the procedures of the tribunal are not ones that have been developed over many years and have stood the test of time but are merely imposed by someone who turns out to be relatively unbiased and reasonable. Yet to judge the legitimacy of the tribunal's procedures merely in terms of the reasonableness of the judge is not to proceed in the way defenders of the rule of law would advocate. Indeed, since procedural fairness is often said to be the hallmark of legitimacy in courts, the fact that Athena's tribunal achieves procedural fairness, if it does, merely as an incidental effect of who the judge is, leaves many readers justly concerned.

Ultimately, Athena's tribunal succeeds because of the reasonableness and fairness of the judge along with the force of divine sanctions that a god such as Athena can command, especially since she is backed by her fellow gods on Mount Olympus. But succeeding in reaching a fair result and achieving legitimacy are two different things. Indeed, a tribunal could achieve fair results and yet be so flawed procedurally that the putatively fair results themselves would be tarnished. And the sanctions meted out by divine authority hardly answer those who would criticize Athena's tribunal as seemingly foisted upon the mere mortals who were forced to stand before it.

II THE TRIBUNAL AT NUREMBERG

The first, and most important, tribunal in modern times was the International Military Tribunal established by the Allied Powers in Nuremberg for the purpose of trying Nazi leaders at the end of World War II. This tribunal shared with Athena's tribunal a number of characteristic features of tribunals, but also displayed several new problems, especially concerning legitimacy. Chief among the problems were that the tribunal appeared to be little more than victors' justice, where the victorious leaders at a war's end establish a tribunal to prosecute the vanquished leaders. Such tribunals are sometimes seen as little better than other measures used to divide up the spoils of war, especially since the Nuremberg tribunal did not deal with such crimes as mass looting or systematic rape of the women of the conquered peoples.

At the outset of the trial, the U.S. Supreme Court justice Robert Jackson, on special assignment for the U.S. president Franklin Roosevelt as one of the main Nuremberg prosecutors, offered the best justification he could muster for a trial that did not prosecute any of the obvious crimes committed by the victorious parties:

> The privilege of opening the first trial in history for crimes against the peace of the world imposes a grave responsibility. The wrongs which we seek to

> condemn and punish have been so calculated, so malignant, and so devastating, that civilization cannot tolerate their being ignored, because it cannot survive their being repeated. That four great nations, flushed with victory and stung with injury stay the hand of vengeance and voluntarily submit their captive enemies to the judgment of the law is one of the most significant tributes that Power has ever paid to Reason.[8]

Notice that Justice Jackson, speaking for the prosecution team at Nuremberg, offers as his first justification that the Nuremberg tribunal has "stayed the hand of vengeance," just as Athena stayed the hand of the revenge-seeking Furies.

Unlike the tribunal of Athena, those leaders who established the Nuremberg tribunal aimed to stay the hand of those powers that were "flushed with victory." Athena stays the hand of the powerful Furies, who are also "flushed" but not from victory. Instead, the Furies are accustomed to getting their way and are flushed with success at having done so in all previous situations. In both cases, there is a sense of entitlement of the power-wielding to take revenge that is then redirected by the creation of tribunals. The endless cycle of revenge killing is so poisonous to harmony in society that even seemingly unauthorized and illegitimate tribunals are seen as better than what is the alternative.

Like Athena's tribunal, there is also a recognition at Nuremberg that the judges and prosecutors are in uncharted waters:

> This Tribunal, while it is novel and experimental, is not the product of abstract speculations nor is it created to vindicate legalistic theories. This inquest represents the practical effort of four of the most mighty of nations, with the support of 17 more, to utilize international law to meet the greatest menace of our times – aggressive war. The common sense of mankind demands that law shall not stop with the punishment of petty crimes by little people. It must also reach men who possess themselves of great power and make deliberate and concerted use of it to set in motion evils which leave no home in the world untouched. It is a cause of that magnitude that the United Nations will lay before Your Honors.[9]

In a sense, the Nuremberg tribunal is also like Athena's tribunal in that rulers, not small fry, are those who stand in the dock. And the justification of the "experimental" nature of the tribunal is that the great powers of the world eventually come to support it, seemingly similarly to the way in which Athena's

[8] Justice Jackson's opening statement is published in volume II of *Trial of the Major War Criminals before the International Military Tribunal* (Nuremberg: IMT, 1947), pp. 98–155.

[9] Ibid.

tribunal eventually gained support from other gods of Mount Olympus, and even grudging support from the Furies themselves.

One of the chief differences between Athena's tribunal and the Nuremberg tribunal is that there was only very selective prosecution in the case of the Nuremberg tribunal. The only possible similarity is that Athena did not prosecute Clytemnestra for killing her husband, Agamemnon, but it also appears that the Furies did not haunt Clytemnestra. Nonetheless, the Nuremberg prosecutors chose from among contemporary crimes only those committed by Nazi German officials, completely disregarding nearly identical crimes committed by Allied officials – we are thinking of the use of firebombing of civilian centers by both sides during the war. In Athena's case, she is acting on the basis of divine or natural law, and in the Nuremberg case the tribunal is acting on the basis of natural or international law.

Nuremberg creates a significant problem for those who wish to defend international criminal tribunals in terms of the rule of law. While the procedures employed were highly laudable in many respects, the defendants were tried according to a statute that had been drafted just months before the trial commenced. This has been a persistent source of strong criticism in the sixty-plus years since the tribunal sat and convicted most of those who were prosecuted at Nuremberg. And this continues to be a major source of worry about most tribunals, at least in part, especially for those created on an ad hoc basis, although we later also discuss some of the problems of the permanent ICC as well. Yet, like Athena's tribunal, there is a strong sense today that Nuremberg succeeded because of the reasonableness of its procedures and the rulings by its judges. As we will explore later, the question is whether a kind of bootstrapped legitimacy is enough to offset the inherent shortcomings in international tribunals.

III PROBLEMS FROM A LACK OF A LEGISLATURE

Tribunals are generally free-standing in the sense that they are not part of a legal system that has a legislature passing laws that are then interpreted and applied by the tribunal in its prosecutions. There are at least two major problems that result from the lack of a legislature that we will address in this section. First, there is a significant worry, as mentioned in connection to the Nuremberg tribunal, about retroactive prosecutions. Since the laws with which the prosecution proceeds are typically only established at the instigation of the tribunal, those laws are created only after the alleged criminal acts have occurred. In the case of the ICC, however, alleged criminal acts can only be prosecuted if they occurred after the court came into existence, but there remain critics who allege selective prosecution even for cases that fall squarely under the ICC's jurisdiction.[10] Second, the lack of a legislature connected to the tribunal means that the authority of the tribunal is independent of a legal system – free-floating, as it were – and often seemingly has little accountability. Again, the ICC is a partial exception here since it is permanent, although to many it seems nonetheless to be free-floating since it lacks a connection to a legislature.[11]

Retroactive application of law is not always problematic, as Lon Fuller argues in *The Morality of Law*.[12] Fuller points out that certain social goods can only be accomplished by the application of retroactive statutes, such as would be true in the case of a statute that required a seal on a valid marriage certificate, but where the seal had been destroyed or mislaid. Here a retroactive statute validating marriages even without a seal seems to be needed for the common good. Yet, retroactivity is especially pernicious in criminal law. In criminal tribunals, and criminal courts more generally, the defendant is at risk of significant loss of liberty and even loss of life, as was seen at Nuremberg, where more than twenty defendants were hanged as a result of their convictions.

In the debates about the legitimacy of Nuremberg, many legal philosophers at the time, including Fuller, H. L. A. Hart, and Gustav Radbruch, argued that the retroactivity of the Nuremberg statute did not delegitimize that tribunal.[13] And one of the most striking arguments, similar to Justice Jackson's, was that enforcing a retroactive statute was better than not prosecuting the Nazi leaders at all – a lesser evil defense.

In a different vein, one could argue that the lack of a statute at the time the Nazi crimes were allegedly committed is really beside the point. The question is whether or not there were sources of law, knowable at the time, that proscribed the conduct for which the defendants were being prosecuted. And here the record is not terribly clear. Scholars often point to the Kellogg-Briand Pact that Germany ratified, which made aggression by one state against another state illegal as a matter of international law. And other scholars have

[10] See Matthew Happold, "The International Criminal Court and the Lord's Resistance Army," *Melbourne Journal of International Law*, vol. 8 (May 2007).

[11] See Antonio Cassese, "The Legitimacy of International Criminal Tribunals and the Current Prospects of International Criminal Justice," *Leiden Journal of International Law*, vol. 25, no. 2 (2012), pp. 491–501.

[12] Lon L. Fuller, *The Morality of Law* (New Haven, CT: Yale University Press, 1963).

[13] See H. L. A. Hart, "Positivism and the Separation of Law and Morals," *Harvard Law Review*, vol. 71, no. 4, 1958; Lon. L. Fuller, "Positivism and Fidelity to Law: A Reply to Professor Hart," *Harvard Law Review*, vol. 71, no. 4, 1958; see also Gustav Radbruch, "Gesetzliches Unrecht und übergesetzliches Recht [Statutory Lawlessness and Supra-Statutory Law]," 1 *Suddeutsche Juristen-Zeitung* [SJZ] 105 (1946, pp. 105–108) (Ger.), translated in 26 *Oxford J. Legal Stud.* 1, 7 (translated by Bonnie Litschewski Paulson & Stanley L. Paulson., 2006).

pointed to various understandings of customary international law at the time that made mass atrocities committed by a state against its people also illegal. One does not need an explicit statute in order for certain acts to be seen as clearly criminal at a given time.

But as debates about codifying criminal law in the United States have shown, because of what is at stake it is thought that we should not leave it up to the vagaries of custom or common law to be used to prosecute people and put their liberty in jeopardy. And procedurally, it is harder to prosecute especially complex crimes like that of conspiracy, one of the main crimes charged at Nuremberg, if there is not a statute that clearly lays out the elements of such a crime and that is accessible to the defendants at the time that they decide to act.

Of perhaps greater worry is that the lack of a legislature, even for the ICC, calls into question the authority of those who create the tribunal, as well as the accountability of that tribunal. For many societies the legislative branch of government appoints the judges, or confirms their appointments. Since legislative branches are usually elected by the people, where the legislators are thereby authorized to act for the people, the judiciary is similarly authorized by the authority of the legislative branch. Without such authority, courts are worrisome in that they fail one of the main tests of legitimacy – having the authority to rule. Of course, there are other ways to attain legitimacy without authority, but when courts or tribunals are cut off from democratically elected legislatures there is at least a prima facie case for thinking that the courts or tribunals lack legitimacy.

In addition, there is a serious worry about the reach of courts that have not been authorized democratically. The idea that the people will hold the court accountable if it overreaches is defeated when the court or tribunal is not itself authorized by the people. Again, accountability can be achieved without popular oversight either by the people themselves or by their elected representatives, but there is a prima facie case for thinking that the oversight is lacking when courts or tribunals are cut off from democratically elected legislatures. Even in the case of the ICC, many of the ratifying states are not democratically elected, hence raising concerns about whether the people in those states have consented to the rulings by this permanent court.

The ad hoc tribunals, especially the International Criminal Tribunal for the former Yugoslavia (ICTY) and International Criminal Tribunal for Rwanda (ICTR), pose an especially difficult problem for the criticism that international tribunals lack a corresponding legislature. The UN Security Council established these tribunals, and unlike for the ICC there is no assembly of states parties acting as a legislature for the ad hoc tribunals.

There is a sense that the Security Council partially acts like a legislature in that it debates and then passes resolutions that have binding effect on the member states of the UN. But after establishing the ad hoc tribunals, the Security Council did not continue to pass resolutions affecting how the courts were run.

We have two responses to the lack of legitimacy of the ad hoc tribunals based on a lack of a legislature. First, the ad hoc tribunals are wrapping up their trials and the ICTR and Special Court for Sierra Leone (SCSL) are not accepting new cases – only the Extraordinary Chambers in the Courts of Cambodia (ECCC) is still accepting new cases. It is the expectation of all concerned parties that the ICC will now deal with such cases, as the permanent international criminal tribunal that in effect now supersedes the ad hoc tribunals. Second, in ad hoc matters where the jurisdiction is time-bound as well as geographically bound, it is perhaps not as worrisome to lack legislative oversight as when courts with broader jurisdictions are being considered.

IV PROBLEMS OF JURISDICTION AND LEGITIMACY

Legitimacy concerns the right of a government to "rule" by the use of coercive force. Legitimacy in nongovernmental institutions such as international tribunals concerns the right to issue binding "rulings." The right to rule is most clearly grounded in the consent of the "ruled." The right to make binding rulings is most often grounded not in consent but in the acceptance of, or acquiescence in, the "rulings" by those against whom a tribunal or court issues judgment. Of course, it is rare that a person who has been convicted in any court would agree to having the sentence meted out. But it is crucial for legitimacy that the group of which the convicted person is a member assents to these rulings.

John Simmons has provided a highly influential understanding of legitimacy that we will discuss in the context of international tribunals.[14] Simmons sees the issue of legitimacy falling squarely within the social contract theories of Hobbes and Locke, who were interested not merely in what makes states, or their laws, good ones, but rather what gives the state the right, through its laws, to limit the liberty of its citizens.[15] Legitimacy is, in this account, different from justification in that justification only concerns whether a state and its laws are

[14] A. John Simmons, "Justification and Legitimacy," *Ethics*, vol. 109, no. 4 (July 1999), pp. 739–771.

[15] See Christopher Heath Wellman, "Liberalism, Samaritanism, and Political Legitimacy," *Philosophy and Public Affairs*, vol. 25 (1996), pp. 211–212.

morally good, not whether anyone is obligated to do anything in respect to the state and its laws.

One could construe the problem we have been investigating then in terms of the difference between the justification and the legitimacy of international law and its courts or tribunals. And here we can clearly see the central problem with international criminal tribunals that have not been authorized by those people who are subject to their jurisdiction. While these tribunals may be good in the sense that they are better than any of the alternatives on offer, they may not be legitimate in that they do not have a right to rule over those whom they put in the dock or seek to arrest and extradite for this purpose. For some critics, the lack of authorization by the people means that international criminal tribunals are not legitimate.[16]

In this section we will explore the possibility that other than the consent of the people over whom these tribunals operate, some other source could provide legitimacy for international tribunals. The Nuremberg tribunal claimed for itself the legitimacy of the consent of humanity. Such phrases as "civilization cannot tolerate their being ignored" or "the common sense of mankind demands," along with the later charge that various "crimes against humanity" had been committed, were supposed to indicate that the tribunal claimed for itself universal jurisdiction based on the consent of humanity.

Universal jurisdiction and the consent of humanity would not necessarily meet the requirements of legitimacy that a social contract approach would require. It is not enough that others consent to be ruled; what is crucial for the legitimate exercise of coercion over a given person is that he or she consent, or at least would consent, to the court's rulings. Of course, there is some sense in saying that once one chooses to live, or to stay, in a given jurisdiction one tacitly consents to obey the laws of that jurisdiction. And such tacit consent can sometimes substitute for actual consent, as John Locke and his followers like John Simmons have contended.

The question of jurisdiction is a fraught one given that there generally is not a place where one can move in order not to be within the jurisdiction of some state. The problem of having no exit options is exacerbated when the jurisdiction is the entire globe, as is claimed in the case of universal jurisdiction. Until intergalactic travel is a reasonable option for people, it looks as if merely being on the Earth is not enough to show that one has tacitly consented to be ruled by those claiming universal jurisdiction for the scope of international law. The question then arises of whether one would consent to the jurisdiction of these tribunals. Here various points can be stated.

16 See Marlies Glasius, "Do International Courts Require Democratic Legitimacy?" *European Journal of International Law*, vol. 43 (February 2012).

It could be argued, as John Rawls and Allen Buchanan have argued, that we are all under a natural duty of justice to support just institutions. Insofar as international tribunals are just institutions, or perhaps good enough institutions, we should support them. But then the question becomes what this "support" means. Must we feel bound by their dictates even when it appears that our own liberty, or life, is put at risk by such support? Here we are greatly tempted by Hobbes's response to such situations: we are obligated to obey only as long as the institution seems to be concerned with protecting our security. When situations look otherwise, even in cases when the execution sentence is justly imposed, we are not obligated to obey.[17] Of course, in some cases different groups are in competition with each other for just such protection.

Or it could be argued that an international criminal legal order, which has at its pinnacle international criminal tribunals, should be supported since any reasonable person would see the need for these institutions to stand against violations of the most important of international norms, such as that against mass atrocity. But even here, it may not be thought that this is indeed the best way to achieve such a laudable goal, and perhaps favoring a system in which municipal courts and tribunals enforced international criminal law might be more effective. Except in the very rare case when no municipal courts or tribunals are likely to engage in such enforcement, having these reasonable alternatives to international criminal tribunals means that a given defendant would not have a duty to support such tribunals. In general, the normative argument in favor of a duty to obey the rulings of an international tribunal will not easily rest with such positions.

It could be argued that the focus on jurisdiction is misleading in that theorists sometimes fail to understand how even in domestic cases, having jurisdiction is not the same as being authorized to try a given case. Hersch Lauterpacht distinguishes between jurisdiction and justiciability: jurisdiction is a matter of what disputes are cognizable by courts; justiciability is a matter of liability to be tried by a court having jurisdiction. Not all cases that are proper as a matter of jurisdiction are justiciable. For example, the matter may indeed have taken place in the territory where a certain court has jurisdiction, that is, where a court can recognize the parties as potentially bound by the court's judgments. But the matter at issue may be too minor or the harm too distributed throughout a group for the court to offer effective remedy.

Under international law, a given tribunal may have jurisdiction because the matter is one that falls under universal jurisdiction or because the states parties

[17] See Larry May, *Limiting Leviathan: Hobbes on Law and International Affairs* (Oxford: Oxford University Press, 2013).

to a convention have agreed to bestow jurisdiction on the tribunal. Yet, the tribunal may not take the case because of justiciability concerns, for instance, because the case does not have a sufficiently grave matter to be decided.[18]

In Chapter 2 we will explore a host of problems of international criminal tribunals related to the abridgment of sovereignty of states. But there is a legitimacy issue of a different sort that we want to discuss briefly at the end of this section. Not all entities claiming to be states are deserving of that label and the benefits that this status entails. As Vaughan Lowe writes:

> State practice has developed so as to indicate that in addition to having a stable population, defined territory, effective government, and the capacity to engage independently in international relations, a candidate for Statehood is expected to satisfy any additional requirement of "legitimacy." The main implication of the requirement of legitimacy is that the entity must have emerged towards Statehood in a manner that is consistent with the principle of self-determination.[19]

And here adequate representation of the most important groups within the entity claiming statehood must be satisfied.

Political entities that exclude a significant segment of the population from self-determination lack legitimacy and fail to be states. It is important to note that such political entities do not have strong claims under international law and its criminal tribunals. Indeed, international law may be needed for such political entities to achieve statehood. In this sense there are internal and external legitimacy considerations in determining whether or not a political entity can assert its legitimacy as a state.

V LEGITIMACY BY BOOTSTRAPPING

In this final section, we will begin to sketch another way to support the legitimacy of international criminal tribunals. The bootstrapping approach we use to defend the legitimacy of international criminal tribunals acknowledges both the various criticisms and the various sources of legitimacy of these tribunals. We argue that despite the criticisms, the various sources of legitimacy can, at least together, be seen as normatively sufficient. We here argue only for a defense that is achieved when the sources reach a point where the defense is seen as plausible by reasonable people.

[18] See Hersch Lauterpacht, *The Function of Law in the International Community* (Oxford: Oxford University Press, 1933).

[19] Vaughan Lowe, *International Law* (Oxford: Oxford University Press, 2007), p. 159.

In *The Concept of Law*, H. L. A. Hart talks about the idea of bootstrapping in the way in which we will use the term as well.[20] The idea is that in some cases we have primary norms without additional, or secondary, norms that tell us how to interpret, change, or create norms. We have to rely on what seems reasonable and then hope that others will indeed regard the new norms as reasonable. Here is how Brennan, Erikkson, Goodin, and Southwood explain the idea:

> How does some particular interpretation of the rule come to be established, in the absence of any secondary rule appointing authorized interpreters? Again, you simply get enough other people to come to regard it as the right interpretation. Roughly speaking, that is how the common law emerged.... One judge issues a ruling, and other judges go on to rule in like manner.... Or again how do you change the rules, in the absence of any secondary rules specifying how to amend the first order rules? Again you must simply get enough other people around you to say that this is the new rule.[21]

We follow this model of understanding how norms arise, first set out by H. L. A. Hart.

A bootstrapping approach is a self-sustaining process in the sense that one proceeds without external support or input. It relies exclusively on existing resources. The phrase "picking oneself up by one's own bootstraps" appears to date from the nineteenth century and was sometimes used to stand for an impossible task. But today, and in our usage, "bootstrapping" means that legitimacy is achieved by means of already existing and well-established procedures, such as the use of customs or consensus positions that have already achieved a high degree of acceptance. Specifically, in reference to legitimacy, we use the term "bootstrapping" to indicate that we will not rely on normative considerations that are external to the already existing normative framework of international law or that are not already contained as underlying consensus documents.

As in the rest of the book, in this chapter we are employing normative principles for which there is already widespread support, as evidenced by the way these principles are referred to in the various discussions that are themselves critical of international criminal tribunals. As we proceed in this section, we will refer to the underlying normative principles of the documents that were accepted by states as authorizing international criminal tribunals. In this way

[20] H. L. A. Hart, *The Concept of Law* (Oxford: Oxford University Press, 1961).

[21] Geoffrey Brennan, Lina Eriksson, Robert E. Goodin, and Nicholas Southwood, *Explaining Norms* (Oxford: Oxford University Press, 2013), p. 95.

we will follow Lauterpacht in referring to the "authority of legal rules derived from the very nature of international society."[22]

To this end, we will assume without argument that there is indeed an international society. At the very least, this means that we will take seriously large multilateral treaties as well as the underlying principles embedded in many such treaties, as expressing the normative "will" of that international community. By this we do not mean to imply anything especially "spooky" here – the normative will just means what can be inferred as the best explanation for what must have been supported as grounds for various multilateral treaties. To proceed as plausibly as we can, we will refer primarily to those multilateral treaties that have been overwhelmingly supported.

Our book is not meant to be premised on a controversial idea that there is an international community with rough agreement about certain normative principles. Indeed, most of the critics of international criminal tribunals whom we will give much space to in the chapters that follow support the general idea of an international community or society of some sort. In the era of globalization, it is hard to find theorists who do not believe that there are some common normative commitments that extend across states in something like "a society of states."

The idea of a society of states with some rudimentary agreement about normative principles of justice and equity, for instance, has been supported across the centuries as well as manifested in international treaties today. Hugo Grotius and Emer de Vattel, two of the often-cited theorists in international legal discussions today, clearly advocated the position of there being a normative order that could be characterized as a "society of States." In the eighteenth century, Vattel said:

> Since Nations are bound by the Laws of Nature mutually to promote the society of the human race they owe one another all the duties which the safety and welfare of that society require. The offices of humanity consist in the fulfillment of the duty of mutual assistance.[23]

And yet he nonetheless claimed that "of all the rights possessed by a Nation" sovereignty is the most important.[24] States had various duties in this "society of states"; for example, "If a Nation is suffering from famine, all those who have provisions to spare should assist it in its need without however exposing themselves to scarcity."[25]

[22] Lauterpacht, *The Function of Law in the International Community*, p. 6.

[23] Emer de Vattel, *The Law of Nations or the Principles of Natural Law* (1758), translated by Charles G. Fenwick (Washington, DC: Carnegie Institute, 1916), p. 113.

[24] Ibid., p. 131.

[25] Ibid., p. 115.

A century earlier, Grotius had described what he called the society of states:

> But just as the laws of each state have in view the advantage of that state, so by mutual consent it has become possible that certain laws should originate as between all states, or a great many states; and it is apparent that the laws thus originating had in view the advantage not of particular states, but of the great society of states. And this is what is called the law of nations.[26]

With Grotius as with Vattel, we will proceed along the most plausible route by referring to the normative principles that are embedded in the agreements of the society of states.

Before beginning this defense, it should be noted that while not all international criminal tribunals have been set up with the consent of the states where the crimes allegedly took place or where the people who allegedly perpetrated these crimes resided, some international criminal tribunals do have such status. So, at least in those cases, the social contract approach can be satisfied. Consider the case of the Special Tribunal for Sierra Leone. Here is how the mandate of this tribunal is described on the tribunal's Web site:

> The Special Court for Sierra Leone was set up jointly by the Government of Sierra Leone and the United Nations. It is mandated to try those who bear the greatest responsibility for serious violations of international humanitarian law and Sierra Leonean law committed in the territory of Sierra Leone since 30 November 1996.[27]

The issue of legitimacy here is fairly uncontroversial since the Sierra Leone government requested that the United Nations aid it in establishing this tribunal, specifically because Sierra Leone had difficulty doing this on its own.

Of a more complicated variety, consider the mandate of the Special Tribunal for Lebanon. Here is how its mandate is described on the Web site of this tribunal:

> The tribunal was established following a request by the government of Lebanon to the United Nations. The agreement between Lebanon and the UN was not ratified, and the UN brought its provisions into force through UN Security Council Resolution 1757.[28]

Here the UN failed to reach agreement with the host state but decided to pursue its mandate in any event. The Lebanese government did not reject the

[26] Hugo Grotius, *De Jure Belli ac Pacis* (On the Laws of War and Peace) (1625) translated by Francis W. Kelsey (Oxford: Oxford University Press, 1925), p. 15.

[27] *Special Court for Sierra Leone*, accessed 15 June 2015, www.rscsl.org/.

[28] "About the STL," *Special Tribunal for Lebanon*, modified 18 November 2011, www.stl-tsl.org/en/about-the-stl/511-about-the-stl.

UN's mandate and indeed has aided in much of its work. But the cooperation has been haphazard, and significant portions of the Lebanon population are opposed to the work of the tribunal. Nonetheless, the tribunal has applied international criminal law standards to the case involving the assassination of the president of Lebanon.

In the cases of the Sierra Leone and Lebanon tribunals, special international criminal tribunals have been established through the United Nations with participation and (some level of) consent from the state in question. Another model is the Extraordinary Chambers in the Courts of Cambodia. Here is its mandate, as described on the Web site of the tribunal:

> An agreement with the UN was ultimately reached in June 2003 detailing how the international community will assist and participate in the Extraordinary Chambers. This special new court was created by the government and the UN but it will be independent of them. It is a Cambodian court with international participation that will apply international standards.[29]

Here the Cambodian tribunal was set up to be independent of the United Nations, yet it does apply international criminal law to the various cases involving the Khmer Rouge. The Cambodian government was highly motivated to put this dark period of its recent history behind it and hence requested that this tribunal be established.

In contrast with these recent tribunals, the tribunals for Rwanda and the former Yugoslavia were set up by the Security Council of the United Nations *without* the express or tacit consent of the states involved.[30] These tribunals are United Nations ad hoc courts. The authority and legitimacy of these tribunals cannot be established by reference to the consent of the states in question. Rather the authority and the legitimacy are said to be derived from the United Nations itself, under the UN's chapter VII powers, as described in the Charter of the United Nations, which itself was formed as a multilateral treaty being ratified by nearly all of the states of the world. Here the authority of the United Nations is based on this multilateral treaty, which like other treaties is itself grounded in the consent of the states who are parties to the charter.

29 "Introduction to the ECCC," *Extraordinary Chambers in the Courts of Cambodia*, accessed 14 June 2015, www.eccc.gov.kh/en/about-eccc/introduction.

30 See Payam Akhavan, "The International Criminal Tribunal for Rwanda: The Politics and Pragmatics of Punishment," *American Journal of International Law*, vol. 90, no. 501 (1996); see also Victor Peskin, *International Justice in Rwanda and the Balkans: Virtual Trials and the Struggle for State Cooperation* (New York: Cambridge University Press, 2008).

The legitimacy of the actions of the United Nations, including the Charter itself, is seemingly consistent with the social contract doctrine discussed earlier because their initial mandate is based solely on the consent and ratification of the states, which are then obligated by these tribunals. There is a significant wrinkle here, which we will not be able to pursue in this chapter, which concerns the expanding range of customary international law. On some accounts, even those states that have not ratified large multilateral treaties can over time come to be obligated by them as a result of their seeming tacit acceptance of these treaties.

The tacit consent argument also helps in the case of the ICC, given the problem that many ratifiers of the treaty establishing the ICC are not themselves expressly elected by their people. The problem of the expanded reach of the ICC, to include people from states that have not ratified at all, does not seem to be helped by a tacit consent argument. But here our bootstrapping method will have to make reference to the idea of the reasonable appeal of the decisions themselves to buttress the tacit consent argument. This is why today it is so important that the decisions of the ICC appear to be scrupulously fair – a matter we take up in later chapters.

Given these disparate institutional arrangements for international criminal tribunals, it is unlikely that a single line of argument could support the legitimacy of each of these tribunals. But there are various sources of legitimacy of these tribunals that can be seen as normatively sufficient. Let us now end by discussing some of these often disparate sources of the normative legitimacy of international criminal tribunals. The first aspect to mention takes us back to our discussion of the Athena and Nuremberg tribunals. The legitimacy of these tribunals was linked to their normative efficacy, that is, to the fact that the results as well as the procedures of these tribunals seemed to be fair to at least most of the parties concerned. Of course, the parties that do not accept the normative legitimacy will continue to cause legitimacy worries under this strategy of looking to the efficacy of the tribunals to bootstrap the legitimacy of these tribunals.

Second, the seeming fairness of the procedures of international criminal tribunals is another source of their legitimacy. There is a good debate about whether this source is sufficient to establish the legitimacy at issue. It might be argued, in the mode of Simmons's social contract approach, that the fairness of procedures is a feature of what would make them morally good, not a feature that would give these tribunals the authority to rule over anyone. And while this may indeed be a plausible position to take, the bootstrapping approach we are suggesting is harder to refute in this way since the fairness of the tribunals is only one source among others that together establish the legitimacy of the tribunals.

Third, as we have indicated, many tribunals are constituted with the express or tacit consent of the states where the crimes occurred or where the alleged perpetrators reside. As we have indicated, some international criminal tribunals have the express consent of, or were even initiated by, the states involved, as is true of the ICC. Of course, if those states are not themselves legitimate, then they cannot imbue these tribunals with legitimacy. But insofar as the states are themselves legitimate, having been supported by the will of the people and perhaps also being respecters of human rights of their own people and of other peoples of the world, bootstrapping is not needed since the consent of legitimate states that are involved would be sufficient. When it is only tacit consent, as in the case of the Lebanon tribunal, this also may be sufficient as long as the tacit consent is uncontroversial, if the state giving tacit consent is itself a legitimate state, and if the decisions seem fair.

Fourth, most international criminal tribunals are established with authorization from the United Nations. So, insofar as the United Nations has legitimacy, that legitimacy could be at least one significant basis of the legitimacy of these tribunals. Not only would the UN itself have to be legitimate, but its chapter VII powers would have to be a legitimate source of the authority of the tribunals. Let us say something in more detail at this point in the chapter to indicate how one could bootstrap the legitimacy of international tribunals on the legitimacy of the United Nations.

The UN's chapter VII powers are fairly broad but certainly not unlimited. Here are the relevant articles of chapter VII of the UN Charter:

> Article 39 – The Security Council shall determine the existence of any threat to the peace, breach of the peace, or act of aggression and shall make recommendations, or decide what measures shall be taken in accordance with Articles 41 and 42, to maintain or restore international peace and security.
>
> Article 40 – In order to prevent an aggravation of the situation, the Security Council may, before making the recommendations or deciding upon the measures provided for in Article 39, call upon the parties concerned to comply with such provisional measures as it deems necessary or desirable. Such provisional measures shall be without prejudice to the rights, claims, or position of the parties concerned. The Security Council shall duly take account of failure to comply with such provisional measures.
>
> Article 41 – The Security Council may decide what measures not involving the use of armed force are to be employed to give effect to its decisions, and it may call upon the Members of the United Nations to apply such measures. These may include complete or partial interruption of economic relations

and of rail, sea, air, postal, telegraphic, radio, and other means of communication, and the severance of diplomatic relations.[31]

So, in the Charter we have several possible sources of legitimacy for the United Nations to establish international criminal tribunals. These ad hoc tribunals could be provisional measures (chapter VII, article 40) or more long-lasting ways to give effect to its decisions (article 41). Either of these seems to be authorized under the broad powers of the United Nations. There is, however, a small problem in that international criminal tribunals are not mentioned under the list of things that may be done to give effect to the UN's decisions.[32] But the list in article 41 is not meant to be exhaustive, only illustrative. Indeed, in the *Tadic* case, the ICTY appellate court ruled that the Security Council is granted broad judicial powers under chapter VII of the UN Charter despite the fact that the power to create international tribunals is not expressly mentioned as a chapter VII power. Thus, the United Nations appears to have as one of its legitimate powers the right to set up either provisional or more long-lasting tribunals.[33] Of course, this is controversial, and this is one of the reasons we have not sought to base our argument on this point alone. Rather we have employed a group of arguments to support the legitimacy of international tribunals.

When legitimacy is discussed concerning individual states, it is divided into two categories: internal and external legitimacy. Internal legitimacy involves the approval of those people who are bound by the laws of a state who in some sense agree to be so ruled. External legitimacy involves the recognition by other states that a given state is indeed deserving of being seen as a legitimate state. In the case of external legitimacy, many theorists today call for a test concerning the promotion of human rights both at home and abroad.

We could apply this dual test of legitimacy to international criminal tribunals as well. Internal legitimacy can be understood in terms of the member states of multilateral treaties that set up international criminal tribunals. An international criminal tribunal could achieve internal legitimacy when the states that are party to the founding document of the tribunal agree to be

31 U.N. Charter, Chapter VII, 24 October 1945, 1 UNTS XVI, accessed 14 June 2015, www.un.org/en/documents/charter/.

32 Another problem we will not discuss here is that for some the permanent members of the UN's Security Council operate seemingly with impunity when they exercise chapter VII powers over less powerful states.

33 Of course, here a tribunal that has its legitimacy under question asserts that it does have legitimacy from the UN because of the interpretive authority asserted to be true of that very tribunal. This may go beyond bootstrapping – perhaps approaching dangerously close to engaging in self-legitimation.

bound by the decisions of the tribunal. There will remain, as we have indicated already, a problem with those states that are not party to one or another of the treaties establishing international criminal tribunals. And it may be possible still to ask about legitimacy for states that have not agreed to be bound as an internal matter of legitimacy.

From the standpoint of external legitimacy, a tribunal could over time demonstrate that it is entitled to be seen as legitimate because of the effects and fairness of its decisions. As in the case of external legitimacy of states seen in terms of promotion of human rights, one could view the external legitimacy of international criminal tribunals in terms of retributive and deterrent effects of the tribunal's decisions as well as the recognition that the tribunal's decisions were fair. In addition, as we have been arguing in this section, external legitimacy could be achieved by recognition of a tribunal by the society of states, perhaps through the United Nations framework.

The ICC seems to have achieved legitimacy in both senses of this term. Internally, more than 120 states have ratified the Rome Treaty, which is the founding document of the ICC. And other states have already sought to assign cases to the ICC, even though the state that has pressured the prosecutors of the ICC has not yet ratified the ICC's charter. External legitimacy can be seen in the referral of cases from the United Nations, in behalf of all of its member states. But for a corresponding external legitimacy to that of states, we will have to wait until more cases have been decided and the effects of the working of the ICC can be better seen.

So, there is a sense that legitimacy will accrue to the ICC, as well as other international criminal tribunals, as the states of the world begin to respect the decisions from these tribunals. This is why we will spend much time later in tackling persistent criticisms, especially of the ICC, in terms of the fairness of how the ICC decides which cases to take and how defendants are treated during the trials. These considerations are important not only for the reputation of the ICC and other tribunals, but also for the very legitimacy that these tribunals need in order to be effective in the world today, when some powerful states remain skeptical of international criminal tribunals.

We return now to the *Eumenides* and Nuremberg. Athena is able to gain internal legitimacy for her tribunal because of the consent of the Furies and Orestes, as well as Apollo's acting as Orestes' counsel. The external legitimacy was gained by dint of the approval of the gods on Mount Olympus and was also due to Athena's reputation for fairness. But as with all other tribunals, the legitimacy will have to be earned as well by the recognition that there was much gained by the decision of the tribunal. Some have argued that the restraint on the vengeance of the Furies was one important result. This is metaphor for the way that all legitimate criminal trials are supposed to restrain vengeance as well.

Nuremberg had the external legitimacy that the Allied states had bestowed on it, even as this was only true of the states that had been victorious in World War II. Justice Jackson characterized the tribunal as "staying the hand of vengeance" as a way to claim a solid basis for the tribunal's legitimacy. The continuing debate about the "victors' justice" has been about the tribunal's legitimacy and has made many wonder about the external legitimacy of the IMT. If the states of the world had voted, then as in Grotius' "society of States" model, they would probably have supported the IMT over its most obvious alternative, summary execution of high Nazi officials.

The internal legitimacy of Nuremberg is even less clear. There was no multilateral treaty that included the Axis states in establishing the Nuremberg tribunal. Even the very idea that international criminal tribunals could prosecute individuals was itself not well established. Many of the Nazi Germans in the dock demanded that they be prosecuted in domestic German courts with German judges. And given that Nuremberg was the first major international criminal tribunal, the complaints of the high Nazi officials are not easy to dismiss out of hand. Yet, as in most criminal proceedings, the consent of the defendants is often not forthcoming, for the obvious reason that the defendants do not want to be punished. Internal legitimacy of criminal tribunals is easier to establish when there have been multilateral treaties, and where the communities consent, as is largely true for the ICC today.

In this chapter, we have seen an array of overlapping sources of the legitimacy of international criminal tribunals that provide a bootstrapping argument for international tribunals. In some cases, only one of these sources is sufficient, but in most cases some combination of these sources will have to be employed to establish the legitimacy of international criminal tribunals. It is interesting to note in this context that the United Nations did not think that it had the chapter VII authority to establish a *permanent* international criminal court, and so a separate multilateral treaty had to be established for this purpose. Nonetheless, the United Nations did claim to have the authority to establish ad hoc *temporary* international criminal tribunals. While not uncontroversial, we have argued that despite considerable problems, international criminal tribunals can be established as legitimate, at least since the founding of the United Nations.

2

Sovereignty

A commonly expressed criticism of international criminal tribunals and courts is that they usurp the sovereignty of states.[1] Indeed, the United States has refused to ratify the Rome Statute of the ICC[2] primarily because of concerns about sovereignty, especially the possible criminal punishment of U.S. troops that have acted in overseas wars. In addition, it is sometimes claimed, there is an attempt to establish a cosmopolitan state through the backdoor. Rather than inducing all of the people of the world to consent to a world state, institutions such as international tribunals are surreptitious ways to achieve such a state without global consent. In this chapter we address these challenges.

The sovereignty objection to the ICC has been most responsible for the major powers of the world not ratifying the Rome Statute. Indeed, there is a sense that if a state is powerful already, it can only lose power by joining any international compact, which would inevitably lead to the state's restricting its liberty in ways it would not want to do. This sense is exacerbated when the liberty concerns the prosecution of a state's own citizens, historically one of the most significant domains of exclusive control by sovereign states. So, regardless of whether one talks about this issue specifically in sovereignty terms, it is clear that many powerful states see international tribunals as vehicles to be used by weaker states, and not necessarily as beneficial tools for the strong ones. We will address these various sovereignty objections in several ways, most especially by discussing the way that the ICC's structure is able to preempt some of these objections.

1 See Jeremy Rabkin, "Recalling the Case for Sovereignty," *Chicago Journal of International Law*, vol. 5, 2005.

2 Rome Statute of the International Criminal Court, art. 13(c), Jul. 17, 1998, 2187 U.N.T.S. 90 (entered into force July 1, 2002), available at http://treaties.un.org/doc/source/RecentTexts/rome-en.htm [hereinafter Rome Statute].

In Section I we will set out a view of autonomy as a groundwork for understanding sovereignty. In Section II we will explore the way that social contract theorists such as Thomas Hobbes understood state sovereignty from the standpoint of the idea of bindingness through consent. In Section III we will consider the charge that international criminal tribunals contribute to a backdoor attempt not only to undermine state sovereignty but to create a cosmopolitan state. In Section IV we will examine how the doctrine of complementarity helps to answer some of the critics of international criminal tribunals. In Section V we will explore various conceptions of federated sovereignty as another way to respond to the critics of international criminal tribunals. In Section VI we begin to explore the increasing turn away from treaty regimes and toward customary international law – looking first at some of the benefits of such a change. In Section VII we then explore the significant and abiding problems with international customary law concerning sovereignty worries.

I THE CONCEPT OF SOVEREIGNTY

One of the best ways to begin to make sense of state sovereignty is on the model of the autonomy of individuals. Indeed, philosophers such as John Stuart Mill refer to autonomy as a kind of sovereignty: where the individual person is sovereign over his own life.[3] Liberty is seen as one of the chief goods, and any practice such as that of recognizing the autonomy of the individual that advances liberty is seen as of the highest value.

Some have seen autonomy as an absolute concept – where a person is only autonomous if he or she is unconstrained and not dominated by any other person. Of course, if this were interpreted literally, then no person would be autonomous, since we all depend on others for a wide variety of things, and our lives are ruled, at least partially, by police and many other members of our society. Even Henry David Thoreau, who claimed to be utterly dependent only on himself for a year or so at Walden Pond, was dependent on the largesse of his benefactor Ralph Waldo Emerson, who allowed Thoreau to live on his land and cut timber there for the building of his cabin.[4]

It seems that some restrictions on individual choices might be justified for the good of the individual, despite lack of consent. Yet such interferences are often criticized as paternalistic – they still seem to be autonomy-denying since the individual is not allowed to choose for himself or herself. But what if the individual person chooses to restrict his or her preferences by accepting the

3 See John Stuart Mill, *On Liberty* (London: John W. Parker and Son, West Strand, 1859).
4 Henry David Thoreau, *Walden or Life in the Woods* (Boston: Ticknor & Fields, 1854).

interference in his or her life? Can it not be part of an autonomous life that one restricts one's own future choices by promising or contracting to do so in exchange for something considered highly valuable? Nearly everyone agrees that promising or contracting, whereby one places limitations on one's future choices, can be compatible with autonomy.

One of the most striking examples in the debate over personal autonomy has been that of selling oneself into slavery. Here one seems to deny one's own autonomy either for an indefinite or a definite period of time, during which one's choices will not be one's own concerning all matters in one's life. Can one be autonomous and yet be denied the opportunity to sell oneself? The general idea of self-limitation as an abridgment of autonomy is highly contested. It is at this stage that theorists begin to wonder whether autonomy is always of value to the person who has it, or whether autonomy only has value when it is in service of a good for the individual in question.

On a nonabsolutist view of autonomy, it is only of value when there is a good for the individual or some good that is supported by the autonomy of the individual. Selling oneself into slavery seems to be something that is not a good for the person, and hence restrictions on such choices, while autonomy-denying in the absolute sense of autonomy, are not problematic. Self-limitation agreements can be justified as liberty-enhancing in some cases.

Regardless of how one views the self-limitation cases, the idea that will be important for state sovereignty issues is the question of whether or not a state can still be considered autonomous, or sovereign, if it agrees to have some of its choices restricted by some other authority. And we must wonder again why it is that many theorists have unquestioningly accepted the idea that sovereignty must be absolute to be sovereignty at all.

Sovereignty at the state level is highly similar to autonomy at the individual level. There are differences in terms of size and extent of choices, but the general idea is largely the same – being able to make decisions and choices for one's own good, or what is perceived to be so, without interference from others. In the nonabsolutist construal, sovereignty would best be understood as acting without "undue" interference. And then the question for the nonabsolutist is whether "due" influence can be plausibly construed as accepting influence over an important range of choices.

Here the parallel between individual autonomy and State sovereignty would concern the voluntary restriction of choice not over everything in one's life but over a significant part of one's life. If a person voluntarily joins a monastic order, part of this chosen life may be a vow of silence. While there may be many other choices that are restricted as well, let us focus on just the voluntary taking of a vow of silence. Can such a vow be consistent with autonomy? The type of monastic life where one centers one's thoughts on one's relationship with God to the exclusion of all other relationships seems to be a life that can best be lived in silence. If this is a plausible way to live, the vow of silence can be seen as an integral part of that monastic life.

Voluntarily taking a vow of silence is a significant restriction on one's future choices, but it may indeed be a decision consistent with a person's overall autonomy. This is especially easy to see when one realizes that the vow is something that a person chooses. Unlike in the voluntary servitude agreement, a large range of choices are still available to the person. But most importantly, the vow of silence can be seen as consistent with the way a person wants to lead his or her life. Indeed, many of the things that a person may desire and even cherish are choice-limiting but perhaps also autonomy-enhancing rather than autonomy-diminishing. At the very least one can say that such practices as vows of silence within monastic communities, when consent is not based on strong outside influences are aimed at the perceived good of the people making the vows. But we want to suggest the stronger thesis that autonomy can be enhanced by voluntarily relinquishing choice over a range of conduct.

Autonomy can be enhanced, in a seemingly paradoxical way, by voluntary restrictions on future choices. A person may have a very strong desire to lead a certain kind of monastic life – indeed, spending the rest of one's time leading a monastic life may be the clear autonomous choice of the person at a given time. Part of the explanation is that the individual knows that he or she is weak and needs a community of like-minded people to help him or her achieve as near to a contemplative life of prayer as can be accomplished in this case of mutual cooperation. Future choices that one wished to make would be more difficult if not impossible if one could not make a vow of silence that the other members of the monastic order were asked to help enforce.

The requested help of others in restricting our future choices seems to be the kind of infringement of choice that impedes autonomy. Jon Elster talks of the example of Ulysses, who asks his shipmates to tie him to the mast so that when he hears the singing of the Sirens he will not steer his ship into the rocks from which the Sirens beckon. This strategy, Elster argues, is rational in a sense.[5] Ulysses' strategy is rational because it advances his goals and well-being, even as it limits his freedom at the moment. Indeed, Ulysses enhances his liberty and his autonomy since without implementing such a strategy he

5 Jon Elster, *Ulysses and Sirens* (Cambridge: Cambridge University Press, 1979).

and his shipmates will perish. And part of the request for help from others is that they act against a person's current choices, so as to attain the goal of surviving.

On the model of personal autonomy we have been exploring, there is a plausible way to view state sovereignty that is quite similar to the personal autonomy case. One of the main problems concerning international law is that it is thought to be an infringement on sovereignty, just as the vow of silence with the request for help in enforcing it can be thought to infringe on one's autonomy

International law is on strongest grounds when it is based on multilateral treaties that states ratify requiring the parties to the treaty to restrict themselves in various ways in the future. Treaties are often rightly said to be a form of contract where the states parties to a contract agree to give up something they might otherwise choose to do in the future in order to gain certain benefits of the cooperation of other states. Indeed, states generally do not ratify treaties unless they expect to gain significantly from the cooperation of the states parties who also ratify the treaty.

In many treaties states bind themselves to other states by making certain promises and then recognizing the authority of other states to act to enforce the keeping of these promises. The question that we are pursuing in this chapter is whether such behavior of states severely limits or dissolves their sovereignty. We will discuss several strategies for answering this question in the negative in the following sections. Let us end this section by pointing out some of the similarities and dissimilarities between this question and the question of whether an individual's promising and binding himself or herself to a community severely limits or dissolves individual autonomy.

We have already suggested some of the similarities, so before turning to additional ones let us say a few words about dissimilarities between the individual and state cases. Individual humans are unlike states in that they can have very uncomplicated desires and interests. Because states are collections of individuals but not individuals in their own right, except by stipulation, it is harder to know what are the desires and interests of states than to know an individual's desires and interests. For this reason it is harder to know whether liberty-limiting treaties will achieve what states desire in the long run than it is for individuals.

In addition, it could be claimed that even though individual autonomy cannot be plausibly held to be absolute, state sovereignty lends itself much better to being thought of as an absolute concept admitting of no limitations. Sovereignty involves being the final arbiter of matters that affect the state, and as such sovereignty would be infringed if for a certain realm of conduct an international body were the final arbiter.

Hersch Lauterpacht has presented a forceful defense of international law in general and international tribunals in particular. He takes an approach that we do not share but that is instructive at this point for us to consider. He urges that we think of law in the international domain as embodying "law's impersonal sovereignty."[6] Lauterpacht argues that we move away from the legal positivist idea that law must be understood as the command of "someone." In Lauterpacht's view, law and the state are virtually synonymous – laws are not the commands of the state; rather, law's commands constitute the state. In this sense, the positivists have given us a misleading metaphor. Indeed, in his view, there could be, and probably were, tribunals before there was (statute) law in domestic contexts.

We agree with Lauterpacht that too much can be made of the idea of law as being given as a command by one person who has authority, to another person who must obey. Yet, we also see that the model of the state of nature scenario and its personalization of the coming of law can have its uses, as we will show in Section II. And so while we disagree with the strong thrust of Lauterpacht's remarks, we do agree that sovereignty could be understood, and perhaps should be understood, impersonally.

In our view, state sovereignty and individual autonomy are actually closer to one another than they may initially appear. Sovereignty is not best understood as an absolutist concept – it is best seen, like autonomy, as restrained by what is in the interest of the state or what the state's good is. Sovereignty does not have high value in and of itself since it, like autonomy, can be used in a way that is harmful or even destructive to the state.[7] The exercise of liberty is not of high value in itself – for a person can cause harm to himself or herself as when one exercises liberty by drinking too much alcohol and then driving in an intoxicated state. What is of high value concerns what good the exercise of liberty can achieve. In addition, at least some of the interests of states are indeed quite similar to those of individuals; that is one of the reasons why we can intelligibly talk of states as if they were individuals. We will discuss this issue in greater detail as this chapter progresses. Our next task, though, is to discuss some of the most prominent views of state sovereignty understood in terms of consent and contract.

6 Hersch Lauterpacht, *The Function of Law in the International Community* (Oxford: Oxford University Press, 1933), p. 422.

7 See Joseph Raz, *The Morality of Freedom* (Oxford: Oxford University Press, 1984); and Joseph Raz, "Human Rights without Foundations," in Samantha Besson and John Tasioulis (eds.), *The Philosophy of International Law* (Oxford: Oxford University Press, 2010), pp. 321–337.

II STATE SOVEREIGNTY AND CONSENT THEORIES

As we have suggested, a common understanding of state sovereignty is the right of a state to be the final arbiter of matters that most directly affect that state. Being a final arbiter means that no other state, or organization, can override the decisions of a sovereign state concerning the pursuit of its core interests. State sovereignty has its clearest manifestation in the exclusive control of criminal matters within that state's territories. If another state, or non-state actor, can usurp the power of criminal prosecution from a state, the state ceases to be sovereign in the sense that it has lost control over that which is most significant for its citizens' lives.

The classic statement of modern sovereignty was provided by Jean Bodin in 1576:

> Sovereignty is the absolute and perpetual power of a commonwealth … a commonwealth is a just government, with sovereign power, of several households and of that which they have in common … The person of the sovereign, according to the law, is always excepted no matter how much power and authority he grants to someone else; and he never gives so much that he does not hold back even more. He is never prevented from commanding, or from assuming cognizance – by substitution, concurrence, removal, or any way he please – of any cause that he left to the jurisdiction of a subject.[8]

Bodin sees that any permanent loss of absolute power eliminates sovereignty, or transfers it to the one who now has the absolute power.

Notice that for Bodin, concurrence is one way to transfer sovereignty, although this understanding is quite different from that of Hobbes writing a half-century later, as we will see. For Bodin, even a consensual abrogation of power so limits the sovereign that sovereignty is lost, whereas for Hobbes such consensual arrangements as leagues of states do not necessarily abrogate the sovereignty of each of the state parties.

Today, most of the critics of international tribunals who focus on sovereignty seem to follow Bodin rather than Hobbes in that the critics take as their charge to defend the rights of states and their governments.[9] It is thought that any increase in the power of international institutions must entail a diminishment in the power of individual states. And this is especially asserted with respect to any type of sovereignty that is assumed by these international institutions.

[8] Jean Bodin, *Six Livres de la Republique* (1576), translated by Julian H. Franklin as *On Sovereignty: Four Chapters from the Six Books of the Commonwealth* (Cambridge: Cambridge University Press, 1992), pp. 1–2.

[9] See Jeremy Rabkin, *Law without Nations* (Princeton, NJ: Princeton University Press, 2005).

As theorists from Bodin to Hobbes have shown, when power can be asserted against another, the other has lost autonomy, or its political equivalent – sovereignty.[10] Yet, as we have said, Hobbes has a position much more palatable to international law and its criminal tribunals.

Indeed, Hobbes thought that leagues of states could be defended as not jeopardizing sovereignty. Hobbes believed that consensual arrangements among states were an especially good way for them to increase rather than lose power. Hobbes recognized that it would be rational for states to form themselves into associations. In chapter 22 of *Leviathan* he says:

> For a league being a connexion of men by covenants, if there be no power given to any one man, or assembly, as in the condition of mere nature, to compel them to performance, is so long only valid, as there ariseth no just cause of distrust: and therefore Leagues between commonwealths, over whom there is no human power established, to keep them all in awe, are not only lawful, but also profitable for the time they last.[11]

Here Hobbes seems to accept the possibility of leagues of states and to regard them as profitable and in some sense legal.

The Hobbesian position links the decisions of an individual to enter civil society to the decisions of a state to enter what could be called international society. In both cases, voluntarily relinquishing some rights in order to gain more security is, from a Hobbesian standpoint, a reasonable thing to do. What a Hobbesian, and Hobbes, would be leery of is a world state where the previously sovereign states were now subjected to review and overrule by a higher power. But the international tribunals that are the subject of our book do not have the authority to overrule states and so can be consistent with the views of even a very strong defender of state sovereignty.

The crucial issue for many critics of international tribunals is that once a state has given up certain rights to an international body, that state cannot easily reclaim those rights and is hence diminished by the relinquishing to the point where its sovereignty is jeopardized. Here there are two issues that are often confused. The first is a worry that the decision to enter into an international agreement precludes the later decision to abrogate the agreement. The second is the worry that even in the short run the state that voluntarily enters into an international agreement has thereby lost sovereignty.

Hobbes was especially concerned about the problem of reneging on an agreement one had previously made, and what he says on this topic could be useful for addressing the first issue. Initially, Hobbes struggled to explain

[10] See Bodin, *The Six Books of the Commonwealth*, 1576; and Thomas Hobbes, *Leviathan*, 1651.

[11] Hobbes, *Leviathan*, EW III 223, Tuck 163.

why an individual driven by self-preservation and self-interest would not be motivated to break his agreements. Hobbes reflects on "the Foole" who sees

> that every man's conservation, and contentment, being committed to his own care, there could be no reason, why every man might not do what conduced thereunto: and therefore also to make, or not make; keep, or not keep covenants, was not against reason, when it conduced to one's own benefit.[12]

Yet Hobbes argues that there are indeed good reasons to keep one's covenants and agreements, arguing that

> there is no man who can hope by his own strength, or wit, to defend himself from destruction, without the help of confederates; where every one expects the same defense by the confederation, that any one else does: and therefore he which declares he thinks it reason to deceive those that help him, can in reason expect no other means of safety, than what can be had from his own single power.[13]

It is clear that Hobbes thought that one could back out of one's agreements, but that there were prudential reasons that normally militated against this act.

Hobbes also argued that there is a kind of self-contradiction or absurdity in going back on one's word. The Hobbesian position is that individuals and states should not lightly decide to renege on their agreements, but that if the agreements did not serve the interest of security of the state's own citizens, it would sometimes be prudent to do so.

The United States has already set several precedents for backing out of international agreements when they seemed not to be in the U.S. interest any longer. Most recently, George W. Bush revoked the signing of the Kyoto Protocol, and while many environmentalists complained, Bush claimed that unsigning was a reasonable thing to do given his perception of the interests of the United States at that time. The United States had not irrevocably relinquished sovereignty by signing the protocol, as the revocation seems to have shown. Of course, it is hoped that states do not revoke their agreements lightly, but it is certainly true that such revocations can occur. (Of course, if states generally felt that they could revoke treaty agreements at will, the system of international law grounded in treaties – which has existed since at least the second millennium BCE – would be jeopardized.)

The worry about short-term loss of sovereignty is perhaps harder to deal with. On one level it is true that by entering into an agreement, an individual or a state is restricted from doing certain things it would wish to do. But here it

12 Hobbes, *Leviathan*, ch. 15, 5th paragraph.

13 Hobbes, *Leviathan*, ch. 15, 6th paragraph.

is important to note that the restriction is a self-imposed restriction. And given this fact, states generally do not enter into these arrangements unless they think that there is more to gain than what is lost in terms of short-term interests. Here we can again turn to Hobbes, who puts the point quite succinctly in relation to the individual's agreement to create and be bound by the sovereign:

> he that complaineth of injury from his Sovereign, complaineth of that whereof he himself is Author; and therefore ought not to accuse any man but himself.[14]

If a state complains that its sovereignty is being infringed by an institution that it has authorized to act, that state really complains about itself, since on this Hobbesian understanding of sovereignty and authority the state should not complain at all except to complain about its own past actions.

Another consideration is that perhaps too much emphasis has been placed on the consent dimension of sovereignty. Evan Fox-Decent and Evan J. Criddle have argued that sovereignty is better established by a fiduciary theory than a consent theory. They draw on an analogy from Kant concerning children. When parents procreate, they create children and they establish rights for these children. The children have not consented to the relationship; nor have the parents. But the rights have been acquired by the act of procreation. On this analogy, the state creates a situation where legal order is established and the citizens acquire rights to protection, along with duties to obey the state. If the state is not protecting the rights of its citizens, it cannot complain if another (international) institution intervenes to protect those rights. Whether one follows the fiduciary or consent model, states do not have a basis for complaint when international institutions protect the rights of that state's citizens.[15]

III BACKDOOR COSMOPOLITANISM

A variation of this sovereignty objection against international criminal tribunals and courts is that promotion of international tribunals attempts to create a cosmopolitan order by stealth in a piecemeal manner.[16] Such a

[14] Hobbes, *Leviathan*, ch. 18, 6th paragraph.

[15] See Evan Fox-Decent, *Sovereignty's Promise: The State as Fiduciary* (Oxford: Oxford University Press, 2012); Evan Fox-Decent and Evan J. Criddle, "The Fiduciary Constitution of Human Rights," *Legal Theory*, vol. 15 (2009), pp. 301–336.

[16] See Julian Ku and John Yoo, "Globalization and Sovereignty," *Berkeley Journal of International Law*, vol. 31 (2013), pp. 210–234, and Julian Ku and John Yoo, *Taming Globalization: International Law, the US Constitution, and the New World Order* (Oxford: Oxford University Press, 2012). Also see Darryl Robinson, "A Cosmopolitan Liberal Account of International Criminal Law," *Leiden Journal of International Law*, vol. 26, no. 1, (2013), pp. 127–153.

view takes on greater credence once it is recognized that customary international law, especially in the domain of international criminal law, has been claimed to apply against even those states that did not ratify the respective treaties such as the Rome Statute that created the ICC. If international law, even international criminal law, can be said to spread by means of custom rather than explicit treaty, then it may happen in the near future that the ICC claims to have jurisdiction over nationals of states such as the United States that have not ratified the Rome Statute. U.S. soldiers who operate abroad will be put in jeopardy in ways that clearly violate U.S. sovereignty. Indeed, the very idea of universal jurisdiction, which supposedly is the basis of the jurisdiction of the ICC, is already an acknowledgment that the State's sovereign jurisdiction will not be respected by international tribunals.[17]

In this section we will deal with the various concerns about freestanding international tribunals bringing in a de facto cosmopolitan state. Of course, the increasing reach of globalization could also be cited as a reason to worry about backdoor cosmopolitanism. Globalization connects parts of the world, including states, in spite of whether anyone consents to this or not. This may be regrettable but it also seems to be inevitable. In comparison with globalization, considerations such as universal jurisdiction are fairly minor influences of an emerging cosmopolitan legal order.

No one doubts that politics is increasingly international in focus. But the worry is that law is also becoming increasingly international and usurping what is traditionally the domain of politics. This worry links to sovereignty in that unlike the internationalization of politics, the internationalization of law is supposed to diminish state sovereignty. The objection is often somewhat confused, but we will try to address the clearest form of the objection in what follows in this section, leaving for a later chapter a full discussion of the worries about politics infringing on the domain of law.

In some sense, politics has always had an international component. Ancient city-states waged war against other city-states in order to settle various disputes, as well as to gain territory or access to natural resources. Some claim that law is only recently international in scope and that this development has occurred at the expense of settling disputes by political means. Yet, this is an odd objection when we compare dispute resolution by war with dispute resolution by means of courts. Far fewer people are killed, wounded, or enslaved when settlements are reached by law rather than by war.

[17] See John Bolton, "Universal Jurisdiction: Too Easily Sweeps Political Differences into Legal Arena," *Legal Times*, January 11, 1999.

However, the objection is not fully joined by this obvious response. That objection is often stated more subtly as one involving the inappropriate interference in the political sphere by courts. The heart of this worry is that international courts will operate in a way that is not accountable and is hence unrestrained by the good influences of political considerations. Politics, on this view, carries a heavy dose of realism and prudence into the interactions of states, whereas law tends to operate at the ideal and utopian level. When law usurps politics, the result is one that is often more destabilizing than before law's intrusion.

We would begin to mount our response by pointing out that the dividing line between politics and law is often very difficult to see. Courts are normally created by political processes. And this is surely true of the creation of international tribunals today. Multilateral treaties, which are the basis of many international tribunals, are hard to characterize in any other way than as political settlements reached by states. It is true that war is not employed to reach these agreements, but surely that cannot serve as a fundamental flaw. Indeed, negotiations among states that reach a settlement that creates a legal body such as a court are often best seen as a straightforward way for states to try to influence the likelihood of war as a means of dispute resolution in the future.

Now, if courts are somehow able to coerce states to enter into agreements that are against their own wishes, then there is perhaps room for worry. But again we would return to Hobbes's point that if certain states feel that these courts are not in their interests, those states can withdraw from the treaty regime, as is true for any contractual relationship. Yet for some, the obligations over time become grounded in customary international law, not merely in the consensual law of treaties. And here is where the worry about the rise of international customary law comes to the fore. If international customary law is moving toward being nonconsensual, then states will not have the recourse of simply withdrawing from the auspices of the jurisdiction of international law. Later we will say more about this objection as well as indicate what the advantages of the growth of international customary law are.

The backdoor cosmopolitan objection gets its traction when what were once merely consensual norms become nonconsensual norms. We seem to have moved away from a loose league of states that are involved in the international realm only to the extent that they currently choose to be involved. We seem to be entering a realm where states will find themselves bound by international law even though they no longer wish to be so bound, or perhaps even if they never indicated that they wanted to be so bound. And another dimension is that we have an increasing number of international tribunals being established in a way that begins to look like a system of international courts even though no one has authorized such a major component of a cosmopolitan state.

IV THE PRINCIPLE OF COMPLEMENTARITY

Our response to these serious challenges to international courts and tribunals is to argue that many sovereignty concerns are based on a failure to understand the nature of the ICC, which will now be a model for international criminal tribunals in the future. In particular, the principle of complementarity is such that state sovereignty is to a large extent preserved – the ICC will only intervene if the state is not willing or able to prosecute. We recognize that as with any international institution, there is the appearance that we are moving progressively toward a cosmopolitan state. But so far the various international institutions, and especially the international criminal tribunals and courts, have enjoyed the strong support of states. And these courts and tribunals have been careful not to act in such a way as to betray that support. Indeed, even the ICC can be severely restricted, even disbanded, if a sufficient number of states grow unhappy with how it is functioning.

In light of this point, a question can arise about the ad hoc tribunals that do not operate according to the principle of complementarity. The primary jurisdiction of the ICTY and ICTR, for example, originated with the Security Council directly. By comparison with the ICC, the ad hoc tribunals have a deficit of legitimacy. But it is important to note that these international criminal tribunals are ad hoc in that they have been instituted for a specific geographic domain and a specific time frame. And more importantly, the ad hoc tribunals have arisen where there has been a failed or failing state. There is here an implicit complementarity in that the target of the ad hoc tribunal cannot mount criminal trials for the perpetrators of mass crimes, or at least cannot do so without near-universal condemnation of any trials organized by the failed or failing state as being corrupt. And one last point is that ad hoc tribunals have now lost their usefulness with the establishment of a permanent international criminal tribunal, the ICC. It is hoped that we will see few if any ad hoc tribunals in the future.

Complementarity is especially important for our argument that sovereignty is not being abrogated by international courts and tribunals. Complementarity is merely an attempt to allow international courts to engage in gap-filling – operating only if a state cannot or will not prosecute. If states do not want to have a case handled by an international court, those states only have to take on the case themselves or at least indicate that they are willing to do so in the not too distant future. If a state cannot handle a case that it nonetheless does not want to be handled by an international court, there is still a problem, but one that is solvable by that state's diverting resources from other matters so that its own court system can handle such cases.

One might still object that the idea of gap-filling only makes sense if we think of a legal system that needs to have its gaps filled. In this view, the recourse to gap-filling is actually an admission that there is a cosmopolitan state that has emerged without the consent of the states of the world. Indeed, the response often heard is that not all issues can be dealt with through criminal trials. Yet this is not the way matters appear from the perspective of small or weak states that urge international courts to take up high-profile cases that those states want to have prosecuted but lack the resources to prosecute. Here there are cases that show that some of the states of the world look to international courts and tribunals to fill in the gaps that are left by their own domestic legal systems.

Consider the situation that led Sierra Leone to invite courts in the Hague to take the case of Charles Taylor, former president of Liberia. Not only did Sierra Leone lack the court infrastructure to prosecute such a high-profile case, but it also did not have the security resources to protect the population in the city where Taylor would be prosecuted or, for that matter, to protect the life of Taylor. There are also recent cases involving the Lord's Resistance Army (LRA), which ravaged large parts of the Democratic Republic of the Congo and Uganda. The trial of the LRA leaders was so dangerous that no state in central Africa was willing to prosecute the LRA in their domestic legal systems.

Let us look a bit more closely at the relevant documents describing the principle of complementarity before proceeding with the arguments that could depend on that principle to blunt the sovereignty worries. Here is the relevant part of the Rome Statute:

> Article 17
> Issues of admissibility
>
> 1. Having regard to paragraph 10 of the Preamble and article 1, the Court shall determine that a case is inadmissible where:
>   (a) The case is being investigated or prosecuted by a State which has jurisdiction over it, unless the State is unwilling or unable genuinely to carry out the investigation or prosecution;
>   (b) The case has been investigated by a State which has jurisdiction over it and the State has decided not to prosecute the person concerned, unless the decision resulted from the unwillingness or inability of the State genuinely to prosecute;

(c) The person concerned has already been tried for conduct which is the subject of the complaint, and a trial by the Court is not permitted under article 20, paragraph 3.[18]

Article 17 continues by discussing how the "unwilling or unable" determination is to be made, trying to ferret out cases where there is a total collapse of the national judicial system or where the state may be claiming to investigate or prosecute but is not really interested in bringing the alleged perpetrator to justice.[19]

The ICC claims that it is interested in making sure that justice is in fact done, and that the ICC will only step in if it is clear that a state is not really pursuing justice. The idea of one kind of justice for all states is indeed a cosmopolitan idea, but it is not necessarily the kind of cosmopolitan idea that interferes with state sovereignty. Yet there will be interference with state sovereignty in some cases.

A state that chooses not to prosecute its citizens for clear-cut violations of international criminal law will run afoul of the ICC if the ICC determines that the state's decision was not based on a good faith acceptance of the terms of the complementarity principle. Two factors are important in assessing this situation. First, we are only talking about states that have ratified the ICC's Rome Statute, so there is a presumption (and in fact evidence) that the state has agreed to the application of the principle of complementarity. But we also note that it is the ICC that decides whether the state is acting in good faith, and hence determines whether or not the ICC can interfere with the state.

The fact that the state has ratified the Rome Statute, with its complementarity principle, seems to mean that the state has agreed to let the ICC overrule it in certain matters. But the fact that it is the ICC that decides whether the principle of complementarity has been satisfied means that the ICC does indeed overrule the decisions of the state, seemingly placing itself procedurally above the state and apparently abridging the state's sovereignty. So, it is not easy to say that a member state's sovereignty has been abridged when the ICC decides to prosecute that state's citizen over the objection of the state.

The fact that the ICC seems to be reluctant to prosecute when a state has indicated that it is investigating a case means that the abridgment of sovereignty, if it is to be so understood, has so far not been much of an issue. It appears that only when a state is clearly not engaging in good faith efforts to prosecute would the ICC contemplate prosecution without state consent. But it remains a good question why such a state does not simply withdraw from

18 Rome Statute, Art. 17.
19 Ibid.

the Rome Statute. And it is a bit of mystery why a state that strongly believes that one of its citizens should not be prosecuted for violations of international criminal law does not either launch a legitimate investigation or simply withdraw from the ICC's jurisdiction. Given these live options for a state, it is hard to see that a state has had its sovereignty abridged when it remains in the ICC's orbit and finds that one of its citizens is being brought before an international criminal court in the Hague.

V FEDERATED SOVEREIGNTY

Another part of our response is that sovereignty does not need to be understood as it was in the sixteenth and seventeenth centuries at the time of Bodin and Hobbes. We can conceive of a kind of federated sovereignty, promulgated in the eighteenth century by the founders of the American Constitution. Federated sovereignty allows for zones of jurisdiction over which different entities can claim sovereignty without upsetting the sovereignty claims concerning other zones.[20] Universal jurisdiction is only a serious problem for sovereignty if it means that it can allow international institutions to intrude into the zone of jurisdiction that is clearly the prerogative of states. But that is not how international criminal tribunals have acted or are supposed to act.

Indeed, one way to understand the Rome Statute is that it creates a zone of sovereignty over a very limited number of cases of criminal law. And the zone that is created remains subject to the complementarity principle. It is true that the zone of sovereignty of the ICC does overlap with the traditional zone of jurisdiction of states, namely, criminal prosecution of the state's own citizens. Yet it is possible to separate domestic criminal jurisdiction from international criminal jurisdiction. Indeed, if a state has not incorporated relevant international criminal laws in its own constitution, there is no conflict if the ICC prosecutes these crimes because the state in question could not do so in any event. This response is not open to the ICC defender if the state in question has incorporated international criminal law in its constitution.

Federated sovereignty is not the same as divided sovereignty. Sovereignty arguably cannot be divided, at least not in a way that makes two different entities sovereign over the same territory or jurisdiction concerning the same matters. But sovereignty can be federated in the sense that different matters can be subject to different rules and rulers, even if the domain of territory or jurisdiction is the same. Various models for federation can be conceived. One model is the way a national state government rules over certain matters

[20] See generally *The Federalist Papers*.

affecting the whole state, but where a province's government rules over matters that only, or largely, affect the particular province.

On the basis of either of these models one could have something like universal jurisdiction and yet not have clear violations of sovereignty. In the model of a state and its province, it could be said that all people of the state are governed by state laws, and also that all people of the province are governed by laws of the province. "Universality" is a term that can be limited by restrictions on the universe of jurisdiction. It is true that the principle of universality is most typically meant to apply to the domain of all people in the world. In this usage of universality, there cannot be two universal domains or jurisdictions. But there certainly can be one domain, the domain of international tribunals, that governs everyone in the world, and another domain of domestic tribunals that govern only those who are citizens or members of a given domestic state.

Yet, there are worries about the principle of universality that we have not yet addressed. In particular, the very idea of universal jurisdiction seems to presume that there is a jurisdiction covering the whole world. And in some respects that is correct, although this idea of universal jurisdiction does not yet convey who is to prosecute. The ICC's jurisdiction, as explained in the discussion of complementarity, is modest in that it will not prosecute on the basis of universal jurisdiction unless the state whose citizens are involved is not willing or able to prosecute, according to the conditions laid out in article 17 of the Rome Statute. The worry about the abridgment of sovereignty because of a kind of federated model of jurisdiction is offset by article 17's explicit prohibition of the ICC from prosecuting unless the state has demonstrated that it is unwilling or unable to do so.

Following a federated model of sovereignty in terms of universal jurisdiction should minimize the worries about the abridgment of state sovereignty by the ICC when it prosecutes international crimes. It is true that some states will feel pressured to send cases to the ICC if their judicial system is rudimentary. But this will only be the case for states that have already ratified the Rome Statute, and that could revoke the ratification if the state considered the international pressure to send cases to the ICC too intrusive.

Finally, let us consider the effect on sovereignty of the international pressure the ICC can mount, especially against already weak states, to transfer defendants to the Hague rather than to prosecute these defendants in the state's domestic courts. We recognize the gravity of this concern, whether actually a concern today or a concern that could easily manifest itself in the future. Weak states may indeed face strong pressure to send defendants to the ICC, if they are not already facing such pressure. We believe that it is not appropriate for the ICC or its supporters to put such pressure on weak states.

The concerns about sovereignty are important, and for the ICC to prevent such concerns it must not pressure or coerce weak states to send defendants to the Hague. This is one of the recommendations that we would make for avoiding even the appearance that state sovereignty is not being respected by the ICC.

VI THE BENEFITS OF INTERNATIONAL CUSTOMARY LAW

Customary international law is law that meets two conditions. First, there must be state practice where many states act as if they are bound by customary international legal norms. Second, there must be *opinio juris*, where states act as if they are bound for the reason that they find customary standards to be binding on them. When enough states have satisfied these conditions, then a standard is declared to be binding not only on the states that indicate that they feel bound, but also on all other states. There is a controversial way for a state to attempt to exempt itself from a customary international legal norm – namely, by persistently declaring that it does not regard itself to be so bound. But this doctrine of persistent objection remains controversial, especially among the strongest advocates of expanding the reach of international customary law today, and most especially concerning *jus cogens* norms.

In principle, we believe that there is no clear loss of sovereignty because of the rise of international customary law. Customary international law is, in the end, still tethered to that to which states have indicated that they consent. And so if a state has been a "persistent objector," it is, in our view, not bound by the customary norms to which it has objected. This is especially true in the domain of international criminal law. Again, even if a state has ratified the Rome Statute, the principle of complementarity allows for a state to block the jurisdictional claim of the ICC by demonstrating that the state is willing and able to prosecute the crime in its domestic courts and tribunals. And states that have not ratified the Rome Statute are not bound by its terms – their citizens are blocked from prosecution as a result of lack of jurisdiction of the ICC. In these ways, most states can block any possible usurpation of sovereignty by the ICC's attempting to prosecute their nationals in the Hague. But there will remain some states that lack the means to prosecute in their domestic courts and tribunals or feel under increased pressure to extradite their citizens to the Hague, and for these few states there is still a sovereignty concern.

In addition, there is a worry about how weak states might be pressured by advocates of an expanded domain of international customary law. At least in part, this is because there is a strong current of support for extending universal jurisdiction even to those states that have not ratified the ICC. States such as the United States, China, Russia, and Israel will easily be able to resist such pressure and fend off attempts to prosecute their nationals in international courts or in the domestic courts of other states. But weak states, especially those that depend on the generosity of strong states, will not be able to avoid such pressure easily. Again, we would argue that this kind of pressure is inappropriate and can ultimately undermine the support for the ICC.

So, there are both clear cut problems with and clear cut advantages to the increasing scope of customary international law today. We will indicate some of the advantages of that increasing scope. In Section VII we will continue this topic by discussing the serious disadvantages of the expanding reach of customary international law. At this point let us contrast the role of the common law in domestic Anglo-American legal systems with the role of customary international law in the international legal system – for in both systems we have customary law that rises to a higher level. In Anglo-American law the common law is a way for court decisions to supplement and fill in the gaps of existing legal statutes, often by reference to customary norms. By their very nature, statutes are general in form, and yet there are often gaps insofar as the statute-makers cannot easily anticipate all of the likely cases that will fall under the general statute.

By contrast with statutes, court decisions are highly specific. The common law is the set of court decisions that addresses the application of the general statutes to highly specific facts of particular cases. As Oliver Wendell Holmes said, the common law creates "a path" for judges to follow as they try to make the statutes fit the facts.[21] The common law also provides a path for the citizenry to attempt to anticipate how courts will rule on cases that concern them. Referring to the path of the common law, citizens can anticipate what they will be held responsible for, especially when the likely application of the statutes is unclear. There would be much less certainty to the law if there were no common law in Anglo-American legal systems.

In international law, there are even more gaps in the "statutes" than is typical in domestic law. International "statutes" are primarily treaties that hold only for those states that have in fact ratified the treaties. There are treaties between just two states, but what is of most interest are multilateral treaties among large numbers of states. Yet even very large multilateral treaties do not have the same scope as domestic statutes, which apply to all of the provinces or states within a domestic state. So, at least in this sense, the international legal system is more fragmented and more gap-filled than typical domestic legal systems.

[21] Oliver Wendell Holmes Jr., "The Path of the Law," *Harvard Law Review*, vol. X (1897).

Customary international law increasingly fills gaps by pulling into the domain of large multilateral treaties even some of those states that did not ratify the treaty. This is a clear advantage for the path of international law as well as for the idea that all states are bound to follow international law. And if there is an advantage to having a single system of law across humanity, it is much easier to achieve it through the auspices of customary international law than by having to convince all states to ratify each of the multilateral treaties positively.

We believe that there are significant advantages in having a nearly gapless system of international law by adding customary legal norms to fill gaps, even as we recognize that there are major problems when such a system is extended to criminal matters. One of the most significant advantages of expanding the reach of customary international law is that we move ever closer to a true international legal system. Not only does a treaty-based system leave out many states – namely, those who have not, for whatever reason, ratified the treaties in question. But there is also the problem of states that do ratify a given treaty, but who then decide to "unsign" it once this state's own citizens face the prospect of prosecution at the Hague.

There is little that can be done about the problem of "unsigning" treaties unless there is another source of binding international law that can be appealed to that is not itself consensual, such as customary international law. This is the clear advantage of customary international law, insofar as it provides a basis for blocking states from doing what they said they would not do, namely, "unsigning" the treaties they have already ratified. A state clearly could not satisfy the conditions of being a persistent objector to a customary international law by "unsigning" a previously signed treaty. There is, however, another strategy that appeals to us more, although it is not without significant problems as well. Mark Janis has proposed that there are procedural as well as substantive *jus cogens* norms in international law.[22] One such *jus cogens* norm in his view is the norm undergirding *pacta sunt servanda*, the norm that posits the bindingness of what a state has agreed to do. We thus agree that *jus cogens* norms are not subject to the persistent objector problem, but we do not see those norms as primarily customary norms in any event.[23]

Relying on *jus cogens* norms has, in our view, fewer normative problems than relying on customary international law to block states from reneging on their treaty agreements. One reason the *jus cogens* strategy is more acceptable

[22] See Mark Janis, "The Nature of Jus Cogens," *Connecticut Journal of International Law*, vol. 3 (1988), pp. 359–363.

[23] See Larry May, *Crimes against Humanity: A Normative Account* (New York: Cambridge University Press, 2005), especially chapter 2.

normatively is that like a promise, the idea that one is bound to do what one committed oneself to do is a natural extension, and indeed a constitutive element, of the idea of engaging in voluntary self-binding. Two drawbacks should be noted. First, the idea of procedural *jus cogens* norms is itself highly controversial. And, second, this only solves the problem of blocking states from withdrawing from international agreements that they have already ratified. This strategy does not create a binding norm for those states that have not agreed to be bound by an international legal regime. But given the problems with the strategy of extending customary international law, as we outline next, the *jus cogens* strategy is in our view normatively the least problematic.

VII THE ABIDING PROBLEMS WITH CUSTOMARY INTERNATIONAL LAW

The disadvantages of the increasing scope of customary international law should also be apparent from what has already been said. States that did not agree with the terms of a given multilateral treaty and who explicitly chose not to ratify the treaty could now find themselves bound by the terms of a treaty that they find unacceptable. Even those states who have been persistent objectors to a given treaty may nonetheless eventually find themselves swept up into the treaty regime not by ratification but by application of customary international law. If merely the passage of time is enough to make of a limited-scope treaty one that extends to all states, then the will of the state and its people can be thwarted in ways that have potentially grave consequences for state sovereignty.

As we have said, the least controversial way to institute international law from the standpoint of sovereignty worries is by multilateral treaties. Only those states that consent to be governed by a particular international legal regime will be bound by it. But the strong and wealthy states have often failed to ratify large multilateral treaties such as the Rome Statute. Yet, without these states' agreeing to the regime of international criminal law, international criminal tribunals have faced a number of practical and normative problems. This is a dilemma for those who support international criminal tribunals, and it is no wonder that many have signed on to the agenda of supplementing multilateral treaties with international customary law.

Customary international law could be compared to the common law or customary law in domestic jurisdictions, as we indicated. Customary or common law is not ratified by legislatures in the way that statutes are. And so one could argue that customary or common law is not as clearly binding as is statutory law. But in the domestic case there is a system of law that has itself been accepted by the populace, at least tacitly, which includes both statutory as well as customary or common law. In the international arena there has not been a similar acceptance, tacit or otherwise, that states are bound by customary international law.

Indeed, there is not even a general acceptance among all states at the present that there is an international community or society that is governed by law. From the standpoint of sovereignty concerns, the main subject of this current chapter, those who are critical of international criminal tribunals are also critical of the idea that there is an international community or society governed by law. This is why the least controversial basis for international criminal tribunals is multilateral treaties.

But it will be a challenge for criminal law to succeed at achieving its aims, practically as well as normatively, if it must rely on the consent of those who are to be subject to it. Criminal law is generally a nonconsensual form of law. So, if a state feels bound by criminal law only as a matter of consent, that state can seemingly withdraw consent whenever its citizens are indicted or arrested by an international criminal tribunal. And matters are worse yet if the state never consented to the criminal regime in the first place – its citizens will not have to recognize the jurisdiction of the tribunal even when it is clear that these citizens had violated international criminal law.

In our view, the increasing scope of customary international law is more of a threat to state sovereignty than is the rise of international criminal courts and tribunals. Insofar as international criminal law remains consensual, sovereignty worries can be addressed. But with the rise of nonconsensual customary international law, sovereignty worries move front and center again. One of the central sovereignty worries is that international courts could trump domestic courts, or that international criminal law could trump domestic criminal law. We leave unresolved the question of whether preserving strong state sovereignty is good or bad and merely indicate that the threat to state sovereignty is indeed real as universal jurisdiction and customary international law increasingly are employed to justify the prosecution of people whose state objects to these prosecutions.

So, we are now in a position to make another recommendation about state sovereignty. To counteract the rise of universal jurisdiction and customary international law, we recommend a counterweight – a return to the doctrine of persistent state objection. According to this doctrine, now somewhat lapsing, a state can block its being swept up into a treaty regime that state finds unacceptable by continuing to voice opposition to that treaty regime. Persistent objectors should not be overcome by the length of time or strength of the coalition of states that supports a given treaty regime. International law should thus remain to a certain extent fragmented in order to accommodate the sovereignty worries especially of states that are relatively weak or that hold strongly different views from the majority of states about what is the best legal regime for states.

Let us finally consider some of the problems that will still have to be addressed in a system of criminal law that is fragmented in the way we have discussed. One issue that looms large, and that we will address in greater detail in a later chapter, is the fairness of a checkerboard system where citizens of some states are liable for serious punishments and citizens from other states are not liable at all, at least under international criminal law, even though they have committed the very same crimes. Of course any system of law will be somewhat checkerboard in that prosecutors will only pursue a fraction of the defendants who could be prosecuted, largely as a result of scarcity of legal resources. But in international criminal tribunals the situation will be worse, since whole categories of defendants will not be pursued for lack of jurisdiction, and there may not be prosecution under some other jurisdiction either, leaving some defendants who have committed horrible mass crimes off the hook.

Here is where cooperation by states in pursuing domestic prosecutions for violations of international criminal law can be so important. It is not our view that there is a legal obligation that such prosecutions must take place, given that some states have not ratified the Rome Statute. But it is of increasing importance that especially the strong and wealthy states who have not signed or ratified the Rome Statute nonetheless adopt the main international criminal laws in their own body of domestic law.

Of course, relying on the powerful and wealthy states to subject themselves to international criminal law voluntarily is not an ideal situation since these states will undoubtedly continue to be skeptical about the risks of binding themselves to international criminal law. But there are less obvious problems when states employ international law in their own prosecutions than when states are subjected to an international criminal law regime where prosecutions take place in the Hague.

As we said earlier, the principle of complementarity is supposed to make states less hostile to international criminal law, but this principle has still raised worries that states might be subject to prosecutions in the Hague if they refuse to prosecute crimes domestically. At least in this sense, states should find the idea of passing their own statutes about genocide or crimes against humanity preferable, since these states will have greater control over whether prosecutions for violations of such crimes should occur than if they are part of a regime that is centered in the Hague.

There remains an abiding problem about international criminal tribunals concerning sovereignty worries that are exacerbated by the growing strength of international customary law. The more general sovereignty worries can be addressed successfully, as we have shown in this chapter. Sovereignty is not absolute, just as autonomy is not. And in any event a state's treaty agreement to block certain future options is not clearly a violation of sovereignty; indeed it can be rendered entirely consistent with increasing a state's options in the world, just as is true of other agreements and contracts. But the same cannot be said of strategies that bind states against their wills, such as is found increasingly in the expansion of customary international law. Critics of international criminal tribunals have often misidentified the source of legitimate worry grounded in sovereignty – following Bodin, who failed to see that state sovereignty could be divided in such a way that sovereignty of the state could actually be enhanced by supporting certain consensual collective arrangements. Philosophers such as Hobbes and Locke could easily admit room for international leagues as not violating state sovereignty. Only when there are nonconsensual international tribunals is there truly cause for alarm. But we have nonetheless proposed various strategies for alleviating some of these worries.

3

Punishment

Critics have pointed out that there is not and is unlikely to be a deterrent effect of international criminal punishment since the likelihood of being punished is so remote. A retributive effect is also highly suspicious since the military and political leaders in the international dock think that what they have done is praiseworthy, not something for which they should suffer guilt or shame. Even the expressivist rationale for punishing has been criticized because we cannot assume that the values expressed by a court in the Hague will be taken sufficiently seriously by the rest of the world.[1] So, then, how can the use of international criminal tribunals to punish those who have been convicted of atrocities be justified? Even if we see international criminal tribunals as the appropriate bodies for assigning responsibility, we must be able to identify a rationale for punishing the responsible parties. In Chapter 3, we will attempt to construct and defend such a rationale.

In Section I, we begin with a brief overview of the various theories of punishment that exist in domestic law and consider which of these have had the most influence in the international arena. In Section II, we explore deterrence as a possible rationale for punishment in international law and conclude that this is unlikely. Section III considers retribution as another possible rationale for punishment in international criminal law; Section IV examines expressivist justifications for punishment in international law. In Section V, we claim that the best way to think about international criminal punishment is through a combined approach, where each of these three justifications plays a role in collectively justifying international criminal punishment. Section VI identifies several other philosophical problems related to the practice of punishing in international law. Finally, we argue in Section VII that despite the

[1] See Mark Drumbl, *Atrocity, Punishment, and International Law* (New York: Cambridge University Press, 2007).

criticisms leveled against each justification for punishment of international crimes, and the practical problems the international criminal courts and tribunals have faced thus far, an international scheme of punishment can be normatively defended on the basis of the cumulative benefits of having international criminal courts and tribunals.

I PUNISHMENT AND INTERNATIONAL CRIMES

Punishment involves the intentional incapacitation or infliction of pain by an authoritative institution on one who has been deemed liable to such treatment. The purpose of punishment can be seen as either forward-looking or backward-looking. On a backward-looking view of punishment, a law has been broken and punishment is inflicted as part of the system of law enforcement. Punishment is *deserved* by the person who breaks the law and is inflicted on the basis of the mental state and the acts taken by the person who has broken the law. On the forward-looking view, punishment is inflicted in order to prevent future harms from occurring.

Historically, the primary justifications for punishment are retribution, deterrence, rehabilitation, and incapacitation. We will not address rehabilitation here, as it has not been propounded as a justification for punishment in international criminal law. Any discussion of incapacitation will fall under our discussion of specific deterrence. Thus, we focus on retribution, deterrence, and the newer justification of expressivism as possible justifications for punishment by international criminal tribunals.

Retributivism, a backward-looking justification for punishment, is the justification most directly linked to the actor. Punishment is inflicted as retribution for the specific harm caused by the actor. Immanuel Kant argued that this was the only legitimate form of punishment, as the use of a criminal as a means to promote some good for society or the criminal himself was impermissible.[2] The principle of proportionality requires that the punishment for an offense must be relative to the harmfulness of the actor's behavior. Thus, for the retributivist, a system of punishment must reflect the imposition of more severe penalties for more severe crimes.

Jeremy Bentham was one of the most prominent advocates for a system of punishment based on deterrence rather than desert. Bentham argued that the duty of the state was "to promote the happiness of the society, by punishing and rewarding."[3] All penalties, for Bentham, were only permissible insofar as

[2] Immanuel Kant, *Metaphysics of Morals*, section 49.

[3] Jeremy Bentham, *An Introduction to the Principles of Morals and Legislation*, edited by and with an introduction by W. Harrison (New York: Macmillan, 1948), p. 125.

they were used to avert greater evil, i.e., violations of the law.[4] The preventative aims of deterrence are directed at individual actors and also at society as a whole. While the punishment itself is inflicted only on an individual actor, the penalties are intended to deter all potential law violators, including but not limited to the individual actor. Deterrence is thus also premised on the principle of proportionality, but while the retributivist claims that punishment must be measured in relation to what an actor deserves, deterrence-based accounts maintain that the proper amount of punishment is that which will prevent any amount of harm greater than that inflicted by the punishment itself.

The expressivist account of punishment identifies the purpose of punishment as serving as an articulation of the appropriate reaction to criminal acts, on the part of a society, government, or other institution. On this account, the imposition of punishment "says something," or communicates emotions such as anger, resentment, or frustration to the criminals themselves and to a broader community. The result of punishment is, for the expressivist, the garnering of respect for the laws themselves.

When we move to the international scene, we are confronted with two important and interrelated questions. First, we have to identify a different source of authority for punishing than those sources that are readily apparent in domestic arenas. This authority is a subject we consider more fully in other chapters. However, we briefly note that universal jurisdiction over individuals (and a corresponding ability to punish individuals) is quite new in international law. Historically, only pirates were considered individual criminals under international law.[5] The International Military Tribunal at Nuremberg was the first international criminal tribunal to expand the reach of international criminal law and assert the authority to punish individuals for crimes committed in any jurisdiction in the world.

Assuming we can identify a body with the authority to punish, we then ask, "For what purpose do we seek to punish?" Even if an international institution has the requisite authority to punish, there should still be an identifiable purpose or goal of punishment. These justifications may look similar to those given by domestic institutions in some cases, but in others the domestic rationale may not translate to international criminal acts. While the ICC's Rome Statute is clear in stating its purpose for existing, namely, to "put an end to impunity for the perpetrators of these crimes and thus to contribute to the prevention of [the most serious crimes of concern to the international

4 Ibid.

5 Charles C. Hyde, *International Law, Chiefly as Interpreted and Applied by the United States* (Boston: Little, Brown, 1945), pp. 768–770.

community]"[6] and "to guarantee lasting respect for and the enforcement of international justice,"[7] it does not state a specific purpose for imposing punishment on those who are convicted under its authority. The Rome Statute merely lays out the permissible penalties for convicted international criminals, which are limited to (a) "imprisonment for a specified number of years, which may not exceed a maximum of 30 years,"[8] (b) "life imprisonment when justified by the extreme gravity of the crime and the individual circumstances of the convicted person,"[9] (c) a "fine under the criteria provided for in the Rules of Procedure and Evidence,"[10] or (d) a "forfeiture of proceeds, property and assets derived directly or indirectly from that crime, without prejudice to the rights of bona fide third parties."[11] The ad hoc tribunals contain similar wording related to their purpose and the punishment of duly convicted criminals.

Given the ambiguity of the foundational documents of international criminal tribunals, the international community is left to construct its own narrative justifying punishment of international criminals by international criminal tribunals. Sections II–IV will focus on the possible rationales of deterrence, retributivism, and expressivism for international criminal tribunals.

II DETERRENCE

International criminal courts could serve as a deterrent for future atrocities. The punishment imposed by the courts could create either a general deterrent effect or a specific deterrent effect, or both. As a specific deterrent, punishment imposed by international criminal courts on international criminals would prevent those criminals from reoffending merely in virtue of their incarceration. Once the specific criminals have served their time and been allowed to reenter society, the experience of past incarceration and the threat of future punishment could prevent reoffense even after release. The reoffense of a given individual is virtually guaranteed not to occur during their incarceration. But given the collective nature of most international crime, it is hard to assess the specific deterrent effect on that individual upon his/her release from prison.

As a general deterrent, punishment imposed by international criminal courts on international criminals stands to deter other would-be

6 Rome Statute, preamble.
7 Ibid.
8 Ibid., art. 77, 1(a).
9 Ibid., art. 77, 1(b).
10 Ibid., art. 77, 2(a).
11 Ibid., art. 77, 2(b).

criminals from planning or participating in atrocities through the threat of punishment. If punishment is consistently imposed for certain types of crimes, potential criminals are on notice that they are likely to face punishment if they are convicted of such crimes. The overwhelming focus of international criminal law has been on general deterrence.[12] In 2005, as the UN secretary-general encouraged member states to cooperate with international criminal courts and tribunals, he noted the importance of "increas[ing] avenues of redress for the victims of atrocities and deter[ring] further horrors."[13]

Accordingly, proponents of deterrence as a justification for punishment by international criminal tribunals point to the existence of judicial systems with the support of the international community and the legal authority to punish as an institution capable of deterring future crimes. Indeed, the preamble of the Rome Statute, which, as noted, states its goals of ending impunity and contributing to the prevention of atrocities as goals of the ICC, can be read at least to intend such a deterrent effect. Supporters of the ICC identify a direct link between ending impunity and deterring future atrocities.

Mark Drumbl and others have argued that because it is so unlikely that any given individual will be prosecuted for his participation in atrocities, international criminal law is unlikely to be a successful deterrent.[14] Domestic criminal law has a deterrent effect to the extent that a potential criminal sees similarly-situated individuals called to account for their crimes in a predictable and consistent manner. International criminal law, on the other hand, is applied selectively, as only certain conflicts result in criminal prosecution and only certain individuals are called to account for their crimes within a given conflict. The size and complex nature of these conflicts force international criminal courts and tribunals to limit the scope of their prosecutions to those thought to be most culpable for the violence, and these restrictions may allow many guilty individuals to live on in impunity

However, this should not be a reason not to support international criminal law. Rather, it should support its development and acceptance. The Nuremberg tribunal was established to ensure that we never again would face the scourge of mass violence. We continue to face it, and there continues to be impunity. As Drumbl notes, "To the extent that international criminal law pins blame for atrocity on a small number of horrible individuals, who generally control a state apparatus, it achieves some justice and curbs atrocity as a

[12] Drumbl, *Atrocity, Punishment, and International Law*, p. 169.

[13] Report of the Secretary-General, In Larger Freedom: Towards Development, Human Rights, and Security for All, UN Doc. A/59/2005, ¶ 138 (March 21, 2005).

[14] Drumbl, *Atrocity, Punishment, and International Law*, p. 169.

tool of a state's foreign or domestic policy."[15] But he goes on to express concern that focusing on international criminal prosecutions for a few may allow us to shift "our gaze away from the many other actors involved in the tapestry of atrocity" and prevent us from rooting out other causes of violence.[16] It seems to us, however, that international criminal prosecutions are necessary, if not sufficient, for achieving justice and producing a deterrent effect. Either we must give up on international criminal law altogether, or we have to recognize that it will take time (and successful prosecutions) for certain aspects of international criminal law to be effective. We prefer the latter option.

Deterrence (both specific and general) only works if the possibility of punishment actually affects actors' decisions to participate in criminal activities. This means that for a system of punishment to deter a would-be violator, she must know the rule, perceive any possible punishment as worse than the benefit of the violation, and have the capacity to use the knowledge to affect her decision making.[17] If we assume that would-be violators act rationally and with knowledge of the law, our main concern in assessing possibilities for a deterrent effect is the cost–benefit analysis. Economic accounts of deterrence are generally premised on the idea that people engage in wrongdoing for personal gain and that they will be less likely to do so if there is an additional cost to their wrongdoing, namely, that they will face prison time if caught and convicted.[18] Economists seek to explain criminal behavior as unrelated to the specific preferences of individuals, and instead argue that rational actors share fixed preferences.[19] Sociological accounts allow for individual preferences and take a much broader approach to what might influence a potential criminal.[20]

Accordingly, we should focus on what the original motivations of the actors were at the time they acted, as well as what will likely be the motivations of the actors committing international crimes in the future.[21] Here it matters significantly that international criminals act largely out of patriotic or other positive

15 Ibid., p. 173.

16 Ibid.

17 Paul H. Robinson and John M. Darley, "The Role of Deterrence in the Formulation of Criminal Law Rules: At Its Worst When Doing Its Best," *Georgetown Law Review*, vol. 91 (2002), pp. 949, 953.

18 See ibid.; see also Yvonne Dutton, "Crime and Punishment: Assessing Deterrence Theory in the Context of Somali Piracy," *George Washington International Law Review*, vol. 46 (2014), p. 608.

19 Patrick Keenan, "The New Deterrence: Crime and Policy in the Age of Globalization," *Iowa Law Review*, vol. 91 (2006), pp. 505, 516.

20 Ibid., p. 523.

21 See Padraig McAuliffe, "Suspended Disbelief? The Curious Endurance of the Deterrence Rationale in International Criminal Law," *New Zealand Journal of Public and International Law*, vol. 10 (December 2012), pp. 227–262.

motives rather than personal or economic self-interest.[22] Thus, a purely economic cost–benefit analysis will not be useful in the international context. As Margaret deGuzman notes, individuals who commit genocide and crimes against humanity are usually in positions of power, and they believe that their actions are morally appropriate rather than morally risky.[23] They claim to be acting to protect their community or otherwise to pursue religious or political justice. This makes the cost–benefit analysis quite different from that of someone who only stands to benefit personally from committing a crime. Rather, a would-be criminal who thinks she stands on the moral high ground is likely to take great personal risk in order to promote her ends.

So if an individual acts not out of self-interest but out of more noble motives, then any possible deterrent effect within the cost–benefit analysis can only be achieved if the costs are both certain and severe. A change in an individual's self-interested motivations will not necessarily affect the wrongdoer.[24] A wrongdoer who has purely idealistic (and self-sacrificing) motives is unlikely to be deterred by any consideration. But the criminal who has mixed self-interested and idealistic motives may be deterred. A would-be criminal who knows that he will likely be arrested, convicted, and sentenced to substantial punishment may see the expected sanction as worse than the expected benefits and decide to abstain from committing a crime.[25]

Even if we were to assume that the motivations of actors were such that they could be deterred from committing atrocities such as genocide or crimes against humanity by the existence of systems of punishment within international criminal tribunals, we would still be hard-pressed to assess such a deterrent effect. It is unlikely that we could collect empirical data on deterring international crimes because it would be difficult to know that a crime would have occurred save for some intervention. To date, there is some anecdotal evidence supporting a deterrent effect on some actors, but there has been no

[22] See, e.g., Jan Klabbers, "Just Revenge? The Deterrence Argument in International Criminal Law," *Finnish Yearbook of International Law*, vol. 12 (2001), pp. 249, 253; Robert D. Sloane, "The Expressive Capacity of International Punishment: The Limits of the National Law Analogy and the Potential of International Criminal Law," *Stanford Journal of International Law*, vol. 43 (2007), p. 81.

[23] Margaret M. DeGuzman, "Harsh Justice for International Crimes?" *Yale Journal of International Law*, vol. 39, no. 1 (2013), pp. 15–16; see also Klabbers, "Just Revenge?" and McAuliffe, "Suspended Disbelief."

[24] See Martti Koskenniemi, "Between Impunity and Show Trials," *Max Planck Yearbook of International Law*, vol. 6 (2002).

[25] See generally Keenan, "New Deterrence"; see also Julian Ku and Jide Nzelibe, "Do International Criminal Tribunals Deter or Exacerbate Humanitarian Atrocities?" *Washington University Law*, vol. 84 (2006), p. 777.

systematic study of the deterrent effect of growing international criminal institutions on international crime.[26]

What we need is to support and further develop systems of international criminal prosecution in order to achieve the possibility of a deterrent effect. First, the likelihood of criminal prosecution needs to be increased through the predictable and consistent prosecution of international criminals. There should not be an expectation of impunity for genocide and crimes against humanity. The norm should be prosecution and punishment, so that individuals considering criminal activity can weigh the impact of the activity against their own freedom. But additionally, we should recognize the impact of strong international legal institutions on the social norms associated with international crime. If most of the international community can collectively condemn the violence associated with international crimes, potential criminals might be less inclined to claim the moral high ground. It is certainly possible that they will not. But we contend that prospects for deterrence should encourage, rather than count against, the development of international criminal law.

Empirical limitations should not prevent us from analyzing the impact of international criminal tribunals on powerful actors. The ICC, in particular, is in its infancy in terms of successful prosecution of international criminals. Just as we cannot assume the deterrent effect of international criminal tribunals, we also cannot assume its absence. If international criminal tribunals can begin to end impunity through conviction and punishment of criminals, then we can reasonably anticipate some impact on world leaders. Perhaps most actors with religious or patriotic reasons for committing atrocities would not be deterred, but perhaps some lower-level political actors would have a reason to stop and think about the consequences before blindly following their undeterred leader. Again, we cannot demonstrate a statistically significant deterrent effect of international criminal tribunals, but neither should we rule it out.

III RETRIBUTION

Retribution is another justification for punishment at the hands of international criminal courts. The idea that actors who have created massive harms in the world should have to pay for their actions has great intuitive appeal. Those who commit crimes against humanity deserve proportionate punishment, and therefore, all else being equal, they should receive proportionate punishment.

[26] See generally William W. Burke-White, "Complementarity in Practice: The International Criminal Court as Part of a System of Multi-Level Global Governance in the Democratic Republic of Congo," *Leiden Journal of International Law*, vol. 18 (2005), pp. 557, 587.

Proponents of retributivist justifications of international criminal tribunals argue that individual responsibility must be imposed on those who are found guilty of serious wrongdoing in order to vindicate the rights of the victims who have been wronged.

Ad hoc tribunals can be pointed to as places where victims of genocide and crimes against humanity see retribution in the form of the punishment of their attackers. They have thus been hailed by some as successful sources of justice for these victims. Especially in the cases of the tribunals in Lebanon, Sierra Leone, and Cambodia, victims have been able to participate in the criminal proceedings as witnesses or have been able at least to view the criminal process of assessing guilt and assigning appropriate punishment. In these cases, whether or not those convicted are affected by the punishment they receive, the retributive effect of the ad hoc international criminal tribunals may at least exist for the victims.

For retribution to work as a justification for international criminal courts and tribunals, we must be able to establish what any given individual *deserves* in terms of punishment. The actor should be punished based on the seriousness of the harm and his individual culpability for the harm caused.[27] The more serious the crime, and the more culpable the individual, the more punishment is deserved. Legal scholars have moved in the direction of promoting community norms as the appropriate foundation for retributive punishment.[28] However, retributivist international criminal law scholars generally argue for a cardinal ordering of desert.[29] Jens David Ohlin has argued that proportionality suggests international criminal courts and tribunals should not consider the relative desert of criminals, but should impose sentences in accordance with the inherent gravity of crimes.[30] Ohlin states that "prison sentences for severe crimes need to be long to capture the moral depravity of these acts adequately, consistent with Kantian and deontological inspirations."[31] This would result in many international criminals' receiving similarly harsh sentences for a wide range of crimes, but Ohlin claims that this is what retribution requires: a recognition of the seriousness of the crime and corresponding punishment.[32] It

27 See deGuzman, "Harsh Justice," p. 10; see also Adil Ahmad Haque, "Retributivism: The Right and the Good," *Law and Philosophy* 32, no.1 (2013), pp. 59–82.

28 Paul H. Robinson, "Competing Conceptions of Modern Desert: Vengeful, Deontological, and Empirical," *Cambridge Law Journal*, vol. 67 (2008), pp. 145, 162.

29 deGuzman, "Harsh Justice," p. 12.

30 Ibid.; see also Jens David Ohlin, "Towards a Unique Theory of International Criminal Sentencing," in Göran Sluiter and Sergey Vasiliev (eds.), *International Criminal Procedure: Towards a Coherent Body of Law* (London: Cameron May International Law & Policy, 2009), pp. 381, 390.

31 Ibid., p. 377; see also Immanuel Kant, *Philosophy of Law*, translated by W. Hastie (1887).

32 Ohlin, "Towards a Unique Theory of International Criminal Sentencing," p. 377.

should be noted that Ohlin and others who defend a retributivist justification for international criminal punishment do not claim a particular understanding of individual desert; rather, they appeal to the gravity of international crimes in arguing for corresponding harsh punishment, despite the lack of international consensus about crime severity.[33]

Critics of international tribunals argue that retribution only succeeds if individuals have a sense of guilt or shame when they have done something wrong. Retribution generates reactive attitudes that can, in turn, motivate individuals to have remorse for having done wrong.[34] Yet international criminals, such as military and political leaders who wage an ethnic cleansing campaign against an ethnic minority within their state, do not even have a preliminary sense that they should feel guilty for participating in such acts. As noted, international criminals may see their crimes as morally correct rather than as morally reprehensible actions. This could be for several reasons, including the community's particular norms and values, political circumstances causing moral outrage, naïve realism, or other judgment errors.[35] In some cases, legal condemnation may force an international criminal to reassess her moral judgments and feel remorse for her actions. But assuming each of these mistakes in moral judgment is uncorrected, particularly if the individual remains enmeshed in her community of like-minded individuals, legal avenues will be unlikely to generate the appropriate reactive attitudes. Thus, even if the retribution is deemed necessary, a court should locate this necessity in recognition of the harms done to the victims, rather than in the actions of the international criminal.

Another problem that follows from the retributivist justification is the proportionality principle, as alluded to previously. Critics argue that the proportionality principle is meaningless for someone who, say, ordered the death of thousands of human beings. Given that the international criminal tribunals can issue no punishment greater than life imprisonment (assuming that a defendant has no financial resources to redistribute to his victims), punishing on the basis of proportional desert seems meaningless. If a soldier who murders one member of a particular religious sect receives the same punishment as his commander, who helped orchestrate the death of thousands of members of the religious sect, in addition to killing some personally, the severity of the crimes may be different while the punishment remains the same. Yet failing to punish the soldier in order to accentuate the severity of

33 deGuzman, "Harsh Justice," p. 14.

34 See Peter F. Strawson, "Freedom and Resentment," *Proceeding of the British Academy*, vol. 48 (1960).

35 See Andrew K. Woods, "Moral Judgments and International Crimes: The Disutility of Desert," 52 *Virginia Journal of International Law*, vol. 52 (2012), p. 633.

the commander's sentence does not solve the problem. It may be that sentences for international crimes cannot be meted out in a way that looks proportional to other international criminal sentences, but that does not mean the proportionality principle has been ignored.[36] Rather, it is probably the case that almost all international crimes are severe enough to warrant long prison sentences, and any comparison should be made with sentences for less serious domestic crimes. Minimal prison sentences are simply unlikely in the realm of international criminal law.

For victims, their main concern with respect to international prosecution might be to achieve justice for wrongs committed against their family or community, and "in this sense the victims are frequently motivated by retributivist sentiments."[37] This means that whether or not the perpetrators experienced appropriate reactive attitudes, victims and survivors could still benefit from having their own retributive beliefs vindicated, either purely psychologically or even by providing a reason for the victims not to seek personal vengeance. Regardless, it is important that the victims see international criminal courts and tribunals as sites of justice, and their understanding of what constitutes justice will be largely retributive.[38]

Yet the location of international criminal tribunals can negate their possible retributive impacts, at least for victims. Even where deserved punishment is imposed on international criminals, the victims can have a tough time understanding or accessing the intended impact of the punishment when the tribunal is not located in their community. The ICC and the ICTY are located in the Hague, far away from the communities in which most of the prosecuted atrocities have occurred. The ICTR, located in Arusha, Tanzania,[39] is at least on the same continent as the site of the Rwandan genocide, but the trip from Rwanda to Arusha is just as prohibitive as a trip to the Hague for most of the survivors. As Elizabeth Neuffer noted from an interview with survivors of the Rwandan genocide, the location of the ICTR "deprives genocide survivors of something they need in order for reconciliation: the need to confront those whose orders left them mutilated or robbed … of their

[36] Ohlin suggests that we could differentiate among severe crimes by ceasing to impose life sentences and instead imposing sentences of determinate (and defendant-relatively proportionate) length, which extend beyond natural life expectancies. The sentences would, in effect, "all yield life imprisonment, but they would preserve a relative distinction among defendants, even if that distinction does not yield concrete benefits for the lowest level perpetrators." See Ohlin, "Proportional Sentences at the ICTY," in Bert Swart, Alexander Zahar, and Göran Sluiter (eds.) *The Legacy of the International Criminal Tribunal for the Former Yugoslavia* (2011), p. 338.

[37] Ohlin, "Towards a Unique Theory of International Criminal Sentencing," p. 390.

[38] Ibid., p. 391.

[39] S.C. Res. 977, U.N. Doc. S/RES/977 (Feb. 22, 1995).

families."[40] If the accusers cannot confront the accused, they may be deprived of opportunities for reconciliation, but lack of access to the trials also deprives survivors of a sense that their attackers received what they deserved. If victims cannot hear the testimony of witnesses or watch the presentation of evidence or listen to the sentencing of a convicted *génocidaire*, they will likely experience a lesser retributive impact from the trial.

Unfortunately, the location of international courts and tribunals is determined by balancing a lot of goals, not just retributive goals. In the case of the ICTR, the Security Council stated that the location of the ICTR would be determined through

> considerations of justice and fairness as well as administrative efficiency, including access to witnesses and economy, and subject to the conclusion of appropriate arrangements between the United Nations and the state of the seat, acceptable to the council, having regard to the fact that the International Tribunal may meet away from its seat when it considers it necessary for the efficient exercise of its functions and decides that an office will be established and proceedings will be conducted in Rwanda, where feasible and appropriate, subject to the conclusion of similar appropriate arrangements.[41]

Thus, it is necessary first to consider the legal system of Rwanda in determining its ability to host the international tribunal, and whether fair trials could be obtained for defendants in a state overwhelmed with recent tragedy. But the Security Council also had to consider the infrastructure capacity of Rwanda, and Arusha was arguably much better suited to handle the logistics of an international tribunal. It may be that in the future, considerations will weigh in favor of housing international tribunals in the location where the atrocities were committed, as in Cambodia. But the retributive aims will not always outweigh other considerations in determining the location of trials. Even so, retributive aims are not negated by the distance between the victims and the trials. Most of the trials have taken place in a secondary location, and the retributive feelings of the victims, while perhaps moderated by the distance, do not disappear.

The goal of ending impunity seems to suggest that retribution is necessary, but not sufficient, as a rationale for imposing punishment on international criminals through the work of international criminal tribunals. Punishment

[40] Elizabeth Neuffer, *The Key to My Neighbor's House: Seeking Justice in Bosnia and Rwanda* (London: Bloomsbury, 2000), p. 377; see also Phil Clark, *The Gacaca Courts, Post-Genocide Justice and Reconciliation in Rwanda: Justice without Lawyers* (Cambridge: Cambridge University Press, 2010), p. 166.

[41] S.C. Res. 955, U.N. Doc. S/RES/955 (Nov. 8, 1994).

under international criminal law may be able to respond appropriately to the retributive beliefs of some victims, and this reason is very important for the continued legitimacy of international criminal courts and tribunals. But it will not guarantee the reactive attitudes we seek from the perpetrators of violence as a result of their particular motivations for acting. Additionally, international criminal prosecutions are perhaps less able to uphold the proportionality principle of retributive punishment than their domestic counterparts, if only because calculating what constitutes proportional sentencing in international criminal law remains quite challenging. Yet as we have shown, retributivism still can be utilized as at least a partial justification for international criminal punishment.

IV EXPRESSIVISM

Expressivism has become a common punishment rationale of choice for many defenders of international criminal law and international criminal tribunals. And it does seem to have fewer problems than either a deterrence or retributive rationale for international criminal punishment. Under an expressivist rationale, the purpose of punishing criminals through international criminal tribunals is to tell the world that these crimes are unacceptable. This rationale has developed naturally out of the International Military Tribunal at Nuremberg, where the existence of the tribunal was largely touted as necessary to condemn the atrocities of the Holocaust, if nothing else.

Expressivist theories of punishment are much newer than retributive or deterrence-based theories of punishment and may be particularly well-suited to the newer international system of criminal law and its large audience. Joel Feinberg argues that punishment is distinguished from other kinds of penalties by its expressive function, in that it is a "conventional device for the expression of attitudes of resentment and indignation, and of judgments of disapproval and reprobation, on the part either of the punishing authority himself or of those 'in whose name' the punishment is inflicted."[42] Feinberg goes on to note that the significance of punishment is symbolic, in that it expresses both the disapproval of a community and their feelings of resentment toward the criminal.[43] Cass Sunstein takes this idea further, arguing that since certain laws can influence social norms and "push them in the right direction," we should support the expressive function of law in producing the best outcomes.[44] In the realm of punishment, if it can be used to change norms that are "obstacles to

[42] Joel Feinberg, *Doing and Deserving* (Princeton, NJ: Princeton University Press, 1970), p. 98.
[43] See ibid., pp. 98–100.
[44] Cass R. Sunstein, "On the Expressive Function of Law," *University of Pennsylvania Law Review* (1996), pp. 2025–2026.

well-being," such as a norm of impunity, it seems that Sunstein would support the use of punishment to avoid such an obstacle.[45]

Robert Sloane defends an expressive account of punishment by international criminal tribunals by claiming that it best captures "both the nature of international sentencing and its realistic institutional capacity to make a difference given the legal, political, and resource constraints and will continue, for the foreseeable future, to afflict international criminal tribunals."[46] The goals of an expressivist account of punishment in international criminal law are broader than deterrence or retributivism and can capture aims that include "the crafting of historical narratives, their authentication as truths, and their pedagogical dissemination to the public"[47] in addition to the more traditional legal goals. Whether or not international criminal courts and tribunals can actually succeed in crafting accurate (or even useful) historical narratives is a separate question, but they are certainly in a unique position to do so. Expressivist justifications of international criminal punishment are also valuable because they work well in concert with other justifications for punishment. Expressivism is less focused on the instrumental value of punishment and more focused on the "long-term normative values" that are developed within the international criminal legal systems.[48]

There is evidence that the international criminal courts and tribunals have identified the possibilities for the expressive force of their judgments. At Nuremberg, Justice Jackson spoke of showing the defendants to be "living symbols of racial hatreds, of terrorism and violence, and of the arrogance and cruelty of power" through the collection of a record of their crimes and their corresponding punishment.[49] Diane Marie Amann claims that the international criminal courts and tribunals do in fact "reinforce pronouncements of norms, such as the proscription against genocide in the 1948 Convention."[50] She argues that even though there were no enforcement mechanisms for several decades, the international recognition of norms against genocide, torture, war crimes, and crimes against humanity grew in force in the years following Nuremberg.[51] The appearance of enforcement mechanisms, in the form of

[45] Ibid., p. 2053.

[46] Sloane, "Expressive Capacity of International Punishment," p. 42.

[47] Drumbl, *Atrocity, Punishment, and International Law*, p. 173.

[48] Sloane, "Expressive Capacity of International Punishment," p. 71.

[49] Opening Statement of Supreme Court Justice Robert H. Jackson, Chief Prosecutor for the United States, November 21, 1945, reprinted in *Trial of the Major War Criminals before the International Military Tribunal*, vol. 2 (1948), p. 99.

[50] Diane Marie Amann, "Group Mentality, Expressivism, and Genocide," *International Criminal Law Review* 2.2 (2002), pp. 93–143, 94.

[51] Ibid., pp. 121–122.

international criminal courts and tribunals, has played a significant role in solidifying these norms through judgments with "expressivist flavor."[52]

But expressivism has its own problems as well. For expressivism to succeed there must be an audience that takes seriously what is expressed by a particular source. As discussed in relation to retribution, it is unclear how much of an effect international criminal law will have on actors who are singularly focused on what they see as morally correct (or required) acts of violence. Additionally, many have criticized the quality of the historical narratives generated by international criminal courts and tribunals, arguing that the records produced by the judicial bodies are limited by evidentiary procedures, human memory, and conflicting goals.[53] As we noted in relation to retributivism, the location and audience of the international criminal tribunals may be preventing the expressive impact of the tribunals on victims and on potential future criminals. And finally, a justification grounded on the expressive function produces worries about maintaining rule of law, as prosecutorial selectivity could be used to further social norm production rather than ensuring fair prosecution of the accused.[54]

Other problems that have afflicted the ICC that we saw in earlier parts of this book have also affected the ICC's ability to provide highly valued expressions of condemnation for war criminals and other actors who break international criminal norms. Yet we maintain that the expressive potential of punishment in international criminal law remains one of its greatest strengths. We have seen the incredible expressive impact of Nuremberg and the place it maintains in the narratives we tell our children. But it is the enforcement mechanisms, in the form of permanent and temporary international criminal courts and tribunals, that give international criminal norms their teeth. Consequences have to follow from an assessment of behavior in order for a community to comprehend the law backing the assessment. Punishment of international criminal actors "internalizes – and even reinforces – social norms among the public and, thereby, from the expressivist perspective proactively promotes law-abiding behavior."[55]

But we need the judicial structures in order to promote these ends. As we discuss at length in Chapter 8, the fact that international criminal prosecutions are selective does not mean they are unfair. And the fact that the

52 Ibid., p. 123
53 See Drumbl, *Atrocity, Punishment, and International Law*, p. 176.; see also Koskenniemi, "Between Impunity and Show Trials," p. 33.
54 Alexander K. A. Greenawalt, "International Criminal Law for Retributivists," *University of Pennsylvania Journal of International Law*, 35 no. 4 (2014), pp. 987–988.
55 Drumbl, *Atrocity, Punishment, and International Law*, p. 174.

historical records generated by international criminal judicial bodies may not be 100 percent truth-apt does not mean they have failed to serve a historical or social purpose. It will take time for norms and practices to develop, and it will take time for these to have an impact on global actors and would-be violators of international criminal law. As long as the courts and tribunals continue to strive for best practices and recognize the multiple (and sometimes competing) goals at play, international criminal punishment can serve an unmatched expressive function. And as we will see in Section V, it can do so in concert with other justifications for punishment.

V A COLLECTIVE RATIONALE FOR INTERNATIONAL PUNISHMENT SCHEMES

All three of the most commonly cited justifications for punishment in international criminal tribunals present serious problems. Therefore, our response to the punishment-oriented critiques of international tribunals must have multiple prongs. As in other parts of this book, we argue that the critics of international courts and tribunals have made their task too easy by focusing on various aspects of punishment without looking to the sum of the parts. Rather, as we argue, the best way to think about international criminal punishment is through a combined approach, where each of these three justifications plays a role in collectively justifying international criminal punishment.

Ohlin argues for a two-tiered collective justification of international criminal punishment.[56] As discussed previously, Ohlin defends the retributivist model to justify individual punishment on the grounds that it "most closely tracks the policy goal of international criminal justice,"[57] which is that of meting out punishment based on desert. However, Ohlin suggests that at the collective level, there are also consequentialist considerations. He notes that in many cases, the aim of international criminal courts and tribunals is "to convince victims to put down their arms and forgo reprisal attacks, and to submit their grievances to the rule of law."[58] So for Ohlin, the retributivist justification and the consequentialist justification (notably distinct from mainstream deterrence-based justifications) work together to utilize criminal justice for individuals as a way of promoting "international peace and collective security."[59]

56 See Ohlin, "Towards a Unique Theory of International Criminal Sentencing"; see also Ohlin, "Proportional Sentences at the ICTY."

57 Ohlin, "Towards a Unique Theory of International Criminal Sentencing," p. 388.

58 Ibid., p. 391.

59 Ibid.

In criticizing the three justifications for international criminal punishment, Drumbl also recognizes that these theories are not mutually exclusive.[60] He notes that "courts often refer to them overlappingly when it comes to punishing a single defendant" and that this overlap can lead to both tension and cooperation.[61] He goes on to perform a detailed analysis of the empirical successes and failures of international criminal courts and tribunals to achieve the goals of deterrence, retribution, and expression, and concludes that they fall short.[62] We clearly agree that the three theories are not mutually exclusive, but we disagree with Drumbl's conclusion that they may be insufficient. We argue that when all three justifications are considered together, they can stand up to the scrutiny of their critics. Collectively they are normatively sufficient. This is because the problems Drumbl identifies are descriptive. Normatively, where one justification fails, another justification can succeed, and this makes the descriptive problems facing the system of international criminal punishment worth fixing (instead of throwing it out altogether).

There are serious reasons to doubt the deterrent or retributive effects of these tribunals, and to wonder about the expressivist aspect of punishment as well. But as H. L. A. Hart argued, when we look at defending an institution of punishment, we must realize that "different principles (each of which may in a sense be called a 'justification') are relevant at different points in any morally acceptable account of punishment."[63] Accordingly, when we add up the benefits of having international criminal courts and tribunals for each of these aspects of punishment, a normative defense can be successfully mounted.

Concerning retribution, it is important to note that retribution is not just about whether the wrongdoer changes his or her behavior, for this would be to confuse retribution with deterrence. Retribution primarily entails giving a wrongdoer his or her "comeuppance," to use a phrase made popular in theoretical circles by Joel Feinberg.[64] For this to succeed, there must be serious penalties for acts of wrongdoing. And here there is certainly room for improvement in international criminal law today. Often the sentences that are meted out are not considered sufficiently serious as a response to the

60 Drumbl, *Atrocity, Punishment, and International Law*, p. 149.

61 Ibid.

62 Ibid., p. 180.

63 H. L. A. Hart, "Prolegomenon to the Principles of Punishment," in *Punishment and Responsibility: Essays in the Philosophy of Law* (Oxford: Oxford University Press, 2008), p. 3.

64 See Joel Feinberg, *Harm to Others*. Vol. I. *The Moral Limits of the Criminal Law* (Oxford: Oxford University Press, 1984).

nature of the crime. But this would take only a fairly minor set of changes to correct. And in any event, the crimes that are prosecuted in international tribunals, such as genocide, need not have an exactly corresponding sentence to that which the wrongdoer would receive under a domestic regime in order to meet the requirements for retributive success. Murder is not a crime under international law, which of course it is in all domestic jurisdictions. Only killing under certain circumstances, such as killing aimed at destroying a group, counts as an international crime in any event.

Deterrence is much harder to deal with in the international setting than retribution. Initially we would comment that there is mixed evidence about whether or not deterrence is successful in domestic tribunals, in such places as the United States and Europe. So, we should not expect much more from international tribunals than domestic tribunals concerning deterrence.[65] Yet there may be structural reasons to doubt that international tribunals can effect deterrence. In particular, it seems that international criminals are not like normal criminals in terms of their motivations. Yet, while this is true to a certain extent, it is also true that these "criminals" like all other individuals are affected by significant penalties attached to what was previously seen as not too costly behavior. Indeed, here is where even heads of state may think twice before openly persecuting a people – again on the assumption that the penalties really are significant and the prosecutions for such crimes are likely to occur.

Expressivism is the kind of rationale for punishment that does not depend as much as deterrence, on the number of wrongdoers actually prosecuted, convicted, and punished. What is crucial is that some are indeed punished and the world community stands behind the punishment as deserved given the enormity of the wrong. What is needed for expressivism to succeed in articulating the strong condemnation of the international community is a consensus. At the moment that is not always evident. But there is nothing in principle, or in practice, that would prevent such a consensus in support of the judgments and sentences of international tribunals. Of course, the trick is to figure out which reforms of the international tribunals that are feasible could be wholeheartedly endorsed normatively.

Now that we have identified a role for each rationale for punishment to play in defending the international criminal courts and tribunals, let us turn to some of the practical problems of actually punishing international criminals.

[65] See Drumbl, *Atrocity, Punishment, and International Law*, ch. 4.

VI PUNISHING IN PRACTICE

As argued earlier, the deterrence, expressivist, and retributive rationales for punishment are sufficient. Our argument that these three justifications are collectively sufficient appears to generate potential difficulties when we turn to practical problems facing the international criminal courts and tribunals. In practice, it does seem to matter which punishment rationale is playing a justificatory role. However, we would argue that the collective approach actually gives the courts and tribunals more flexibility in allowing them to make effective choices, rather than trying to mold their punishment practices to fit one punishment rationale.

While there are certain international standards and norms of punishment, domestic practices vary widely. In this section, we will discuss some features of punishment in international criminal tribunals that are particularly tricky to handle given the range of global practices. We will consider problems that international criminal tribunals face with respect to penalties, detention, and child soldiers. Other practical issues related to punishment are considered elsewhere in this book, especially those related to collective responsibility and the superior orders defense, as well as issues related to evidence.

One aspect of punishment in international criminal law that causes problems for international criminal tribunals is determining the appropriate penalty for an individual actor. In accordance with the requirements of each of the three punishment rationales discussed previously, international criminal courts and tribunals, like domestic courts, seek to impose penalties that are proportionate to the gravity of the crimes committed. However, international courts and tribunals have had to make these decisions with little formal guidance, in stark contrast to most domestic courts.

The Statutes and Rules of the ICTY and ICTR require the trial chambers to take into account the gravity of the crime and any relevant aggravating and mitigating factors,[66] but they do not lay out exactly how this should be accomplished.[67] The result is that sentencing practices vary, but do in fact rely heavily on both aggravating and mitigating circumstances.[68] The use of aggravating factors in sentencing, including the gravity of the offense or

66 See ICTY Statute, at art. 24; ICTY Rules, at rule 101; ICTR Statute, at art. 23; ICTR Rules, at rule 101.

67 See Andrew N. Keller, "Punishment for Violations of International Criminal Law: An Analysis of Sentencing at the ICTY and ICTR," *Indiana International and Comparative Law Review*, 12 (2001), p. 53.

68 Marisa R. Bassett, "Defending International Sentencing: Past Criticism to the Promise of the ICC," *Human Rights Brief*, 16 (2009), pp. 22–60, 23.

abuse of authority, supports a retributive approach to punishment in international criminal law.[69] The use of gravity of the crime as an aggravating factor (particularly in cases where the defendant is charged with genocide) is inconsistently applied in practice, given that all of the crimes charged under the ICTY and ICTR statutes are grave.[70] Other factors are easier for the judge to use in making a statement about the culpability of a defendant, as in the case of Jean-Baptiste Gatete, who received a harsher sentence due to "the abuse of his general authority vis-à-vis the assailants who carried out the killings."[71]

Mitigating factors may also help achieve the correct level of retribution. However, they may also serve an expressive function in undergirding the fairness that legitimizes international criminal courts and tribunals, or in demonstrating to the global community that good deeds within a conflict will be rewarded. An example of the use of mitigating factors is found in the case of Augustin Ndindiliyimana, the chief of staff of Rwanda's gendarmerie. His conviction for genocide was ultimately overturned,[72] but his initial sentence was determined by considering the personal risks he took to protect Tutsis and his personal beliefs opposing the violence.[73]

Critics argue that the leeway gives judges almost unlimited discretion in sentencing various convicted defendants.[74] The benefit of allowing judges to consider aggravating and mitigating circumstances is that judges can be more precise in imposing punishment commensurate with the crime committed. This is a virtue, despite the fact that it could be abused in practice. However, the problem of judicial discretion in considering mitigating and aggravating factors is not unique to international criminal sentencing. This is an issue faced by any domestic legal system that seeks to allow for individualized sentencing. Thus, it may be necessary for international courts and tribunals to provide more guidance in how to view mitigating and aggravating factors,

69 Barbara Hola, Alette Smeulers, and Catrien Bijleveld, "Is ICTY Sentencing Predictable? An Empirical Analysis of ICTY Sentencing Practices," *Leiden Journal of International Law*, 22 (2009), pp. 79–97, 82.

70 William R. Pruitt, "Aggravating and Mitigating Sentencing Factors at the ICTR – An Exploratory Analysis," *International Criminal Law Review*, 14 no.1 (2014), pp. 148–176, 159.

71 *Prosecutor* v. *Gatete*, Judgment, ICTR-2000-61-T Tr. ch. III, 31 March 2011, paras. 678.

72 *Ndindiliyimana et al.*, Judgment, ICTR-00-56-A, 11 February 2014, Appeals Chamber.

73 *Ndindiliyimana et al.*, Judgment, ICTR-00-56-T, 17 May 2011, paras. 18–19, 22–23, 2242, paras. 2183–2242; see also Jean Galbraith, "The Good Deeds of International Criminal Defendants," *Leiden Journal of International Law* 25 (2012), pp. 799–813, 799.

74 See Mirko Bagaric and John Morss, "International Sentencing Law: In Search of a Justification and Coherent Framework," *International Criminal Law Review*, 6 (2006), pp. 191, 193; Allison Marston Danner, "Constructing a Hierarchy of Crimes in International Criminal Law Sentencing," *Virginia Law Review* 87 (2001), pp. 415, 501.

particularly in the realm of offense gravity. But the underlying structural concerns are not worrisome.

A related sentencing issue is the matter of capital punishment and comparative sentence severity in domestic legal regimes. There are very few nations that still impose the death penalty or other harsh punishments; China, North Korea, and the United States are a few of them.[75] There is no capital punishment permitted in any of the international criminal courts or tribunals.[76] But when domestic regimes can impose the death penalty for murder or other crimes we might think of as more minor than genocide, what is the expressive force of sentencing a *génocidaire* to twenty-five years in prison? How are retributive and deterrence-based concerns about proportionality being satisfied?

The solution to this problem would certainly not be to allow for capital punishment in international criminal courts or tribunals. We agree with the assessment that capital punishment is a human rights violation. But this is a concern when we think about proportionality under any of the justifications given for punishment in international criminal law. We concede that this problem may have no easy answer, at least in practice, until the global community can reach a better consensus in their domestic criminal systems about what constitute appropriate punishment practices. We argue that all domestic systems should be moving toward more humane conditions, and in the meantime, the humane conditions that can be imposed on international criminals can serve a different expressive purpose: that of demonstrating what sorts of punishment are appropriate for any criminal, regardless of the gravity of his or her offense.[77]

A largely practical concern still exists in figuring out how and where to incarcerate accused and sentenced individuals, and this too relates to the humaneness of punishment. Victims have criticized the conditions under which criminals are held when they are being tried by the international courts or tribunals, in comparison to the prison conditions for those being tried by domestic courts. The disparities are unfortunate, but they should not lead the international criminal courts and tribunals to alter the humane treatment of prisoners. A greater problem exists with where to locate the prisoners. Prison terms are served based on agreements between the sentencing court

75 deGuzman, "Harsh Justice," p. 5.

76 Ibid., p. 7, citing S.C. Res. 827, U.N. SCOR, 48th Sess., 3217th mtg., Annex, art. 24(1), 24(3), U.N. Doc. S/Res/827 (1993); see also, e.g., Rome Statute of the International Criminal Court art. 77.1(a), July 17, 1998, 2187 U.N.T.S. 3, at art. 77(1)–(2).

77 See William Schabas, *The Abolition of the Death Penalty in International Law* (Cambridge: Cambridge University Press, 2002).

or tribunal and states that have agreed to house convicted individuals.[78] This means that the conditions under which individuals are imprisoned can vary widely, depending on the facilities available in a given state, in spite of the international standards that must be met. But it also means that those serving prison terms may be required to serve their terms in countries with which they have no connections, and it may be prohibitive for them to receive visits from family or friends.

Again, these concerns are not dissimilar to those faced by domestic courts. We should encourage the international criminal courts and tribunals to uphold the highest human rights standards, by ensuring adequate prison conditions and appropriate concern for housing criminals within the reach of their family members.

A final and somewhat different concern is how to determine the appropriate punishment for child actors who are simultaneously victims. This presents its own unique challenges as none of the three punishment rationales we endorse in this chapter seems to be appropriate for punishing children. In cases where the accused are child soldiers or pirates, international law tends to present children accused of crimes as deserving either of "perfunctory release (the faultless passive victim image) or criminal trials regardless of age (the demon and bandit image)."[79] The first of these options does not serve any deterrent or retributive purpose, and regardless of any other expression, impunity seems to be the only guaranteed expression. Yet the second option is much too harsh. Drumbl argues that the deterrent effect of punishment is unclear for children, and that retribution is too heavy-handed and/or incomprehensible to a young person.[80] The expressive function of punishing children, Drumbl claims, is minimal, given that criminal trials of children "yield superficial explanations of the etiology of mass atrocity."[81]

We agree. International criminal trials are not an appropriate venue for prosecuting child soldiers or child pirates. This does not undermine the system of international criminal punishment. Rather, it makes clear the limitations of the system for particular kinds of criminals, namely, those who can be held most fully responsible for their actions. Children who have participated

78 See Steven Arrigg Koh, "Geography and Justice: Why Prison Location Matters in US and International Theories of Criminal Punishment," *Vanderbilt Journal of Transnational Law* 46 (2013), p. 1267.

79 See Mark A. Drumbl, *Reimagining Child Soldiers in International Law and Policy* (Oxford: Oxford University Press, 2012), pp. 6–11; see also Mark A. Drumbl, "Child Pirates: Rehabilitation, Reintegration, and Accountability," *Case Western Reserve Journal of International Law* 46 (2013), pp. 235, 244.

80 See ibid.

81 Ibid., p. 273.

in international crimes should be dealt with in a manner focused on rehabilitation and reintegration into a community.[82] Thus, while the concerns about child actors in international crimes are not easily dealt with, we are convinced that the international criminal courts and tribunals that currently exist are not the appropriate venue.

In this section, we have considered a variety of practical problems facing international criminal courts and tribunals in how to punish fairly those who have been convicted of international crimes. But we have shown that none of these problems should leave us disillusioned about the prospects for achieving the aims of retribution, expressivism, and deterrence. Most of the problems are similar to those faced by domestic courts, and the issues caused by the others can at least be mitigated through further development of oversight practices for the courts and tribunals.

VII INTERNATIONAL CRIMINAL TRIBUNALS AS SOURCES OF PUNISHMENT

We have argued that a fair and accurate assessment of punishment by the international criminal courts and tribunals requires recognizing the value of all three of the most commonly cited justifications for punishment. International criminal punishment can serve a retributivist function, generating feelings in the perpetrator and victims that the perpetrator got what she deserved. International criminal punishment can serve a limited purpose in terms of specific deterrence, and we are hopeful that it can serve a general deterrent purpose as well. Finally, international criminal punishment expresses our condemnation of atrocity crimes and our intent to end impunity for such crimes. Collectively, they can account for the schemes of punishment in international criminal law. Even when we look at some of the most pressing practical problems facing the international courts and tribunals today, we can see that they are not insurmountable. Some of these problems are similar to those faced by domestic courts and are issues that will be faced by any criminal justice system. Others are problems unique to the realm of international punishment, as a complementary system to domestic criminal legal systems.

None of these problems, descriptive or normative, succeeds in derailing the promise of international criminal prosecution and punishment. There is much work to do in improving the practices of international criminal courts and tribunals and making them more consistent, but we see institutional promise for ending impunity and increasing global security.

[82] We agree with Drumbl's approach on this account as well.

4

Responsibility

There are very good critiques of international criminal tribunals in terms of their ability to assign responsibility for mass crimes, including crimes that involve groups as both the victims and perpetrators. The problems center on the idea that criminal trials are, by design, aimed at establishing individual guilt or innocence, whereas international crimes are generally group crimes. The ad hoc tribunals have generated strong criticism for adopting a prosecution strategy of holding individuals responsible as members of joint criminal enterprises. And the ICC is also being criticized for adopting the control of crime theory. In addition, there are questions being raised about the attempt by the ICC to assign responsibility for crimes committed during what might be considered civil wars, where reprisal killings and attempted ethnic cleansing occur on both sides. Ad hoc tribunals are almost always set up to punish one side of a conflict, namely, the losing side, and thus have also been criticized as victors' justice or one-sided prosecution. Another problem of responsibility is how a criminal court can establish responsibility for just one person when so many others are often also involved.

In this chapter we will assess the significant criticisms that have been leveled at international criminal tribunals on grounds of responsibility. In Section I we set out a plausible view of responsibility that will help us understand the criticisms of international tribunals and how best to respond to those criticisms. Section II discusses the complex question of whether individuals or states should be held responsible for mass crimes. In Section III we examine which individuals should be blamed or punished for international crimes. In Section IV we discuss the problems that have arisen concerning how individual defendants are selected to be held accountable for their actions. In Section V we wade into the quagmire that has been created by the ad hoc criminal tribunals' use of the theory of joint criminal enterprise liability, as well as the use of the control of crime theory by the ICC. Section VI discusses the further complexities that arise when the crimes are committed in a civil war as opposed to an international war, and Section VII tackles the so-called responsibility dilemma, which Mark Osiel has proposed in order to criticize international criminal tribunals. Section VIII examines the problem of bystanders, especially whether and how they should be prosecuted for mass crimes. Section IX briefly concludes with some thoughts on various jurisdictional critiques of international criminal tribunals related to who is accountable to whom for international criminal behavior.

I AN ACCOUNT OF RESPONSIBILITY

The concept of responsibility is rooted in the idea that when an untoward event has happened, an account is needed of how the event occurred, who brought it about, and what should be the upshot of attributing liability. Since the beginning of ancient legal thought, causal responsibility and moral responsibility have been distinguished, and it is this distinction with which we will begin.

Causal responsibility provides the answer to the question of how a particular event or state of affairs occurred. In one sense, this task is to show what the sufficient conditions were that together produced the event. Causal responsibility is not yet normative responsibility since there may be wholly natural forces that produced a given event, such as a tornado or lightning strike. Typically, moral or legal responsibility is not assigned unless there was a voluntary intervention by a human that at least partially caused the event.

H. L. A. Hart and A. M. Honore provide the canonical account of responsibility in their book *Causation in the Law*:

> In the moral judgments of ordinary life, we have occasion to blame people because they have caused harm to others, and also, if less frequently, to insist that morally they are bound to compensate those to whom they have caused harm. These are the moral analogues of more precise legal conceptions; for in all legal systems liability to be punished or to make compensation frequently depends on whether actions or omissions have caused harm.[1]

In law, responsibility is primarily assigned for harm that a person has caused. The kind of causation at issue is referred to as "but for" causation. Here the responsibility will not be attributed unless the harm would not have occurred without the intervention of the person held responsible. So while causal

[1] H. L. A. Hart and A. M. Honore, *Causation in the Law*, 2nd ed. (Oxford: Oxford University Press, 1985), p. 62.

responsibility and moral or legal responsibility are different, normally moral or legal responsibility will not be assigned unless a person is causally responsible in the "but for" way.

While legal responsibility or liability is assigned to individual persons primarily for harm caused to other persons, there are exceptions, such as when one person is held responsible for the harm caused by another person. But in such cases, as in an employer's being held responsible for the harm his employee has caused, there is some special relationship such that the one held responsible is thought to have control over, or to be able to control, the actions of the person who actually caused the harm.

Of special concern to international criminal law is the situation where several people acting in concert cause harm to another person or group of persons. One plausible strategy is to assign legal responsibility to each person based on his or her causal contribution. But there are other alternatives, such as assigning responsibility to each for the entire harm that the group has caused, or assigning responsibility only to the member of the group who was the leader, whether or not the leader played the main causal role. We will take up each of these alternatives in the next few paragraphs.

In some sense the fairest way to assign responsibility to the members of a group that has jointly caused harm is to apportion guilt or blame to each member of the group on the basis of his or her causal contribution to the harm. This strategy assumes that a given harm can be divided into parts and that we can determine who the cause of each part is. One problem with this approach is that if the harm is truly caused by a joint venture, we may not be able to figure out who is causally responsible for which part. Indeed, it may be that in terms of "but for" causation, each of the parties caused all of the harm.

So, in some cases it may seem that we have no other choice but to assign responsibility for a jointly caused harm to each person for the whole harm. After all, that is what it means to be a member of a group that caused harm – one is responsible for the harm that results from joining a group with the knowledge that the group is causing or is likely to cause harm. The mens rea for the whole harm is the individual's intention to join a group knowing that it is likely to cause this harm, and the *actus reus* is satisfied in that the individual did something, or omitted to do something, that was part of the joint causal process. Yet, it has seemed to many that holding each person responsible for the whole harm is potentially unfair since normally the roles of the members of such a group are different from one another.

But in other cases, even if we cannot figure out who caused which part of the harm, we may nonetheless be able to identify who is the leader of the group. This strategy can be defended in that the group is the appropriate focus of the causal responsibility, but it may not be fair to hold each member of the group responsible for all of the harm. We can recognize that there are distinct roles in the group, even if we cannot say precisely how to assign causal responsibility to each person in that group. Given that the group is the most appropriate agent of the harm, then by looking at all of the members we may be able to distinguish one person whose role was so important that it may not be unfair to hold him or her responsible for the harm, and this is often the leader of the group.

Responsibility and liability differ in some respects that are worth noting at this point. Responsibility does not have the same connotation as does liability in terms of what follows from a person's having been ascribed responsibility. Liability means that the person has opened the door for treatment that would not otherwise be permitted, such as being punished or executed. Being liable to be punished is of a different character than being responsible for being punished. Indeed, the phrase "being responsible for being punished" sounds wrong – it is far more common that one is responsible for what one has done, such as causing a harm, rather than being responsible for a punishment. So, one could say that responsibility calls for an accounting, but does not necessarily call for a punishment, whereas liability goes directly to the call for some sort of punitive response.

A relatively uncontroversial account of individual legal responsibility is one that links causal elements with liability elements. An account of group responsibility is harder to characterize uncontroversially, as we will next see. And it is the mixture of individual and group responsibility that is the main terrain of international criminal law, which generally deals with the responsibility of individuals for crimes that are nearly all group crimes. In this respect, individuals are being prosecuted for the part they played in a group's actions, whether that group is a state or a looser collection of people who take joint action to cause harm.

A recent criticism has been advanced by James G. Stewart concerning the causal element of collective crimes. In some, if not many, collective crimes, the individual in the dock did something that played a role in the perpetration of the crime, but was not itself necessary for the crime. The reason for the lack of necessity is that the crime was overdetermined, in that there were several sufficient sets of conditions, at least one of which did not include the accused individual's act.[2] Stewart uses the example of a firing squad to illustrate one version of the overdetermination problem – any of the firing squad members

2 James G. Stewart, "Overdetermined Atrocities," *Journal of International Criminal Law*, vol. 10 (2012), pp. 1189–1218.

is sufficient to cause the death, but no one's act is necessary. This problem raises questions about whether we should continue to think that causation is an essential component in international crimes as is currently done in international criminal tribunals. Yet, as Stewart himself points out, the problem of overdetermination is much larger than merely as it exists in international criminal law. Whenever there are individuals enmeshed in collective enterprises, overdetermination may occur, and yet there is value in holding individuals responsible for the role they played, as we will see. We next turn to how best to characterize the relationship between the individual and collectivities such as the state.

II INDIVIDUAL V. STATE RESPONSIBILITY

What does it mean to say an organization or a state has committed a crime? There are at least two things that can be meant. First, a state may commit a crime as a state, full stop. Here, one would have to show that the state has taken illegal action (*actus reus*) and that it has taken this action with a guilty mind (*mens rea*). Of course, this would require a showing that a state can take actions and have intentions in its own right that are different from the actions and intentions of the individual humans who make up the state. One strategy here would be to show that there are actions and intentions at work that are "of the state" in the sense that they cannot be reduced to the actions and intentions of the individual humans who make up the state. Another strategy is to see state action and intention as strongly analogous to individual human action and intention, much as the way we talk of such matters as the United States' deciding to retaliate against North Korea for its cyberattacks on U.S. businesses. We will briefly explore each of these views.

Some might believe that only individual persons should be held responsible. But then the question becomes which individuals are the ones who should be bearers of responsibility. Some collectivities so resemble individual humans that they might count as "individuals" who can be held responsible. The state has a decision making structure much like the individual human person's. The decisions of the state are made according to rules (often specified by a constitution) where the individuals who occupy various roles within the state often vote in ways that they would not if they were deciding matters outside the context of the state. And the actions that are taken by the state, often involving many individual persons acting jointly, are also quite different from the ways any individual or any group of individuals acting outside the state would act. In this sense there are actions and intentions of the state that cannot be reduced to the actions and intentions of individual humans.

Some theorists have analogized state action and intention to individual action and intention. Indeed, we often talk of the state's taking actions and having intentions as if it were a person. And the analogy, if not also the reality, is that the state does seem so remarkably like an individual human person that such corporate entities have been called "persons" in law for millennia. States and other collectivities are recognized as legal persons because of how much like individual human persons they are. As we pointed out, states have decision-making capacities much like individual humans', and states can act in the world in ways that are often best captured by talking as if they acted as a person would. The International Court of Justice regularly speaks of the responsibilities of states and has suggested, as in the case of Serbia, that states could commit crimes such as genocide. So according to some variations on this first strategy, we might be able to treat the state even in criminal law as a person. In this view, a state crime is then one that is committed by the state, full stop.

A second meaning of state crime would begin where the first strategy left off, by thinking of the state as a group of individual humans, where there is something important in the way these individual humans are related to each other. In this view, groups are generally seen as "individuals in relationships."[3] States are individual humans related to each other organizationally, where the organizational structure matters. If we only look at the actions and intentions of individuals, there will be a remainder that is unaccounted for. Some have called this view the group-based view.

On the group-based view of state crime, what will be prosecuted is individual humans who were acting in their various roles, such as their roles as camp guards or commanders of troops. The group-based view of state crime has many advantages when it is applied to the current model of criminal trials that focus on individual defendants rather than groups of defendants. Indeed, as it has often been noted that with respect to corporations, the problem is that collectivities have no soul to damn and no pants to kick.

There is a third understanding of state crime that will not allow for the ascription of responsibility to states as one would to individual humans. Here, one sees state action and intention as simply the aggregate of actions and intentions of certain individuals acting in their individual capacity. This completely reductive strategy would only see state action and intention as placeholders for the actions and intentions of individual humans. Criminal trials could be conducted against these individuals, but the state

[3] See Larry May, *The Morality of Groups* (South Bend, IN: University of Notre Dame Press, 1987), ch. 1.

would disappear since the trials would divide the state into its human components and hence concern the acts of individuals in their individual capacities. This strategy has the advantage that it puts before the criminal tribunal a defendant whom the criminal trial was designed to judge, the individual human person who will now be held responsible for what he or she intentionally did.

Yet, in our view, state responsibility cannot be utterly divorced from individual responsibility. We subscribe to a kind of compromise view, the "group-based model," where state responsibility involves individuals acting and intending in their roles within the state – the group-based roles make a difference. States can be said to be responsible insofar as the state has created the roles that individual humans assume. But states cannot be successfully punished except by punishing its individual members. So, the way that the perpetrators of mass crime are currently treated conforms nicely to our idea of how to understand state actions and intention in terms of responsibility and punishment of individual humans acting in their capacity as members of the state.

What is somewhat harder to see is how to meet the *mens rea* requirement of criminality. The main reason for this is that while individual humans act on behalf of the state, the intentions of the state are often instantiated in different individual members of the state. Moreover, as intention is a state of mind, it is particularly challenging to establish the *mens rea* of an individual person, much less a state. Nonetheless, an individual can be linked to the intention of others in the group by showing that the individual knew of these intentions and intended to perform actions while aware of the intention behind the action taken on behalf of others. Indeed, in international criminal trials the intention of the individual defendant is often hard to connect to the *mens rea* needed for criminal conviction, for example, because many of the individuals who do the state's, or some other organized group's, bidding are acting with the intention to do their duty to the state and not with the additional or specific intention to bring about harm.

In criminal actions of states generally, the intention and action of the state are separated so that the leader of the collectivity may express the intention of the state but does not often do the killing or raping himself or herself. And this has caused many critics to complain that it is unfair to hold an individual human person responsible and liable for harm when that person does not display the right combination of action and intention to meet normal criminal standards. We take up this issue and our response in Section III.

III WHO, OR WHAT, SHOULD BE BLAMED AND PUNISHED?

Given that most international crimes are committed by states or groups that often act as states do, it seems that groups such as states should be the ones held responsible for these international crimes. But courts, even international courts, are not very likely to be able to hold states liable. Indeed, in the few cases when the International Court of Justice (ICJ) has been effective in dealing with states, this has occurred only when states have agreed to allow the ICJ to hold them responsible. This is unlikely in cases of criminal liability. First of all, states would see any criminal judgment against them as a matter of abridging their sovereignty. Second, the ICJ deals primarily with matters of treaty violation, where the law in question has been agreed upon mutually. Criminal law, unlike contract law, for instance, is not grounded in the consent of the parties – one cannot merely decide whether or not to be subject to criminal laws.

Holding states accountable for their wrongdoings is seen by the critics of international criminal tribunals to be a matter of politics, not discretionary law enforcement practices. In this view, if states, or statelike entities, are to be held accountable and deterred from mass atrocities and other international crimes, then either the international criminal tribunals will have to engage in politics or the tribunals will not succeed. And if the tribunals become involved in politics, it might seem that the tribunals will lose their public stature as fair and independent arbiters. As some critics allege, courts hold out the claim that they are not political entities but are seekers of the truth and purveyors of impartial judgments and punishments.

One other point worth considering in this component of the responsibility critique of international criminal tribunals is that states are not the sorts of entities that can be punished easily in any event. It is hard to imagine what it would mean to put the state into the dock, let alone in prison. This aspect just reinforces the critical point that mass crimes committed by states or statelike entities, like all other collective entities, cannot easily be dealt with by criminal tribunals, as has been well-known in domestic jurisdictions for a very long time.

One way to begin to answer these objections is to try to be creative in altering the way that criminal trials are arranged. Some have suggested that instead of holding individual criminal trials, we should be exploring the ways in which a state might actually be a party to a criminal indictment.[4] At

[4] See Anthony Lang, "Crime and Punishment: Holding States Accountable" *Ethics & International Affairs*, 21, no. 2 (2007), pp. 239–257.

Nuremberg, corporations, such as I. G. Farber and Krupps, were defendants before the International Military Tribunal. And there certainly have been attempts to hold other groups, as groups rather than merely their members, criminally liable. States often act very much like individual human persons even if it would be hard for them to appear physically in the criminal dock.

For instance, in U.S. criminal law, corporate presidents, in their corporate role, have appeared in the dock and been punished for what their corporations have done.[5] In the last few years, there has been a sharp increase in criminal prosecutions of corporate leaders, especially for the wrongdoing that caused the collapse of the housing market in the first decade of the twenty-first century. These prosecutions are evidence that individuals can be successfully prosecuted for the wrongdoing of their organizations and could serve as a model for how to prosecute the leaders of states or statelike entities for the wrongdoing of their organizations.

Another strategy is to hold high-ranking leaders of states responsible for what they individually have done or failed to do that contributed to the wrongdoing of their organizations. This is one of the main strategies currently employed by the international criminal tribunals. The general term for this strategy is "command responsibility." The strategy in international criminal law developed from the practice of holding military commanders in the field responsible for the wrongdoing of their troops. But the idea can be extended to encompass all the "commanders" up the chain of command, including the top political leaders of a state. It is true that presidents, for instance, are "commanders in chief" and hence should be held at least somewhat accountable for the wrongdoing of those under their command. Of course, not all wrongdoing down the chain should be the responsibility of the commanders. Acts that are accomplished by means of the organization and where the party does not act *ultra vires* should be acts for which the commander could be held liable. However, the line between *ultra vires* acts and acts that a commander knew or should have known about is not always clear.

There are still questions about whether the commander or other leader is indeed the appropriate person or entity to be put in the dock when an organization has committed a crime. While the commander may have been formally responsible, as a matter of how the organization is structured, it is not clear that such responsibility should translate into criminal responsibility. The hallmark of criminal responsibility is that a person acts in an intentional way to

[5] See *US v. Park*, 421 U.S. 658, 95 S. Ct. 1903 (1975).

cause undue harm to another person. And while the commander may intend various things by his or her actions or omissions, typically he or she does not actually harm anyone. The idea that a commander could be responsible for murder or for genocide seems only to make sense if he or she has personally killed someone else. Criminal responsibility typically requires *actus reus* as well as *mens rea*.

So, in order to address these problems with responsibility in international criminal tribunals directly, some attention needs to be paid to how to conceive of collective responsibility in international criminal law. It is not obvious that holding the highest ranking member of an organization responsible, when all of the others down the chain of command are not held responsible, does justice to the nature of the crime and is fair to the parties concerned. Here, we see that there is a lack of connection in the hunt for "the" responsible party when there are many people who are responsible. And matters get worse when the members of a large community act to facilitate those who actually perpetrate the harms. It is for this reason that international criminal tribunals turned to the idea of conspiracies and other strategies that seem to deal better with the group nature of the international crimes that are prosecuted by international criminal tribunals. We turn to several of these schemes in the following sections. There, we try to address a variety of criticisms of international criminal tribunals on grounds that they unfairly prosecute and hold liable for punishment individuals who may only have played a small role in a large organization. Where the magnitude of the crimes is so hard to fathom, it is hard to apportion responsibility when one focuses on how just one individual person intentionally acted.

IV PROBLEMS WITH HOW DEFENDANTS ARE SELECTED

Before a trial begins, there are elaborate efforts to determine who should be considered a defendant and forced to answer for participating in a particular mass crime. Often there are many potential defendants who could be held accountable. How a particular person is chosen is highly contentious, especially since there are so many who are not selected and hence avoid punishment, while normally only one or two individuals are liable to be punished, and often for very long terms.

It may be instructive to begin with the ICTY's first case,[6] concerning Serb atrocities committed against Muslims in Pritodor in Bosnia and Herzegovina. Dusko Tadic was selected to stand trial, as it has been admitted by the ICTY's

[6] *Prosecutor v. Dusko Tadic*, ITCY-94-1.

chief prosecutor at the time, largely because Tadic was in custody and Serbia was refusing to cooperate to extradite to the Hague any of the major players, including General Mladic, who headed the military units that assaulted Muslims in Bosnia and Herzegovina. So, instead of prosecuting the leaders of the campaign of ethnic cleansing, the first international prosecution was for a very minor player, Dusko Tadic.

There were at least three circumstances that made Tadic an attractive defendant for the prosecution, yet these circumstances were problematic and subject to much criticism. First, Tadic was in custody in a German jail and Germany had indicated that it was willing to extradite him to the Hague. Second, Tadic had confessed to German police his role in the ethnic cleansing and had even said that his intention had been to kill as many Muslims as he could. He admitted that he shared the aim of eventually destroying the Muslim population in Bosnia and Herzegovina. Third, Tadic had committed especially gruesome acts against Muslims that had already grabbed headlines because of their salaciousness.

The first advantage to choosing Tadic was that there were no extradition problems. Yet, this was in part because Tadic had decided to travel to Germany instead of remaining in Bosnia or traveling to Serbia. So, it was largely a matter of luck that he was easy to prosecute and others, perhaps more deserving of prosecution, were not.

The second "advantage" of choosing Tadic was that he had confessed and done so in a way that made it easy to establish his intent to commit an international crime, not just a domestic crime. Here again, this was largely a matter of luck for the ICTY Prosecutor's staff. And as critics pointed out, this made it seem as if it would be a simple matter to connect the defendant's intention to harm his neighbors and countrymen to the intent to commit the larger international mass crime.

The third "advantage" was perhaps the most unfortunate. Choosing a defendant because his crime was especially salacious is not a particularly fair strategy for deciding who is deserving of prosecution. In Tadic's case, the facts were indeed so inflammatory that while the world took notice, it was hard to see how a fair trial could be had. In particular, Tadic had forced one concentration camp inmate to bite off the testicles of another concentration camp inmate and had engaged in especially gruesome acts of rape against inmates as well.[7]

It has been claimed that the ICC has also selected defendants on the basis of their high-profile status rather than on the basis of who most deserved to

7 See Michael Scharf, *Balkan Justice* (New York: Carolina Academic Press, 1997).

be held criminally liable. Here, the case of Kenya is perhaps the most notorious because it appears that a leading politician, who then became a sitting head of state, was chosen to be prosecuted for a massacre that happened after a national election in Kenya. The decision may have been based on the high profile of Kenyatta. But when political pressure was brought to bear on the ICC Office of the Prosecutor, the case was postponed indefinitely and then dismissed. Both of these prosecutorial decisions, first to indict Kenyatta and then to postpone the trial, have opened the ICC to criticism of its method of deciding who deserves to be held accountable for international crimes.

Our response to these criticisms is to admit that they are by and large correct. At the beginning of the life of international criminal tribunals, it seems that bad decisions were made about the first cases to prosecute. The concern about defendant selection does diminish the longer there are prosecutions by any given international criminal tribunal, but it is very unfortunate that the first cases have been so badly selected. The question to consider is whether or not there are structural flaws with these tribunals that make it likely that such problems cannot be corrected.

We understand these concerns but do not see any structural shortcomings that cannot be changed in order to make the initial selection of who is to be held liable of punishment considerably fairer. We will address the general issue of fairness in case selection in a later chapter. For now, we end this brief section with some suggestions about how international criminal tribunals could address the selection problem in terms of those who are held responsible.

Our general position, and one we will argue for at various points later, is that decisions about whom to prosecute should not be made on political or popular-opinion grounds. Defendant selection should be based on who is most deserving of punishment. Now, the difficulty is that we are speaking of deservingness for punishment for an international crime, and those crimes are mainly mass crimes, where there are many people who played roles. So, if for no other than practical reasons of resource scarcity for the Office of the Prosecutor, the selection should be made in terms of who played the most important role in the perpetration of the mass crime, and that will almost always mean that prosecutions should be restricted to leaders of states and nonstate groups. Recent international chief prosecutors have already signaled that they are approaching the selection problem in just this way. We will next examine some of the controversial strategies that have been adopted for such prosecutions.

V MASS CRIMES, JOINT CRIMINAL ENTERPRISE LIABILITY, AND THE CONTROL THEORY

Nearly all international crimes that are under the jurisdiction of the ICC are mass crimes. The central responsibility issue concerns how to hold individuals criminally liable for what a group has done. Indeed, matters are even more difficult when the group is organized under the auspices of a state. As we said, it is not possible, at least at the moment, to put an entire state or other group entity in the criminal dock. So, the question is which individual persons of the state are responsible for what the state has done. The mismatch between the individual in the dock and the enormous extent of a crime such as genocide he or she is charged with has caused some of the sharpest criticisms of international tribunals. And these criticisms have been especially heartfelt when drawn in moral terms.[8]

The response of the ICC and various ad hoc tribunals, at least as controversial, has been to allege that an individual defendant, whether low-ranking or high-ranking, was part of a larger "conspiracy."[9] Controversy about this strategy has grown because over an extended period the international prosecutors have used this strategic device in nearly every case. Various forms of what is called "joint criminal enterprise" (JCE) liability have been devised, with the most controversial holding everyone who took part in the slightest way responsible for all that the criminal enterprise did, whether the individual defendant realized what the rest of the enterprise was doing or not.[10] There is also more recently a turn toward the control of crime theory as a way to respond to some of the criticisms of the JCE liability models.

The first and least controversial of the joint criminal enterprise strategies also covers the fewest cases. In this vein, the ICTY has employed an idea very similar to conspiracy in common law countries. The defendants must have reached an agreement displaying a shared intent with a common design to perpetrate harm. The agreement component of joint criminal enterprise liability is very similar to the agreement component in conspiracy law in the Anglo-American tradition. But showing that there was such an agreement has proven to be very hard indeed in international criminal law cases. The idea of shared intent has received close scrutiny in

[8] See Jens Ohlin, "Second Order Linking Principles: Combining Vertical and Horizontal Modes of Liability," *Leiden Journal of International Law*, vol. 25, no. 3 (2012), pp. 771–797.

[9] See James Stewart, "The End of 'Modes of Liability' for International Crimes," *Leiden Journal of International Law*, vol. 25, no. 1 (2012), pp. 165–219.

[10] See Mark Osiel, *Making Sense of Mass Atrocity* (New York: Cambridge University Press, 2009), chapter 3.

philosophical circles and is also very difficult to analyze let alone to prove. Common design can be inferred from the enterprise itself – but shared intent has remained elusive.

To illustrate this problem, consider how difficult it is to prove the *dolus specialis* (special intent) for genocide. This intent is characterized as the intent to destroy a group in whole or in part. While it is relatively easy to show that an act of murder, for instance, was a hate crime in that it was committed because of animus toward the group to which the victim belonged, the special intent is much more difficult to prove. The prosecutor would have to show that the individual defendant intended the destruction of the group, not merely the persecution or oppression of the group. And yet it is not at all clear what actions would manifest the *dolus specialis*, providing the definitive insight into an individual's intent.

The second form of joint criminal enterprise liability is designed to capture those who participated in detention or concentration camps. Here there must be "organized systems of repression and ill treatment" where "all of the defendants were present or in the immediate vicinity of the murders, and none of the defendants were charged with participation in some larger plan outside of the unlawful treatment of the prisoners."[11] For fairness sake, it is important that no defendants participated directly in another illegal larger plan, instead of the one charged. The existence of a structure aimed at mass incarceration and oppression has made it easier on the prosecutors who want to prove that there was a joint enterprise. But there is still a challenge in figuring out, for instance, how a particular camp guard displayed a shared intent to oppress the inmates, rather than the intention merely to collect a paycheck.

The third form of joint criminal enterprise liability is the most controversial and the most far reaching. Here the joint criminal enterprise includes criminal acts that are beyond the common design but are "a natural and foreseeable consequence of effecting it."[12] Defendants need not authorize or even order the commission of harm.[13] It is for this reason that many critics have said that this third form of joint enterprise liability is criminal liability without *mens rea*. Foreseeing that something will result is not the same as intending that something will result. And in general those who enter into a common undertaking do not necessarily intend everything that could be foreseen to result from that undertaking. Perhaps if this form of joint criminal liability is

11 Tadic Appeal, paragraph 202.
12 Tadic Appeal, paragraphs 204 and 206.
13 See Osiel, *Making Sense of Mass Atrocity*, p. 52.

to remain it should be considered a form of negligence rather than intentional wrongdoing, since there is no commission but only omission on the part of the defendant.

The criticisms of these various forms of collective liability have been strong and long-standing ever since these forms of liability were announced in the Tadic appeal. The underlying claim of the criticisms is that these collective liability schemes punish some people who are not morally responsible. Sometimes this criticism is drawn in legal terms, but the underlying idea remains an argument about moral responsibility, and it is to this argument that we will attempt to reply in what follows in this section. Of course, we recognize that moral and legal responsibility are closely intertwined in criminal law, whether domestic or international.

One way for us to defend international tribunals from such persistent criticisms is to point out that some of these controversial strategies could simply be abandoned by the Office of the Prosecutor, as seems to be true at the moment at the ICC. It is not clear to us that the use of joint criminal enterprise liability is an overall benefit for criminal tribunals given how much criticism they have generated. And so, one clear way to respond is to eliminate this option for international prosecutors. Prosecutors could and should have to show more defendant involvement in mass crimes than they do under the third form of the joint criminal enterprise models of liability. And there is an obvious charge that could be used more widely and is more closely linked to what people actually did: namely, indicting for complicity.

Arguably, the first two forms of joint criminal enterprise liability are already forms of complicit responsibility. Complicity is only a quasi-collective form of responsibility. The idea behind complicity is that individuals should be held responsible for the parts that they played in collective enterprises, but that these individuals are not to be held responsible for all the harms caused by the collective enterprise. It is worth noting that complicity takes many different forms depending on the role that an individual played in the larger collective effort. The most common form of complicity is "aiding and abetting" – providing material assistance to someone else who is the principal perpetrator of a crime. In the classic case, one person plans the bank robbery and another person drives the getaway car, while two others actually enter the bank and steal the money. All might be guilty of the whole crime, but it also could make sense to hold each individual responsible for his or her part, especially in a criminal trial where restrictions on the use and presentation of evidence limit prosecutors to focusing on what the person in the dock actually did alone.

The idea that one can parse a collective effort into the individual efforts of those who are principals and those who are secondary and tertiary participants may itself need some defense. Indeed, it has been argued that this way of proceeding always leaves a remainder, the truly collective dimension, and hence never really comes to terms with the collective crime. We actually agree with this point. But we would argue that dividing the collective crime into the parts played by individuals is still defensible in terms of the group-based roles played by the individual persons, and indeed it is probably the best we can hope for if we are to employ criminal law to assign responsibility and punishment for such crimes. The remainder may be something that still needs to be referred to in order to understand the enormity or the extent of the crime, but this can be done in the written judgments of the court, or perhaps in a separate truth and reconciliation process, even if not in the way that the responsibility and punishment are meted out to individual defendants by that court.

There is a sense in which the first two forms of joint criminal enterprise liability could be reformed, or at least understood anew, that would make them closer to the model of complicity we have just sketched. In order to establish that an event has occurred of that kind that has principal and tertiary participants, some of the conditions of joint criminal enterprise liability of the first variety would have to be shown. But if the collective nature of the event is established, then the individuals will be prosecuted for, and only for, the discrete roles that each person played in that event.

Here is one of the strongest responses to the myriad worries about holding some people responsible for what they have not done, although, to be sure, it would involve changes in how the prosecutors currently operate in international criminal law. The prosecutors could not merely show that a particular defendant was a participant in a collective criminal enterprise, but instead show precisely what was the role of the defendant and why a particular punishment is appropriate for what the defendant did, and only for what he or she did. The move to add elements of complicity to joint criminal enterprise liability will not solve all of the problems involved in seemingly holding some people responsible for what the state or at least other members of the state did, but will move us closer to an acceptable form of responsibility for international criminal tribunals.

The current strategy of the ICC Prosecutor is to employ a wider concept of perpetrator so as to include those most morally responsible, namely, the people who controlled the crime by their planning and persuading others to execute the plan in a hierarchical arrangement. The ICC now sees perpetrators as those who physically "carry out the objective elements of the offense," but also includes "those who, in spite of being removed from the scene of the crimes, control or mastermind the commission because they decide whether and how the offense will be committed."[14]

There have been various criticisms of this new responsibility model, especially because of the inherent vagueness of the core idea of "control" itself.[15] In addition, some have worried that if the control model takes over completely, those who were the mere cogs will escape punishment completely. As of this writing it is not fully clear whether the control theory will completely replace the JCE theory, or merely supplement it.

It is clear that the control theory will work best in those cases where there is organized criminality, such as in concentration camps and criminal political structures such as that of the Nazis. Counting those who control the crime remotely as perpetrators seems to us to be a very good start at finding a more acceptable theory of collective criminal liability than was JCE. But we also think that this is only a start, since other types of collective criminality that were addressed by JCE also need to be developed. There is a need to deal with the complicity cases discussed previously. Those who were not in control should also be prosecuted. This is especially true of the bystanders who have played an outsized role in mass atrocity cases.

VI APPORTIONING RESPONSIBILITY DURING CIVIL WAR

Another responsibility worry is that it is unlikely that international tribunals can apportion responsibility fairly when atrocities occur during a civil war where both sides may have engaged in similar tactics. As Hannah Arendt once argued, "Where all are guilty, nobody in the last analysis can be judged."[16] Judicial apportionment of responsibility is based on the idea that some are guilty, and those who are not guilty are the ones in a position to judge the guilty. When all are guilty at least of complicity, the least guilty can hide because of the complicity of others who are just a bit worse.

When most members of a society are involved as perpetrators (or are at least complicit), it is hard to assign responsibility fairly even if there is not a civil war with similar atrocities committed on both sides. Take the Rwanda case, for example – one group in the society was attacked by another group

14 Lubanga Confirmation Decision, para. 330, discussed and cited in Elies van Sliedregt, *Individual Criminal Responsibility in International Law* (Oxford: Oxford University Press, 2012), p. 83.

15 See ibid., p. 87.

16 See Hannah Arendt, "Organized Guilt and Universal Responsibility," *Jewish Frontier*, 1948, reprinted in *Collective Responsibility*, edited by Larry May and Stacey Hoffman (Savage, MD: Rowman & Littlefield, 1991), pp. 278.

of the society while many of the remaining members of the population stood by and did nothing. There is evidence that atrocities were also committed by individuals who were part of the attacked group in society. As was seen at the time, it was not possible to prosecute all who were involved in the genocide, and it was not clear what to do with those who committed crimes outside the strict genocide narrative. But then how is a judge to decide who should be apportioned responsibility? And can one fairly assign responsibility for "genocide" to what just one person did when there were so many others involved? Is it possible to prosecute individuals who could be considered both victims and perpetrators? Prosecuting anyone, when so many similarly situated others must be unprosecuted cannot but appear so biased as to call into question the very enterprise of holding people responsible amid so much similarly wrongful behavior of other people.

So far the majority of cases adjudicated by international criminal tribunals have involved civil wars and this presents other problems as well. International criminal tribunals must in effect choose who are on the just and who are on the unjust side of these wars. And doing so in the midst of a civil war is often exceedingly difficult or even impossible. Indeed, international prosecutors would be well advised, so their critics say, to stay out of civil wars that can morph a supposedly just defender of security in a society into a defender of oppression instead, as has most recently happened in Egypt.

A similar issue can be seen when the ICTY came under heavy criticism for singling out Serbs for prosecution, when it was clear that Croats engaged in similar tactics, as did some Muslims. Here, there was patent discrimination in the prosecutorial strategy, and the unfairness of singling out only the members of one group for prosecution tainted the proceedings and convinced people who were already suspicious of international criminal tribunals of their valuelessness. Serbs who rightly voiced this criticism of the ICTY were then unable to accept that in places such as Srebrenica there were atrocities that needed to be prosecuted, given their sense of the unfairness of the use of prosecutorial discretion.[17]

Concerning the criticisms of apportioning responsibility in a discriminatory manner, the international tribunals could indict in such a way so as not to give the appearance of discriminating against one group in an ongoing civil war by prosecuting individuals from both sides whenever possible. The ICTY did eventually indict defendants who were not Serbs, but the Prosecutor waited so long that many within Serbia and elsewhere had already become convinced that the international tribunal was biased.[18] Yet, a similar set of indictments

[17] See Aleksandar Jokic, ed., *War Crimes and Collective Wrongdoing* (Oxford: Blackwell, 2001).
[18] See Michael Scharf, *Balkan Justice* (New York: Carolina Academic Press, 1997).

of Tutsis has not occurred at the ICTR and is unlikely to transpire since the ICTR is currently in the final stages of wrapping up its last trials. It is important to give the appearance, if not the reality, of fairness from the beginning, as we will also see in Chapter 8.

Civil wars and other asymmetric wars pose a host of responsibility problems. But part of our response is to point out that these problems are not so clearly different from some domestic responsibility problems. Often prosecutors are faced with the question of whom to indict when many can be indicted but resources for trials are limited. Critics of a given prosecutor will often claim that there has been prosecutorial misconduct because some are prosecuted and others are allowed to walk free. It is very often true that only a small fraction of those who act similarly will be prosecuted. Domestically this is not thought to be the kind of stinging indictment of the whole system of adjudication that should lead us to contemplate disbanding the domestic prosecutor's office. So, again, part of our response is to point out that there is always a problem of having only some indicted, and the question becomes why such a problem is thought to be insurmountable merely because the numbers are greater or the crimes are more heinous at the international level.

Another part of our response is to say that while clear-cut discrimination by prosecutors needs to be eliminated, remedial measures do not necessarily threaten the institution of international criminal tribunals. If more oversight of the Office of the Prosecutor is needed, this can be accomplished in a variety of ways that do not jeopardize the very institution of international criminal tribunals. Civil wars are a challenge to justice on a host of levels. And international criminal justice is strained by such wars. This needs to be admitted and confronted squarely by the Office of the Prosecutor. But we see no reason to think that the best approach to solving these problems is to eliminate international tribunals.

VII RESOLVING THE RESPONSIBILITY DILEMMA

Mark Osiel has argued that there is a dilemma facing defenders of international criminal tribunals.

> When it narrows its lens to the person in the dock, the law risks underestimating the significance of his or her deeds, for their gravity is comprehensible only when seen in relation to those of many others, above and below the accused in the chain of command. Responding to this concern, international criminal offenses are now often defined to widen the narrative frame,

> encompassing a broader picture. A crime against humanity, for instance must be part of a "widespread or systematic attack" on civilians. Prosecutors need to show that the defendant's actions took place within such a context and that he or she was aware of it. Yet here the law almost immediately succumbs to the opposite danger: blaming the defendant for wrongs beyond his or her control or contemplation. Criminal law seems to find itself impaled on the horns of this dilemma.[19]

Osiel clearly formulates a position that many critics of international tribunals have voiced, even as Osiel himself thinks there is a solution to this problem. In this section we will explore various ways to respond to this dilemma faced by defenders of international tribunals.

First, we have already suggested one approach – holding individuals responsible for what they have done "as members" of a collective organization. It is true that merely focusing on what each member did risks diminishing the gravity of the collective endeavor. But by treating the individual "as a member" ineluctably draws the focus to the collective endeavor in order to figure out what role the individual played. Indeed, one cannot hold an individual responsible for what he or she has done as a member of a collective organization without understanding the larger collective endeavor.

If we hold individuals responsible for what they did in their roles, we by and large hold individuals responsible for what they have done. It is true that these individuals could not have created the collective organization on their own, in their individual capacities. So, insofar as what the individual did "as a member" could only occur within the collective organization, holding him or her responsible as a member to a certain extent holds the member responsible for what the organization did. But what the organization contributed is merely the context in which the individual took action – we are not holding the individual responsible for what the organization did that was beyond the individual member's action. We do not, in the end, hold the individual responsible for the context, but rather for action within the context.

A second, related strategy is also suggested in our endorsement of the model of complicity. The idea of complicity as a form of responsibility is well accepted in most societies, both in morality and in law. It is not normally said that if a person is held responsible as an accomplice, for instance, we hold that person responsible for what is beyond her action. Those who are complicit have it in their control to assist the primary perpetrators, or not to assist them. It is true that there can be no complicity without primary responsibility on the part of a perpetrator. And it is also true that the person who is complicit does

[19] Osiel, *Making Sense of Mass Atrocities*, p. 3.

not have control over the perpetrator's responsibility. But the role played by the complicit party is still a contribution to the wrong, even though it is less of a contribution than is that provided by the principal perpetrator. That is why complicity is normally not as strongly punished as is perpetration of the principal crime.

Complicity provides a model of how to assign responsibility when a group of people have each contributed to a wrong. The central idea is that it is possible to distinguish those who are the most responsible from those who are less so, and still be fair to all parties in how their participation is treated. So, here the dilemma is somewhat resolved. In recognizing the group as having done something that often could not have been done by a single person, and recognizing the seriousness of the wrong done, we give voice to the full gravity of what has occurred. But we do not hold the participants in the wrong responsible for everything the group does. The idea of drawing a distinction between principal responsibility and complicit responsibility marks that for which each individual is rightly held responsible.

Third, following Mark Osiel's lead, perhaps some of these issues would be better addressed outside a criminal context. In part, the responsibility dilemma surfaces in trying to fit a group act and collective actor into a criminal trial that is suitable primarily for individual acts and actors. In other domains of law and morality the dilemma does not arise, or, if it does, it has a more ready resolution. Civil law and moral norms can approach issues of responsibility in a more fine-grained manner than can criminal law.

Osiel has suggested that making military officers pay damages for their conduct during atrocities, rather than prosecuting and punishing them, might be a more effective way to deter the commission of atrocities by members of army units.[20] This proposal, which shifts some of our focus away from criminal law and its high burden of proof to civil law, is worth considering, we believe, although there are no comparable international civil law courts to the international criminal tribunals today.

This last strategy raises again the larger question of this chapter – whether international criminal tribunals are indeed the right institution for assigning responsibility in cases of mass crime. It may be possible to design alternative institutions that deal with mass crime better – perhaps in some cases truth and reconciliation commissions or trials of states themselves should be pursued instead of criminal trials of individual human persons. But the problem is that these alternatives are unlikely to come into being in the near future. So, the question is then whether we are better off or worse off with the existing

20 See Mark Osiel, *Obeying Orders* (New York: Transaction, 1999).

brand of tribunals, given that there are not alternative institutions available today. In Section VIII we consider a set of objections concerning responsibility of bystanders that pose an especially difficult question of how best to assign responsibility for mass crimes.

VIII BYSTANDERS AND PERPETRATORS

Mass crimes occur when large numbers of people stand by and do not act to thwart or even to provide disincentives for these crimes. So, it seems reasonable to think that stopping mass crimes in the future will require strategies that affect the bystanders as well as the perpetrators. Yet, international criminal tribunals seem ill-suited to have any effect on the bystanders. We began to address this issue when we discussed civil war, where many are at least somewhat guilty and perhaps only a few are truly innocent. In this section we want to consider a somewhat related question of whether holding international criminal trials can affect bystanders and others who do not act to stop the perpetrators. In Chapter 3 we looked at the efficacy of punishment. Here we want to discuss whether people's sense of responsibility can be affected if there are fewer in the society who do not participate in or support the mass crime.

The problem is especially acute if the majority of the people are not only bystanders but also in some sense complicit in the mass crimes. Here there is a sense of normalcy in not interfering that needs to be confronted, and it is not clear that holding criminal trials, whether domestic or international, is the best way to proceed. Critics have argued that truth and reconciliation commissions are often better than trials if reconciliation is indeed the goal.[21] And other critics have pointed out that trials can actually make conditions worse in that people become even more nationalistic and resistant to change after a contentious international trial than before.

We readily acknowledge that in some cases it is better not to hold criminal trials in the aftermath of mass atrocity, as we said, where it is feasible to institute truth and reconciliation commissions. But in most cases, the adverse effects of criminal trials can be minimized and there are positive effects that are hard to achieve in forums other than criminal trials. We can begin by noting that truth and reconciliation commissions generally do not establish guilt or provide punishment for anyone, no matter how egregious the acts. So, unfortunately the message sent by doing nothing when faced with evidence of

[21] See Robert Rotberg and Dennis Thompson, eds., *Truth v. Justice: The Morality of Truth Commissions* (Princeton, NJ: Princeton University Press, 2000); and Verwoerd and Villa-Vilencia, eds, *Looking Back, Reaching Forward: Reflections on the Truth and Reconciliation Commission in South Africa* (Cape Town: University of Cape Town Press, 2000).

the crime is that the crime was not all that bad. Of course, what criminal trials do best is counter this impression.

Bystanders pose a special problem if they are not indictable for complicity. Yet, they rarely rise to the level of being complicit. They sometimes appear just to "stand around," as the term signifies. Bystanders do not do anything – which of course could be a sign of neglecting to do something they should be doing. But what bystanders fail to do, such as not trying to stop their neighbors from killing each other, typically does not rise to the level of being criminal negligence. And so they are not easily dealt with in criminal law, especially if their failure to act to stop mass crimes does not rise to the level of being complicit.

Yet, the problem is that mass atrocity typically only succeeds when there is a climate of acceptance of discrimination by the majority of the society. And here the fact that bystanders do nothing in the face of a buildup to persecution means they contribute to a climate of accepting persecution, if not as individuals then as a group. And arguably when they do not feel that they share in the responsibility for mass crimes they will not cease to be passive spectators. So, while criminal trials indict the perpetrators and some others who were complicit, there is no specific way to deal with the bystanders who contribute to the climate of acceptance of discrimination and persecution.

International criminal trials could be reformed to include a mechanism for dealing with some of those who are bystanders to mass atrocity, who merely contribute to the climate of persecution. International criminal trials could be reformed in various ways that would minimize their negative effects so as still to allow for them to achieve their positive effects. One of the keys here is to induce multiple parties to see that they did play a role, even though a relatively small role, along with the main players who perpetrated the mass crime.

In addition, international trials have become avenues for telling the larger story of a mass crime in that there is generally a long section at the beginning of the written judgment that provides the context of the crime. And in describing the context of the mass atrocity the role played by minor figures and even bystanders sometimes is documented. In documenting the role, the trial judgment focuses on more than just those who had a direct role in the mass atrocity, shining a light on the minor players. Even more of this than is currently standard could be employed so that the role of bystanders is indeed discussed and there is at least shaming that occurs, although this is still not enough. In some cases, truth and reconciliation commissions are the only way to deal effectively with the large variety of bystanders.

The problem with focusing on bystanders who have not been indicted is that the perpetrators are sometimes tarred with a brush that actually does not include the perpetrators' acts. So, there is a fairly important fairness issue here that we will need to explore in more detail. Yet, there have been trials, including the Tadic trial, where fairness has been preserved even as hundreds of pages of the trial judgment have considered the climate and small actors that contributed to the situation where Tadic was able to engage in persecution of Muslims in Bosnia.

Another response is to point out that criminal trials should not be seen as the entirety of forums used to condemn perpetrators in cases of mass atrocity. It is possible to have criminal trials proceeding at the same time as truth and reconciliation commissions (TRCs). It is true that in South Africa it was thought that criminal trials would impede the work of the TRC. But it has been recognized after the fact that the TRC process would have been easier if the main perpetrators were tried separately. This is what occurred in Rwanda, where the main perpetrators were tried by the ICTR at the same time the Gacaca process was dealing with minor players and even with the role of bystanders.

Criminal trials are not well-equipped to assign responsibility to minor players in large-scale crimes. It is our view that the right conclusion to draw is not that trials, especially international criminal trials, should be disregarded. Rather, there are means to make the international criminal tribunals better at dealing with the problem of bystanders. And in any event, as we have argued, one need not choose between trials and other dispute resolution models such as truth and reconciliation commissions; both can function side by side. But it is indeed important to remember that criminal trials operate best when assigning responsibility to the main perpetrators in situations of mass atrocity.[22]

In this chapter we have tried to deal with a variety of critiques of international criminal tribunals related to responsibility issues. Despite the fact that international crimes are often committed by states, there are plausible strategies for holding individuals responsible for what their states do, and hence for putting individual humans into the international criminal dock. We embrace a theory of the state that sees it as composed of individual humans and their various organizational relationships. Holding individuals responsible for what they do in their roles in the state, along with holding others responsible for how they were complicit, will allow normal criminal proceedings to take place in international criminal tribunals, where it will not be true that these proceedings are unfair for holding some responsible for what others have done.

[22] See Jovana Davidovic, "Timor-Leste and Transitional Justice: Should We Pursue International Prosecutions for the Crimes Committed in East Timor in 1999?" in Larry May and Andrew Forcehimes (eds.), *Morality, Jus Post Bellum, and International Law* (New York: Cambridge University Press, 2012).

But there are still questions about whether domestic courts might not be better than international courts for these complex collective responsibility issues.

IX SOME JURISDICTIONAL ISSUES

We consider various aspects of the jurisdictional critique of international criminal tribunals throughout this book. We will end this chapter on responsibility by highlighting how responsibility worries exacerbate the jurisdictional worries. Those who are said to deserve to be held accountable have raised the question of whether they are truly deserving of international rather than domestic prosecution. Often the evidence is strongest that a given person has killed or raped, but the evidence is not as strong that the person intended to do so as part of a mass crime of the sort that international criminal tribunals prosecute. Indeed, the first case before the ICTY raised a significant jurisdictional challenge to the prosecution of Tadic by an international criminal tribunal.

The problem is not that international crimes could be tried in domestic tribunals – since most theorists are happy with that eventuality. Instead, the problem is that what most international defendants do, without the larger context, looks so much like a garden-variety domestic crime that it is hard to see why anyone should think that it is best prosecuted as an international crime at all. The small fry are often engaging in standard domestic criminal conduct. And while the leaders are doing something different than the small fry, they also are often not doing anything different from what the leaders of groups do who are involved in criminal conspiracies. Indeed, this is why, as we have seen, the international criminal tribunals have had to follow domestic conspiracy and complicity law in prosecuting international criminal leaders.

One of the most prevalent reasons given for international prosecutions is that the harmful act in question would not have been prosecuted domestically because it is not considered a crime in domestic jurisdictions. But this is problematic since the underlying act is much more commonly also a domestic crime. The issue then becomes why it should be prosecuted under international law, no matter where the prosecution takes place.

Our response is to admit that some crimes should indeed be better prosecuted as domestic crimes under domestic jurisdictions. But there are still cases that fall into one of two categories that are best prosecuted as a matter of international law. The first category involves those few cases where the crime, such as genocide, is distinctly different from the underlying acts of murder upon which the genocide is based. The other category concerns matters that need a high-profile prosecution that the whole world will take notice of because of the gravity of the crime. We will explore each of these categories in the remainder of this section.

First, genocide and crimes against humanity, as well as aggression, are not domestic crimes in many jurisdictions. If aggression is to be prosecuted by the ICC in the future, this will be the only forum where it will be prosecuted. Some states have amended their criminal codes to add genocide, and a small number of states have done the same for crimes against humanity. But many states do not have criminal statutes about such matters. Murder, even mass murder, is different from genocide in that genocide has a distinct intent requirement, the intent to destroy, in whole or in part, a social group. Aggression is a crime that only a state or statelike entity can commit, and it would be odd and hugely problematic for such crimes to be prosecuted by a state's domestic criminal courts.

Second, crimes such as genocide and crimes against humanity are by their nature crimes that affect the whole world and should be prosecuted on the world stage, as it were. The expressive function of international criminal prosecutions is best suited to these crimes. This is especially true when the crimes would otherwise be prosecuted by states that have a weak judicial system or where the case is likely to be not well publicized.

In this chapter we have generally defended the role of international criminal tribunals in assigning responsibility and liability in some mass crimes. We have, as in earlier chapters, recognized the problems of international prosecutions, but have not seen these criticisms as requiring an abandonment of the international criminal tribunal as a locus of trials for mass crimes. We would note, though, that the models that have been developed, especially the joint criminal enterprise models, are indeed so problematic that it would be best that they were abandoned in favor of more standard models related to conspiracies and especially complicity. And the selection of whom to prosecute is also in need of major overhaul, in light of the missteps by various tribunals as they have started the process of sifting through the many individual acts that could be the basis of international prosecutions. A defense of international criminal tribunals cannot be tone deaf to the often excellent and heartfelt criticisms that have been offered by leading legal theorists. Indeed, we have found merit in many of these criticisms, even as we have not seen them as warranting the abandonment of the development of international criminal tribunals.

5

Economic and Other Practical Issues

Some authors who take a law and economics perspective, or some other social scientific perspective, have criticized international criminal courts and tribunals for having weak compliance and for being inefficient in terms of the way their resources are spent. Eric Posner and his various coauthors, including Jack Goldsmith and Alan Sykes, have offered an extensive critique of international law that is highly relevant for the specific case of international criminal tribunals. They argue that there is no sense of obligation that moves states to participate in the international domain. At best, there is a weak compliance by states concerning their supposed obligations in international law. When that tendency is extended to international criminal law, Posner and his colleagues foresee that international tribunals only succeed insofar as states see it to be in their interests to comply, but that in a nonconsensual area of law such as international criminal law achieving such success has been difficult.[1]

In Section I of this chapter we discuss the general idea of compliance and its relation to law, and to international criminal law in particular. Section II introduces the critique of international criminal tribunals offered by several economic theorists that challenges the feasibility of sanctions. In Section III we examine the larger question of whether anything other than appeals to the self-interests of states will solve the problem of compliance. Section IV discusses some claims of these critiques that actually favor international criminal tribunals. In Section V we reflect on why critiques of legal or moral obligation drawn in terms of self-interest have proved so problematic. In Section VI we examine critiques that focus on how few international criminals have actually been prosecuted. And in Section VII we examine the critiques that have

[1] See Jack Goldsmith and Eric Posner, *The Limits of International Law* (Oxford: Oxford University Press, 2005); and Eric Posner and Alan Sykes, *Economic Foundations of International Law* (Cambridge, MA: Harvard University Press, 2013).

focused on the sheer amount of money it has cost to prosecute individuals in international criminal tribunals.

I COMPLIANCE AND LEGAL SYSTEMS

Let us begin by considering whether a legal system can be considered practically legitimate if the laws of that system are not routinely followed. First, one might think that laws that are validly propounded bind regardless of whether or not anyone actually obeys them. It might be that satisfying the procedural requirements alone, such as having been passed by a majority of legislators, is sufficient. Second, one might think that legitimacy of a legal system is merely the aggregate of all laws once considered to be valid laws in a particular jurisdiction, even though there might be many ways that laws could once have been considered valid. Third, one could think that legitimacy follows from what is agreed to be binding by those who would be subject to the legal system, where regarding something as binding does not yet mean that one complies with these laws. Or, fourth, one might think that legitimacy is due to what the officials of the system accept and set out to enforce. Any of these four understandings of the practical legitimacy of a legal system leaves out any mention of whether the laws of a legal system are in fact obeyed.

Yet, it would be very odd indeed if a system of law considered to be legitimate nonetheless lacked compliance among the population that was subject to the laws of that system. The question would arise: why are the laws not being complied with if those laws are considered part of a "legitimate legal system"? Of course, it is possible that the populace disagrees with the officials of the legal system. Or the populace may have interests that override the obligation to comply with the law. But if the laws of the legal system were routinely not complied with, and by a substantial section of the populace, it would be very odd to say that the system of law is legitimate. We will first try to explain the oddity here before turning to issues in international law.

Legitimacy in law is different from other normative categories in that it depends on the acceptance or at least the acquiescence of those who are governed by the laws. As we discussed in Chapter 1, legitimacy concerns the right of a government to "rule" by the use of coercive force. This right cannot be grounded merely in the value of the laws. The strong liberty interests of the populace are such that the populace can only be legitimately coerced if they have in some fashion agreed to be so coerced.

And so we arrive at the nub of the problem of the practical legitimacy in law: if the populace is not complying with the laws of a given legal system, it would seem that the populace is by these acts of noncompliance indicating that it has not consented to be coerced by the laws, and the laws are thereby rendered illegitimate. On this understanding, a populace could render a previously legitimate system of law illegitimate by its acts of defiance of or at least noncompliance with that legal system. Or if the populace does not generally comply with the laws, then regardless of how those laws were formed, the legal system will not have legitimacy.

The legitimacy of a legal system is thus a curious combination of factors: formal conditions concerning how the laws of the system are enacted and compliance conditions concerning whether the laws are followed. But it is not fully clear how the compliance condition is to be established as having been fulfilled. There are at least two ways that compliance can be established: by observing whether the populace follows the laws, or by ascertaining whether the populace feels bound to obey and then does so for this reason. We could, following H. L. A. Hart, discuss these as external and internal perspectives on compliance. The external perspective approaches compliance by taking an outsider's perspective, whereas the internal perspective approaches compliance from the perspective of the people who are under the laws.

If compliance is to ground the legitimacy of a legal system, it would seem that it does so in that a populace feels bound to obey, not merely that it does in fact obey, the laws of a legal system. The feeling that a person has of being bound, combined with the formal legitimacy of the source of the bindingness, overcomes the liberty problem and establishes that the use of coercive force in a legal system is legitimate. If compliance is due to something that is itself normatively weak or even questionable, it is not clear how the state would have the right to use coercive force over the populace.

This leads us to a consideration of the motivation that a populace expresses in its compliance with the laws of a legal system. If a populace acquiesces and generally obeys the law, but does so out of fear, can the acquiescence count as establishing the legitimacy of the legal system? And if the populace over time ceases to fear the rulers, could that fact render the legal system illegitimate? For a legal system to be legitimate it seems that it must "achieve" and maintain legitimacy as something fairly stable for it to be efficacious.

A problem that we will take up in more detail later in this chapter concerns a populace that complies but for self-interested reasons. Critics of international criminal tribunals have argued that it is true that many states seemingly comply with international law, but unless this is done out of a sense of obligation there is no reason to think that the states are bound to obey. If this kind of compliance does ground the legitimacy of a legal system, it is nonetheless problematic since the interests of a population can shift over time and thereby render illegitimate a system previously legitimate. For this and other reasons, theorists are troubled by the idea that a legal system could be legitimate even though the populace only complies with that system's laws out of self-interest.

Indeed, it seems more plausible to think that compliance must be based on a feeling that the law is worthy of obedience before compliance can partially ground the legitimacy of a legal system. But, of course, there are nearly always mixed motives when individuals act. So, it should be no surprise that members of a populace would obey the law because they feel that the law is binding on them, and obey the law out of self-interest. But if they only obey out of self-interest, then the law will not achieve what it needs to be effective in stabilizing a society and providing a consistent basis for people's expectations about what is legally required of them.

In Chapter 2 on sovereignty, we were critical of the expansion of customary international law. We were not critical of the central idea behind this type of law that state practice, in conjunction with compliance based on a sense of obligation, are the main normative elements of customary international law. One can see a similar structure to the role of compliance in the legitimacy of a legal system: actual compliance on the part of a populace motivated, or significantly motivated, by a feeling of being bound to comply. But in both cases, there has to be a populace and there has to be a way for some members of the populace to opt out.

Opting out of a largely customary basis for the use of coercive force is crucial given the liberty interests that are at stake. Unless there is a strong sense that each is bound by what the majority decides, customary practice cannot be a ground for obligating those who are dissenters or objectors. And even where there is a strong majority-based society, an opt-out proviso is necessary, even if it only means that folks must be allowed to exit the society when they disagree with the laws of a legal system.

Compliance, or its lack, plays a large role in how we assess the legitimacy of a legal system. And so the economic critique of international law, in terms of the lack of compliance, must be taken very seriously. But the compliance issue, as we have discussed, is multifaceted – whether there is de facto compliance, and whether there is motivation to comply based on a sense of bindingness of the law.

The issue of compliance is especially important in criminal law, including international criminal law, since criminal law is meant to be nonconsensual. If the state can coerce a person concerning criminal standards, such as not murdering or raping, regardless of whether or not a person agrees to these standards, then the general issue of compliance with a system of law is of the utmost importance. There must be compliance with the system of law even when the enforcement of that law opposes what the person would agree or acquiesce to at the moment.

II INCENTIVES TO CONFORM TO LAW

Here is a fairly simple dilemma that Posner and Sykes have provided that neatly captures one of the main criticisms of international criminal courts and tribunals such as the ICC. Posner and Sykes argue:

> Most states have ratified the Rome Statute, but the ICC has limited resources and cannot investigate all of the atrocities being committed around the world. Most of the major powers have refused to ratify the Rome Statute. And the ICC does not address the basic problem with international criminal prosecutions. When states are willing to prosecute international crimes committed by their nationals, the ICC is not necessary. When states are unwilling to launch prosecutions, the ICC has no capacity to compel them to turn over indicted suspects.[2]

Here the economic emphasis on incentives leads to the concern that the ICC and the ad hoc criminal tribunals do not have the enforcement power to make international criminal law work the way that domestic criminal law works.

In light of our discussion in Section I, the question of the practical legitimacy of international criminal law is raised by such cases of noncompliance. It appears to some critics that there is compliance with international criminal arrest warrants only when states see it as in their interest to comply. And this seems to undermine the idea that international law is considered normatively binding by states.

Economists postulate that actors are rational and that they only behave in a certain way, especially if it is otherwise against their interests, when there are incentives to do so. And for the economic model, international criminal tribunals, unlike domestic criminal tribunals, are problematic since they lack effective enforcement mechanisms of their own, and many states are indifferent to the enforcement of international criminal law. President al-Bashir of Sudan was indicted several years ago, and yet so far no state has been willing to arrest him in the name of the prosecuting authority, the ICC. This was most recently seen in 2015 in South Africa's unwillingness to extradite al-Bashir, who was in the country for a conference.

This economically inspired critique raises the larger question of how to regard a freestanding court that does not have either a legislative body that

[2] Posner and Sykes, *Economic Foundations of International Law*, p. 108.

creates its laws or an executive body that arrests those who have been indicted, let alone a clearly defined society with norms that extend to all of its members. One does not have to endorse the rational choice model of many economists to see that there is a problem when a court lacks clear enforcement mechanisms. Indeed, this larger critique has arisen from realists and other theorists as well.

Realists in international relations have attempted to diminish the standing of international "law," seeing international affairs governed by the exertion of power, or its threat, by states. Realists have denied a role for morality as well in international affairs.[3] But recent theorists have seen the realist position as not tenable since it is perfectly possible and indeed likely that states act out of a variety of motives, including ones that are moral and legal. This is largely an empirical question that is beyond the scope of our book. But we have mentioned these ideas merely to show that the recent economic critique of international law is certainly not unique.

Our first response to the economic critique is to agree that international criminal tribunals operate at a distinct disadvantage compared to domestic criminal courts. The ad hoc criminal tribunals, which were set up by the Security Council, had a more direct link to a possible enforcement mechanism than the ICC. But even here there were serious enforcement problems, especially in getting indicted criminals to the tribunals. The United Nations in general, and the Security Council in particular, are practically challenged in that they do not have their own police force or army, and hence must rely on the forces and political bodies of their member states. Enforcement is thus something that varies with the willingness of states to support a particular decision of the United Nations.

While we acknowledge this problem, we also acknowledge that states often have cooperated in the arrest of those indicted by the ICTY, such as in the case of former president Slobodan Milosevic. Milosevic was extradited to the ICTY in the Hague after he had stepped down from power and after extensive economic incentives were provided to the then current government of Serbia. Various leaders in Rwanda, as well as in Serbia, were also successfully arrested and delivered to the respective ad hoc tribunals. So international criminal tribunals have had some success, although it is true that much remains to be done to bring about better enforcement of international criminal law.

As to the dilemma that Posner and Sykes have posed, we would respond that the ideal is to have international crimes prosecuted in the countries where

3 See Charles Beitz, *Political Theory and International Relations* (Princeton, NJ: Princeton University Press, 1979).

they occurred, so that the local population does not see its former leader whisked off to a foreign locale to stand trial. If in the future it is true that states are willing and able to prosecute all international criminal cases, there is no problem with that. In the meantime, the international criminal tribunals will fill rather large gaps created by the lack of enforcement at the domestic level of international crimes. Here we confront the second horn of the dilemma – when states do not want to prosecute, there is an enforcement problem with respect to prosecutions at neutral sites by international criminal tribunals. And it is here that we agree with the economists that there must be increased incentives for states to assist the ICC in handing over indicted defendants to the Hague.

What seems odd is for critics of the ICC to point to the problem of incentives without proposing solutions – given that this is just the kind of problem for which rational choice theorists would normally be good at offering solutions. We will address this issue here in terms of structural factors. It is true that there are some structural problems with enforcement in international criminal law. In particular, we would point to the lack of full support by the Security Council for the ICC. In many ways the fact that the ICC is not closely allied with the Security Council has helped with its legitimacy problems, but the ICC's enforcement problems have been exacerbated.

Posner and Sykes surely overstate the case when they say that "when states are unwilling to launch prosecutions, the ICC has no capacity to compel them to turn over indicted suspects."[4] There is a telling ambiguity here. The states that are unwilling to prosecute are the ones whose nationals have been indicted. But the states that can help compel the arrest of those who have been indicted can be different states from those whose nationals have been indicted. This is what happened with Slobodan Milosevic and other high ranking Serb leaders – it was the United States and Western European states that pressured Serbia to make the arrests. In terms of compliance, most states do indeed seem to comply with international criminal norms. What is not so clear is whether these states so conform because of respect for these norms. It is possible to explain some of the compliance in terms of the self-interests of states, but quite a lot of international criminal law cannot be so understood on the self-interest model. And while it is true that states often act from mixed motives, there is reason to think that states are compliant, when they are, out of a concern for their international obligations, as we will attempt later to show. Indeed, such a dispute is hard to adjudicate because most courts, as with most individuals, operate with mixed motives.

4 Posner and Sykes, *Economic Foundations of International Law*, p. 108.

III SUASION

At the core of the economic critique of international criminal tribunals is that the practice of international law has been overly influenced by those who do not take a rigorous approach but are instead too strongly influenced by moralists. This is the clear impetus of such critics as Eric Posner, Jack Goldsmith, and Alan Sykes. And at the center of this critique is the charge that international lawyers believe, contrary to social scientific evidence, that states are influenced by the mere fact that something is an obligation in international law. From the law and economics perspective, only nonmoral incentives are recognized as effective. And those who do not appeal to economic reasoning are simply not rigorous thinkers.

As Richard Posner has argued, many other goals than efficiency "(various conceptions of 'fairness' and 'justice') are labels for wealth maximization, or for redistribution in favor of powerful interest groups, or else they are too controversial in a heterogeneous society."[5] But justice and fairness are not merely alternative names for wealth maximization, no matter how broadly that term is understood. And while it is true that the international community is even more heterogeneous than any domestic society, there are norms nonetheless that are not so controversial. Indeed, there are actually controversial aspects of the law and economics approach as well, as we shall see.

It should initially be pointed out that there is a lack of connection between the economists who take a rational choice approach and social scientists who do not make rational choice assumptions but rather look closely at the data and form more restricted hypotheses of what could explain the data. Rational choice theory is not social science, and indeed the assumptions that are made by rational choice theorists are self-effacingly counter empirical. No one is perfectly rational and that includes institutions of all sorts. And no one is only influenced, or even always most strongly influenced, by self-interested considerations. It is not rigorous to make such assumptions, because they are patently false. We make this controversial claim at the outset because various critics often assume otherwise, as Eric Posner and Allen Sykes do at the beginning of their recent book.[6] In what follows we will try to unpack the criticism in its more subtle form, rather than in the way it is often portrayed, and we will

5 Richard Posner, *The Problems of Jurisprudence* (Cambridge, MA: Harvard University Press, 1990), pp. 391–392, reprinted in *Philosophy of Law*, edited by Larry May and Jeff Brown (New York: Blackwell Publishers, 2010), p. 133, column 1.

6 Their criticisms are very similar to those of Richard Posner, ibid., who has argued that rigorous approaches to international law, as well as to the rest of law, must include economic assumptions such as that of the "rational man" and the idea that all of us are "wealth maximizers."

begin with the idea that states are not the kind of entities that are likely to be influenced by moral suasion.

Moral suasion operates, when it does, in influencing individuals, not institutions directly. But of course institutions are run by individuals who are by and large able to be influenced by moral argumentation and persuasion. Yet, in fact, the kind of suasion that results from obligation imposed on states is not merely moral in the individual conscience sense. There is an institutional sense of obligation that arises from the interplay of individuals and their institutions. When individuals are part of institutions, they have a somewhat different sense of their motivations. The roles that individuals play, in institutions and elsewhere such as in parental roles or lifesaving roles, carry an enhanced sense of obligation.

While it is possible to understand the motivation one has to act out of a sense of obligation in "self-interested" terms, it is often misleading to do so. Self-interest is best understood as different from altruistic and other moral motivations. And in the case of institutional moral motivations, rational choice theory would have to provide an extended sense of interest if it is to be successful in taking account of the self-reported moral motivations of states and the myriad individual actors who control states. Yet, it seems to us that it is better simply to admit that there are motivations other than self-interest at play, especially when dealing with institutions and states.

In a more conceptual vein, H. L. A. Hart has argued that it is a mistake to think that interest and obligation are the same or can be reduced to one another. In *The Concept of Law*, Hart argued that "the standing possibility of conflict between obligation or duty and interest is, in all societies, among the truisms of both the lawyer and the moralist."[7] It seems to us that Posner and Sykes are looking for a "psychological" explanation of why states would respect international law when they should be looking for what Hart understood as a "normative" explanation. This is best seen in Hart's distinction between the external and internal points of view. The psychologist or social scientist wants to be able to explain from the outside, from a standpoint external to those who are the members of a given community. But there is another dimension that is actually more important. Quoting Hart again:

> To feel obliged and to have an obligation are different though frequently concomitant things. To identify them would be one way of misinterpreting, in terms of psychological feelings, the important internal aspect of rules.[8]

7 H. L. A. Hart, *The Concept of Law* (Oxford: Oxford University Press, 1960), chapter 5.
8 Ibid.

For states and the individual actors who control states, to act as a matter of obligation does not require that there be some interest of states that can be seen from the external point of view.

Suasion of various forms, the more the better, needs to be enlisted to move states and their leaders to accept responsibility for meeting their international obligations to act to prevent and prosecute mass atrocities. The idea here, again following Hart, is to increase the internal point of view of states – to induce them to see themselves as part of a system that is governed by rules that define the relationships among those who are members of that system or society. We do not claim that all states see themselves as members of the world community. But even states like the United States, that have been most opposed to international criminal tribunals, are being convinced by globalization that there is an emerging "society of states" (to use the term made famous by Hugo Grotius in the seventeenth century and that permeated the work of Hersch Lauterpacht in the twentieth century).[9]

Cosmopolitan suasion of the moral variety is premised not on the idea of a "rational man" but instead on that of an "international society." Indeed, there are those who do not call themselves cosmopolitans who still, like Grotius and Lauterpacht, accept the idea of a society of states, which has rules from which motivation and suasion can gain traction, when they are adopted from the internal perspective. Insofar as there is motivation stemming from this basis of obligation, one could tell a story involving extended interest, perhaps "enlightened self-interest," but such a view is not easily reducible to the economic terms of the critics we have been discussing.

The economic and practical arguments against international criminal tribunals nonetheless have some merit, especially when these arguments are limited to matters as they stand at the current moment. But they do not have clear purchase about what is achievable into the future. And the economic critique does not go to the underlying idea of the clear need for such criminal tribunals. In Section IV we will provide some countervailing arguments, also drawn in practical terms, for increased support for such tribunals. Those who care about providing incentives against mass crime should support international criminal tribunals, not oppose them.

IV PRACTICAL ARGUMENTS FOR INTERNATIONAL CRIMINAL TRIBUNALS

To see why international criminal tribunals are, as a practical matter, worth preserving, we will investigate what the world would look like without such

9 See Hugo Grotius, *De Jure Belli ac Pacis*, "Prolegomena," 1625 and Hersch Lauterpacht, *The Function of Law in the International Community* (Oxford: Clarendon Press, 1933).

tribunals. We will here focus on the expressive and symbolic effects of having such highly public trials; in Chapter 4 we examined the deterrent and retributive effects of such trials. In this section we will also discuss some "economic" reasons to support international criminal tribunals, although perhaps not reasons that the espousers of the law and economic perspective would find to be persuasive.

David Luban has argued that international criminal trials are primarily to be valued in expressive terms, in that these trials call the world's attention to those who perpetrate mass atrocity, torture, and other heinous crimes.[10] While we do not agree with Luban that expressive capacity of international criminal trials is the primary value of such trials, it does speak rather clearly to the practical advantages of such trials.

As can be seen by the label of "crimes against humanity," there are certain crimes that assault all of humanity, all of us, and are best prosecuted as international crimes, rather than merely as domestic crimes, where those most affected are the nationals of a particular state. Genocide and the crime of aggression are also "crimes against humanity" in that they also assault all of humanity, by which we mean harms that could have been felt by nearly any human as well as harms that undermine the livelihood of large groups of humans. And many war crimes, such as those that are especially widespread or systematic, are also, to an extent, crimes against humanity as well, or at least crimes against humaneness.[11]

Crimes that adversely affect humanity can be distinguished from, and should be treated differently from, crimes that only affect the members of a particular state or society. International criminal tribunals are established precisely to prosecute crimes that adversely affect humanity. The penalties affixed to such crimes need not be the same as or stronger than those that attach to similar domestic crimes. The point is to express the outrage of all of humanity by having separate punishments issued by international criminal tribunals, or by domestic tribunals applying international law. The separate punishments are expressive of the international community's outrage at the severity of the assault.

The practical point that is largely missed by the critics of international criminal tribunals is that there is need for the international community's condemnation of crimes that are so egregious that they affect all of the members of the international community. And this is not always evident when such crimes are prosecuted in domestic criminal courts. Indeed, one can give a

[10] See David Luban, "A Theory of Crimes against Humanity," *Yale Journal of International Law*, vol. 29, 2004, pp. 85–167.

[11] See Larry May, *War Crimes and Just War* (New York: Cambridge University Press, 2007).

good economic reason for international prosecutions – they hold out the hope of changing the incentives of those who perpetrate egregious international crimes such as genocide.

Changing the incentives of harm perpetrated by international actors is clearly consistent with the economic model of how to approach and evaluate legal institutions. We have seen that various economically oriented theorists doubt the current ability of international courts to affect the incentives of international criminals. But there is no good reason to doubt that changing these incentives is indeed a practical priority of international criminal tribunals, as it should be.

Incentives in the real world are not necessarily governed by rationality, and certainly not by anything like perfect rationality. But if we are going to speak of rational incentives, then providing additional possible costs to what people are thinking of doing is indeed a way to affect the actions of these people. And long prison sentences would seem to have this effect, unless there were offsetting benefits that international actors thought they would achieve by their wrongful behavior as well.

So, on the level of incentives, it is hard to understand why the economic critique of international criminal tribunals has been so strident. One reason seems to be that there has been a dispute between those who take an economic perspective and those who take a moral perspective. The moralists tend to be cosmopolitans and the economists tend to be nationalists. But there is no good reason why this is the case or has to be the case. A cosmopolitan international order would solve various coordination problems and would regularize the system of incentives in international cases that would seemingly gladden the economists. It is true that a cosmopolitan order is not yet even close to being realized and so it is unclear how it will manifest itself. But the critique of international criminal tribunals is seemingly misdirected in its stridency if it is grounded merely in the worry about uncertainty.

It should be noted that moralists do not need to be cosmopolitans in providing their moral arguments concerning international law. Grotius, perhaps the greatest theorist to write on international law, did so from a self-consciously moral standpoint and yet espoused a view that he called a "society of states" position rather than a cosmopolitan position. Such contemporary philosophers as Michael Walzer and Joseph Raz have also engaged in moral argumentation about international law and yet are much more communitarian than cosmopolitan.[12]

12 See Michael Walzer, *Just and Unjust Wars* (New York: Basic Books, 1977); and Joseph Raz and Avishai Margalit, "National Self-Determination," *Journal of Philosophy*, vol. 87, no. 9 (September 1990), pp. 439–461.

Indeed, one of the clearest solutions to uncertainty at the international level is to have coordinated and uniform procedures for addressing international criminal actions. We readily acknowledge that the ICC has not achieved that yet. But the critics often seem to move too quickly to the conclusion that we cannot reach uniform treatment of international criminal acts merely because it is not taking place at the moment.

This is not quite fair to some of these critics, especially those who are social scientists trying to grapple with the phenomena of international criminal tribunals that the world has seen in the last several decades. We are primarily critical of those economically oriented legal scholars who have tried to use social science methods to draw normative conclusions.[13] The social science critique of the lack of actual compliance with international law, and other empirical issues, is not the subject of our own critical comments.

Let us return to the simple and seemingly persuasive dilemma from Eric Posner and Allen Sykes with which we started this current chapter. The dilemma is persuasive insofar as the near future resembles the current impasse of establishing clear-cut enforcement mechanisms especially for the ICC. The idea is that if states recognize the need for such prosecutions they will establish them without the ICC; and if these states do not recognize this need there are not incentives to extradite the wrongdoers to the Hague. The assumption is that the current problem with international criminal tribunals will continue into the indefinite future.

But we have tried to show that the plausible critique of where matters stand at the moment is not a good reason to oppose international criminal tribunals in the future rather than a reason to try to change some of the incentive structures in the way that they have been effectively changed in some other areas of law. Indeed, here again we can look at U.S. mass tort litigation, which was once seen as too unwieldy and is now recognized as very effective, perhaps too effective for those who are now caught in its enforcement web.

In this chapter we consider a range of economic and practical criticisms of international criminal tribunals. It sometimes seems that the other criticisms we consider at length in this book are driven by practical worries, especially where it appears that the project of international criminal law has failed or is about to fail. When these arguments are confronted, if not refuted, then it is perhaps easier to see the other criticisms in a clearer light. The economic criticisms seem to be so pragmatically compelling and hard-nosed that they are hard to resist. But we have seen that matters are not nearly as clear as the

[13] On this point see Jens Ohlin, *The Assault on International Law* (New York: Oxford University Press, 2015).

economic critics have claimed. Indeed, there are even competing positive arguments from a practical or economic position that support international criminal tribunals.

V WHY SELF-INTEREST CRITIQUES ARE PROBLEMATIC

At the moment it is undeniable that the world's greatest powers, measured in terms of military might or economic productivity, have not ratified the Rome Statute. And these powers have shown disdain for international criminal law in many of their dealings, including the United States' attempt to persuade its military and trading partners to sign agreements that they will not bring actions against U.S. troops or other U.S. citizens at the Hague. But it is also undeniable that international law generally and international criminal tribunals in particular have flourished in the last twenty years. Indeed, it is hard to deny that international law has become pervasive even in those rich and powerful societies that have failed to ratify the big multilateral treaties. So, how do we square this with the law and economics critique of international law and its courts? Normatively, the question is why states have not simply ignored international law when it suited them to do so – thereby undermining the bindingness of international law.

Let us begin by noting that legal justice has often been assailed by those who think that self-interest is the only reason people even appear to be acting justly. Famously Plato, Hobbes, and Hume all devoted significant energy to the question of why people do not merely pick and choose when to act justly, that is, only when it is in the clear current self-interest of people. In the next few pages we will briefly rehearse some of what these major thinkers thought about this issue and then show how this discussion over the millennia is important today.[14]

Plato devotes a significant section at the beginning of book II of his *Republic* to the question of why people act justly.

> And we'll catch the just person red-handed traveling the same road as the unjust. The reason for this is the desire to outdo others and get more and more. This is what anyone's nature naturally pursues, as good, but nature is forced by law into the perversion of treating fairness with respect.
>
> The freedom I mentioned would be most easily realized if both people had the power they say the ancestor of Gyges of Lydia possessed. The story goes that he was a shepherd in the service of the ruler of Lydia. There

[14] For the most recent philosophical treatment of this issue, see Ohlin, *The Assault on International Law*.

> was a violent thunderstorm, and an earthquake broke open the ground and created a chasm ... peeping in he saw a corpse, which seemed to be more than human size, wearing nothing but a gold ring on his finger. He took the ring and came out of the chasm ... And as he was sitting among the others, he happened to turn the setting of the ring towards himself to the inside of his hand. When he did this he became invisible ... So he experimented with the ring to test whether it indeed had this power – and it did ... When he realized this, he at once arranged to become one of the messengers sent to report to the king. And when he arrived there, he seduced the king's wife, attacked the king with her help, killed him, and took over the kingdom.[15]

Plato then juxtaposes the unjust man epitomized by Gyges' ancestor, who wants to appear just but to act unjustly, with the good man who simply wants to do what is just.

Plato's response is to attempt to show that the just man is generally more likely to be successful than the unjust man since the unjust man must rely on deceit that is very difficult to maintain over the long term: "It isn't easy for vice to remain always hidden."[16] And Plato maintains that injustice is dangerous to everyone including the person who commits it, whereas justice is always beneficial.[17]

In the central discussion of justice in chapter 15 of *Leviathan*, Hobbes also poses the quandary about justice by painting an unjust man as someone who is able to appear just but also to do unjust acts with impunity when he thinks he will not be discovered. Hobbes puts the objection about how we should choose justice when it seems to be against our self-interest into the mouth of a character Hobbes calls "the fool."

> The fool hath said in his heart, there is no such thing as justice; and sometimes also with his tongue; seriously alleging, that every man's conservation, and contentment, being committed to his own care, there could be no reason, why every man might not do what he thought conduced thereunto: and therefore also to make, or not make; keep, or not keep covenants, was not against reason, when it conduced to one's benefit. He does not therein deny, that there be no covenants; and that they are sometimes broken, sometimes kept; and that such breach of them may be called injustice, and the observance of them justice: but he questioneth whether injustice, taking away

[15] Plato, *Republic*, book II, 359c–360b, translated by G. M. A. Grube and revised by C. D. C. Reeve, in *Plato: Complete Works*, edited by John M. Cooper (Indianapolis: Hackett, 1997), p. 1000.

[16] Ibid., 365c, p. 1005.

[17] Ibid., 367e, p. 1007.

> the fear of God, for the same fool saith in his heart there is no God, may not sometimes stand with reason which dictateth to each man his own good.[18]

Hobbes accepts the general legitimacy of the question, even regarding it to be of pressing importance.

Hobbes replies to the fool in two parts. First, he agrees that if covenants are made in such a society where there is no "civil power erected over the parties promising," then it is "not against reason" to break them.[19] But, second, Hobbes points out that even in a "state of war" "there is no one who can hope by his own strength, or wit, to defend himself from destruction, without the help of confederates." [20] Hence the person who "breaketh his covenant, and consequently declareth that he thinks he may with reason do so, cannot be received into any society" and hence will perish.[21]

Finally, David Hume asks roughly the same question and gives a somewhat different answer in his *Enquiry Concerning the Principles of Morals.*

> And though it is allowed, that, without a regard for property, no society could subsist; yet according to the imperfect way in which human affairs are conducted, a sensible knave, in particular incidents, may think, that an act of iniquity or infidelity will make a considerable addition to his fortune, without causing any considerable breach in the social union and confederacy.[22]

Hume responds that the sensible knave will see that he has "sacrificed the invaluable enjoyment of character ... for the acquisition of worthless toys and gewgaws."[23]

So, we have seen that three of the most famous philosophers have considered the question of whether it is rational or reasonable to act justly rather than unjustly, even in the cases when it appears that self-interest will be served by acting unjustly. For Plato, acting unjustly will require deceit, which is difficult to keep hidden, and the injustice is dangerous even to the person who engages in unjust acts. Hobbes argues that the person who acts unjustly will not be able to keep confederates and will not be able to participate in the benefits of society. Hume also argues that there are indeed benefits that the unjust person will not be able to attain, but these are benefits of character and self-regard. In

[18] Thomas Hobbes, *Leviathan* (1651), chapter 15, para. 4, in *The English Works of Thomas Hobbes*, edited by William Molesworth (London: John Bohn, 1839), vol. III, p. 132.

[19] Ibid., chapter 15, para. 5, p. 133.

[20] Ibid.

[21] Ibid., chapter 15, para. 5, p. 134.

[22] David Hume, *Enquiry Concerning the Principles of Morals* (1757) in *David Hume, Enquiries Concerning Human Understanding and the Principles of Morals*, ed. by L. A. Selby-Bigge, 3rd ed. (Oxford: Oxford University Press, 1975), p. 282.

[23] Ibid., p. 283.

each case, philosophers have expressed dissatisfaction with these replies but have often seen that some combination of these responses is hard, although not impossible in the one case at the moment, for the defender of self-interest to rebut.[24] The defender of self-interest in international criminal law also has a difficult job, much more difficult than most of these critics seem to realize. States that feel no obligations of justice and only act in self-interest will have to deceive others, will have difficulty maintaining long-term alliances, and will not be able to benefit from the good that results from having their citizens leading just lives.

Two other brief points should be made. First, since Plato, Hobbes, and Hume wrote, globalization has forced the world to become a much smaller place and has also made it more difficult for states simply to withdraw into isolation in the face of major international upheavals. Indeed, the very idea of self-interest for states has changed because of globalization, because so many events in distant parts of the world will affect the interests of the most powerful states in ways that are often hard to fathom. And, of course, as was also true for Plato, Hobbes, and Hume, self-interest may not, in the end, be in conflict with recognizing obligations, whether legal or moral.

Second, it is important to note that international criminal law has increasingly moved into the constitutional structure of the states of the world. This transformation has not been as public and obvious an indication of the rise of international law, but it is perhaps even more significant than the rise of the international criminal tribunals themselves. States have seen that having laws against international crimes in their own constitutional structures is valuable, or at least not contrary to their self-interests. And this should give the defenders of self-interest reason to pause. It seems thoroughly implausible that so many states would have failed to understand their self-interest – especially since by introducing international crimes into their constitutional structures, states have made it the case that their international obligations cannot merely be "sometimes broken, sometimes kept," to quote Hobbes again.

VI EFFECTIVENESS CONCERNS

Another issue of concern is that there have not been, and are unlikely to be, enough convictions for any positive practical effect (such as deterrence) to occur. Indeed, the evidence seems to be that the ICC has been prosecuting at a slower rate than either the Yugoslav or Rwanda tribunals. In part, this is

[24] See David Gauthier, "Three against Justice: The Fool, the Sensible Knave, and the Lydian Shepherd," *Midwest Studies in Philosophy*, vol. 7, no. 1 (September 1982), pp. 11–29.

by design, in that the ICC sees its role to be increasingly one of pressuring states to prosecute international crimes in their domestic tribunals rather than to mount prosecutions in the Hague. But there is also little evidence that the ICC is yet having a significant effect in accomplishing this goal. As a result, some see the promise of international criminal law fading away for lack of prosecutions of very serious violations of international criminal law.[25]

The effectiveness of international criminal tribunals is not merely to be assessed in terms of the sheer number of cases that are successfully prosecuted. Perceptions are at least as important as actual results. But it is difficult to present the appearance of a well functioning system of criminal justice if there is not a critical mass of cases being prosecuted successfully. And the ICC, so far, has not hit that critical mass. Indeed, the number of cases seems to be dwindling if one compares the ICC to the ICTY or to the ICTR.

As to the charge that the number of convictions is dwindling and so the international criminal justice project is likely to fail as a result of lack of momentum, we must concede that this is a possibility. In and of itself, such a critique should not be all that worrisome. As with any prediction, either it will turn out to be true or it will not. At the moment, we admit the trend is worrisome. But at least one reason may be that the ICC has taken a while to get up to speed, with many cases now in the pipeline. At the same time, the ICTY and ICTR have been concluding work, also with relatively few recent convictions at the end of a very long process.

The failure to prosecute one high-profile political leader, like Assad, will not undermine the ICC or the general efficacy of having international criminal tribunals. But there is a significant worry if it turns out that Assad is not an isolated case. Prosecuting small fry can be important for building a jurisprudence of international criminal justice, as was true in the ICTY's first case involving Dusko Tadic. But there must be prosecutions of the big fish as well. Indeed, many think that the ICC should only pursue important cases, given their limited resources and small number of cases prosecuted overall.

There is an emerging consensus that the ICC should primarily focus on high-ranking rather than low-ranking defendants. The effectiveness of the ICC depends on being able to do so. We would also argue that prosecuting the big fish is normatively more justified than pursuing the small fry. The major defendants epitomize the *mens rea* of state-sponsored crimes against humanity and genocide, for instance. The lower-ranking, by and large, represent the *actus reus*, but they basically do what the big fish tell them to do. Hence it is

[25] See Eric Posner, "Assad and the Death of the International Criminal Court," *Slate*, September 19, 2013.

both conceptually and normatively fair to focus those who are most responsible for international crimes.

As far as we can tell, the ICC Office of the Prosecutor has embraced the strategy of primarily pursuing high-ranking defendants. It remains to be seen whether or not the ICC Prosecutor can obtain indictments and then have arrest warrants served against leading military and civilian leaders. The international community now needs to act to fund the court better, so that the court has a chance of successfully arresting, indicting, and prosecuting the most important criminals. Indeed, it is still possible that the ICC will fail altogether if funds are not forthcoming – but this is surely not a structural problem with the ICC or a normative reason to disband international criminal tribunals.

Effectiveness takes various forms. There is the concern about whether international criminal tribunals are effective at the present in prosecuting those for whom prima facie evidence exists that they have committed international crimes. But in addition, there is the concern about whether prospective international criminals are deterred by what international criminal tribunals do in the present. The latter kind of effectiveness is hard to measure until a sufficient amount of time has passed and a decisive number of judgments have been rendered for one to perceive what the future effectiveness is likely to be.

For the latter kind of effectiveness to be assessed, there has to be a pattern of prosecutions upon which one can make future predictions. The ICC has been accepting cases since 2004, a little more than a decade. But the ICC has only quite recently taken any of its cases to final judgment. Many of the critics ask for results now and clear cut trends for the future. While there is nothing wrong with this type of request in general, it is not reasonable to think that either form of effectiveness could be displayed over such a short period of prosecutions. Of course, one can look back to the ICTY and ICTR to get both a longer period of prosecutions and larger number of cases taken to judgment. But there are good reasons not to judge the ICC, a permanent tribunal that is not linked to the Security Council, on the basis of the ad hoc tribunals that were specifically established by the Security Council and backed by its force. In Section VII, we discuss some of the criticisms of international criminal tribunals in terms of their funding levels and priorities.

VII EFFICIENCY CONCERNS

Some other critics focus on the sheer amount of money that is spent in order to secure a handful of convictions. Quite a lot of money is spent for each conviction in international tribunals such as at the ICTY and ICTR. Even greater resources have been spent for cases before the ICC, where very few convictions have occurred (as of this writing, only a couple of such convictions have occurred before the ICC, but several are wrapping up). For the same amount of money, perhaps truth and reconciliation commissions should be funded instead. And this only scratches the surface of where scarce monetary resources could be spent, such as for alleviating the suffering in humanitarian crises around the world

We should begin by pointing out that it is not unusual for U.S. mass tort cases to take an equally long period before judgment is rendered. More importantly, U.S. mass tort cases often cost millions of dollars because of the sheer size of the cases and the number of companies and individuals that are the subject of the suits. Mass tort cases, like international criminal cases, have hundreds and often thousands of victims whose claims need to be adjudged. Even though there are usually only one or two defendants in the international dock, the act of genocide or crime against humanity in which they are said to have participated is normally very large indeed. Here it is like seeking the conviction of just one coal company for pollution, caused by numerous sources, which harmed thousands of people. Cases with large numbers of victims take a long time and quite considerable resources to pay for the investigation of each of the victims' claims.

The parallels between U.S. mass tort cases and international criminal prosecutions are apt in another respect as well. Typically lots of money is spent to gain a judgment against one or two players. But the aim is to single out the worst offenders, and with successful judgments, to send a message to others who may be contemplating similar actions. Yet, unlike in mass tort cases, international criminal trials are not able to recoup the money spent in investigation and motion writing from the perpetrators. So, the efficiency issue arises in a different, more complex way in international trials than in mass tort cases, where scarce, nonrecouped resources need to be guarded. In international criminal trials the attorneys and investigators are guaranteed payment, which is taken from the same funds that finance other resources for the trial. In mass tort cases in the United States, the attorneys might not be paid at all if they lose. The risk is also different. Some class action suits require a lot of resources that might never be recouped. Yet, this is actually a bad criticism of international criminal law – *génocidaires* are guaranteed good, well-paid legal counsel, while civil rights victims rely on attorneys who might never be paid for their time. However, criminal prosecutors are generally paid fairly well.

Concerning the claim about what the resources spent on international trials could support instead, we are in agreement that this issue needs to be addressed rather forthrightly. Unfortunately, without something like a world state, there will not be maximally rational decisions about the best way to allocate scarce resources. But this problem is not unique to the funding of international criminal law. States always face the issue of the trade-offs of money for the judicial system versus money for schools, health care, and other basic needs.

We largely concede that the ad hoc tribunals have sometimes been inefficient in the way they have used their resources. In the future, the success of the international tribunals will probably be judged in terms of the convictions for international crimes that occur across the spectrum of tribunals, including domestic tribunals. The money spent initially for very high-profile cases should effectively be seen as "seed money." But if in the future the price of convictions continues to be exorbitant, cost-cutting measures would certainly be in order – although of course this is not a reason to urge that international tribunals be abandoned. But what is harder to defend is that some donor groups have had supposedly outsized roles in decision making on the court, especially about which cases to take.[26]

This issue of limited resources and the further charge of bias in how cases are chosen for prosecution at the ICC are very serious charges that we will examine in more detail in Chapter 8 on fairness concerns. Here we wish to highlight how the current funding of international trials does indeed open the door for serious bias. This is again not a reason to abandon international criminal tribunals, but rather an argument to change the way the trials are funded. Indeed, solving the monetary problems that have beset international criminal tribunals since the ICTY and ICTR were founded would also make it possible to increase the number of cases prosecuted. And while such a change will be difficult, we are optimistic that such increased funding from states will be possible in the future.

But even if our optimism is not borne out, the point we have been emphasizing is that international criminal tribunals are, by design, supposed to be only operating when a state cannot or will not prosecute international crimes in its domestic courts. And as globalization continues across a wide swath of areas, it is likely that more and more states will achieve the capacity to prosecute international criminals in their domestic courts. There will still be a residual need for international criminal tribunals in the future, since some states will prefer to send cases to the Hague, as was true of several cases from Africa at the beginning of the ICC's tenure. And there may be some trials that

26 See Sara Kendall, "Donors' Justice: Recasting International Criminal Accountability," *Leiden Journal of International Law*, vol. 24, no. 3 (2011), pp. 585–606.

are so contentious that it is better for all parties for them to be held in the Hague, as was true of the trial of Charles Taylor.

It is thus clear to us that there is and will be a need for international criminal tribunals into the foreseeable future. And it is also clear that the world is better off if there are trials for atrocities in parts of the world where there is not otherwise either capacity or will to engage in these prosecutions. But it is quite likely that this need will diminish over time. Yet, this is not a reason to think that artificial limits should be placed on such prosecutions, before the capacity and will exist across the globe to prosecute those responsible for atrocities.

In this chapter we have explored a series of economic and practical objections to international criminal tribunals. The underlying feature of the various criticisms is that somehow it is not and is unlikely ever to be sufficiently in the self-interests of states to support international tribunals given how inefficient and ineffective these tribunals have been. But we have tried to show that international criminal tribunals are, or can be, both efficient and effective. And that in any event the world's states are actually better off for having international criminal tribunals than being without them.

6

Politics

The international criminal courts and tribunals have been strongly criticized for their susceptibility to political influence. Some have argued that they have a distinctly Western bias and are participating in neocolonialism in Africa. Other critics even argue that history and the complicity of the West should lead us to question whether it is appropriate for the international community to demand prosecution of those individuals participating in conflicts resulting directly from colonialism. Finally, many criticisms have focused on the nature of the creation of the judicial bodies and the inherent political character of any judicial decisions regarding whom to prosecute. In this chapter, we will consider the strength of these empirical and normative arguments and conclude that these ideological criticisms do not defeat the normative value of the international criminal courts and tribunals.

We begin by discussing the (often-fuzzy) relationship between what is political and what is legal in nature. In Section II, we try to piece together how we should understand the relationship between current political leaders in Africa and the past colonial powers. Section III addresses the issue that has instigated much of the criticism of the international criminal courts and tribunals: that the overwhelming proportion of the investigations and prosecutions have been in Africa. We then consider the argument that colonial history alone is a strike against prosecuting individuals for international crimes in Africa. In Section V, we move to claims of Western hegemony and neocolonialism within the international criminal justice system. Sections VI and VII explore the political nature of the ICC's principle of complementarity and other sources of political decision making. We conclude in Section VII by arguing that despite the criticisms leveled against the international criminal courts and tribunals for failing to avoid political influences, none of these criticisms leads us to determine that these courts and tribunals are inescapably political.

I RELATIONSHIP BETWEEN THE POLITICAL AND THE LEGAL

Most attempts to distinguish between law and politics will be met with disagreement. The range of views of the relationship between the two realms is substantial, and recent developments in international law have contributed to the confusion over and interest in this relationship. In Section I of this chapter, we will attempt to carve out our understanding of the relationship between the political and the legal.

Historically, a relationship between politics and the law had to be understood in terms of domestic systems. Law in general, and criminal law in particular, was promulgated by the political institution. International political arrangements were not historically based on legal mechanisms. In fact, most discussions of international obligations referred to nonlegal norms. In certain areas of international relations, this remains the case. But in the realm of international criminal law, a sea change has occurred over the last century.

Carl Schmitt defined the political "in terms of the irreducible opposition between the friend and the enemy."[1] This recognizes the political as necessarily involving a struggle. A state that does not have an understanding of its own internal and external enemies cannot maintain order or function as a state.[2] For Schmitt, this meant that "as long as a people exists in the political sphere, it must have a clear view who its enemies are. Otherwise, the State will cease to exist. What is left may be a set of collective economic or cultural pursuits – sooner or later to dissolve in civil war or by the force of external aggression."[3] While we would not follow Schmitt in most matters, there is a grain of truth in what he says about the future of politics, although the point is clearly exaggerated.

Hans Morgenthau developed a more plausible understanding of international law and politics than did Schmitt, despite the fact that Morgenthau was building on Schmitt's theory. The key for Morgenthau is that law and politics are asymmetrically related.[4] He recognized that while formally mechanisms would allow it, states would refuse to take their disputes to a third party for settlement when those disputes dealt with their vital national interests.[5]

1 Martti Koskenniemi, *The Gentle Civilizer of Nations: The Rise and Fall of International Law 1870–1960*, vol. 14 (Cambridge: Cambridge University Press, 2001), p. 431, citing Carl Schmitt, *The Concept of the Political: Expanded Edition* (Chicago: University of Chicago Press, 2008), p. 26.

2 Koskenniemi, *Gentle Civilizer of Nations*, p. 431.

3 Ibid., p. 432, citing Schmitt, *Concept of the Political*, pp. 45–48.

4 Koskenniemi, *Gentle Civilizer of Nations*, p. 440.

5 Ibid., p. 441.

Morgenthau argued that this showed the difficulty of separating the political and the legal.[6] The idea of something being "political" should be seen as a quality of that entity, and to "say that something was 'political' was to describe it in terms of the degree of intensity with which that entity was linked to the State."[7] Morgenthau thought that "anything might be, and nothing was necessarily political, including any question over which a court might possess jurisdiction," and thus the relationship between the political and the legal could not be symmetrical.[8]

We will now turn to two camps of views about the current relationship between the political and the legal in terms of international criminal justice: on the one hand are those who argue that the legal and political realms must remain completely separate, and on the other hand are those who recognize that all law is political, and the important task is to identify what is impermissibly political in the legal realm.

In the first camp, politics is "portrayed as external to law, as something that needs to be overcome by independent entities acting on the basis of pre-given rules and principles."[9] While Martti Koskenniemi does not think international law can be kept separate from politics, he does note that "the fight for an international Rule of Law is a fight against politics, understood as a matter of furthering subjective desires, passions, prejudices and leading into an international anarchy."[10] Carving out an independent rule of law seems to be a worthy endeavor. But on this first understanding of international criminal courts and tribunals, they are actually held out as immune to political pressures and interests. Bas Schotel argues in this vein, contending that states engaged in a violent or political conflict "may *try* to mobilize the law in their struggle, but that the structure of the law itself escapes the logic of the political: law cannot be 'political' in the Schmittian sense."[11] This view is problematic for a number of reasons, which will become apparent as we begin to discuss the second type of view.

6 Ibid.

7 Ibid., citing Hans Morgenthau, *Die internationale Rechtspflege, ihr Wesen und ihre Grenzen* (Leipzig: Noske, 1929), pp. 70, 105–107, 119 *et seq*.

8 Koskenniemi, *Gentle Civilizer of Nations*, p. 441, citing Morgenthau, *Die internationale Rechtspflege*, pp. 62–72.

9 Sarah M. H. Nouwen and Wouter G. Werner, "Doing Justice to the Political: The International Criminal Court in Uganda and Sudan,"*European Journal of International Law*, vol. 21 (November, 2010), pp. 941–965, 942.

10 Martti Koskenniemi, *The Politics of International Law* (Portland, OR: Bloomsbury, 2011), p. 36.

11 Bas Schotel, "Doing Justice to the Political: The International Criminal Court in Uganda and Sudan: A Reply to Sarah Nouwen and Wouter Werner, *European Journal of International Law*, vol. 22, pp. 1153–1160, 1154.

The first point to note about the relationship between international law and politics is that the international legal system only came about as a result of political consensus among states. Modern international criminal law emerged in the twentieth century in response to the atrocities committed during and after World War II. The Nuremberg Charter, which established the Nuremberg Tribunals to prosecute major war criminals, was created through a political agreement among France, the United States, the Soviet Union, and the United Kingdom and was subsequently ratified by nineteen other Allied States.[12] The ICTY and ICTR ad hoc tribunals were created through political agreement in the UN's Security Council. The ICC came into existence through a large multilateral treaty. The international criminal legal system has grown in large part because of "its promise to make the world a better place,"[13] but this growth has occurred through the promulgation of political agreements.

Sarah Nouwen and Wouter Werner argue, contra Schotel, that the ICC acts politically in the sense of Schmitt's concept of the political, because it has a practice of making the distinction between friend and enemy.[14] They argue that the ICC "adjudicates crimes which are frequently related to politics, and it depends on a mysterious and seemingly magical 'political will' for the enforcement of its decisions."[15]

Even a limited conception of the political cannot be completely excluded from the legal domain. Legislatures make decisions about how courts should function, even overruling court decisions. When you have an international court that is untethered from a legislature, this should not make us think that politics narrowly understood can be kept out of judicial decision making. The legitimate concern is that even narrow political considerations could play too large a role in judicial decisions. In our view, this is a very important concern. The question, of course, is what "too large" means. Once it is recognized that despite rhetoric from lawyers politics and law always intersect, the important question that is hard to answer is whether a given political influence on a court is inappropriate.

We do think, however, that separating legitimate from illegitimate political influence on courts is possible. Given the foundations of international

[12] Agreement for the Prosecution and Punishment of the Major War Criminals of the European Axis, and Charter of the International Military Tribunal, London, 8 August 1945.

[13] See John H. Barton and Barry E. Carter, "International Law and Institutions for a New Age," *Georgetown Law Journal, vol.* 81 (1992–93), pp. 535, 536; see also Laurence Juma, "Unclogging the Wheels: How the Shift from Politics to Law Affects Africa's Relationship with the International System." *Transnational Law and Contemporary Problems, vol.* 23 (2014), 309.

[14] See Nouwen and Werner, "Doing Justice to the Political."

[15] Ibid., p. 943.

criminal courts and tribunals, as well as their functions, we think it is best to view international criminal courts and tribunals as both political and legal entities, at least to some extent. So our response to the charge that the ICC and other international tribunals are political organs is that it would be surprising if this were not so, at least on an expanded understanding of what politics means in the way the term "politics" is typically used in these critiques. Law and politics cannot be disconnected from each other. When lawyers talk about preventing politics from intruding into the domain of law, what they typically mean is preventing judicial decisions from being made by political leaders who are not judicial officers. And yet there is something to the charge that the ICC judges, for instance, themselves, even though they seem to be from all parts of the world, are ideologically biased since they are, after all, judges who have had similar training and are culled from the elites in their societies.

There are certain types of political interference that should be avoided, and we will spend the majority of this chapter discussing these impermissible incursions of the political on the legal. We must admit that there have been cases when political considerations have influenced judicial decisions at the ICC, especially concerning who is to be indicted and left unindicted, when many could be indicted for grave violations of international criminal law. Our limited response is to say that this too does not have to be the case – it is not built into the structure of the Rome Statute that such political interference must occur. And there are plausible changes that can be made to the ICC structure that stand a good chance of being implemented. We are not arguing that the ICC will succeed only in some ideal world. So, to the extent that it can do so, we agree with the critics that the ICC must be scrupulous in how decisions are made, especially at the stage of the issuing of indictments and arrest warrants. In Section II, we will begin to address the political background of the international criminal courts and tribunals.

II WESTERN EUROPEAN EXPANSION AND POLITICS IN AFRICA

To understand the political concerns leveled by critics against the international criminal courts and tribunals in terms of how they have treated African conflicts and African individuals, we must take a step back and look at the progression from colonialism to neocolonialism in Africa. As Matthew Craven points out, during the last three decades of the nineteenth century:

> the visible enthusiasm for colonial acquisitions had led to an estimated 4.5 million square miles and 66 million inhabitants being incorporated

> within the British Empire; France gained 3.5 million square miles and 26 million people; Germany 1 million square miles and 26 million people, and Belgium, through Leopold's Congo Free State, 900,000 square miles and a population of 8.5 million.[16]

He concludes, "Understood as pure jurisdiction, empire knew no boundaries."[17]

In addition, Hannah Arendt, writing a new preface to her landmark study of the nature of imperialism, argued that

> the specifically American version of pre–World War II imperialism that was politically the least dangerous, is definitely over … Foreign aid, even if given for purely humanitarian reasons, is political by nature precisely because it is not motivated by the search for profits. Billions of dollars have been spent in political and economic wastelands where corruption and incompetence have caused them to disappear before any thing productive could be started … The profit motive, whose importance for imperialist policies was frequently overrated even in the past, has now completely disappeared; only the very rich and very powerful countries can afford to take the huge losses involved in imperialism. What seems uncomfortably clear even now is the strength of certain seemingly uncontrollable processes that tend to shatter all hope for constitutional development in the new nations.[18]

But Arendt does not draw a pessimistic lesson in the end:

> To stress the unhappy relevance of this half-forgotten period for contemporary events does not mean, of course, that the die is cast and we are entering a new period of imperialist policies.[19]

The most worrisome situation, as Arendt argues at the end of her study, is that people would be forced to live "outside the common world."[20]

The great promise of international institutions is that they could subsume all peoples under the rule of law where rights are protected regardless of where one comes from. In this ideal, no state or people would be "outside the common world." Yet contemporary critics of international criminal tribunals have argued, as we will see, that a new form of colonialism goes hand in hand with the actual manifestations of these international institutions today.

[16] Matthew Craven, "Colonialism and Domination," in Bardo Fassbender and Anne Peters (eds.), *The Oxford Handbook of the History of International Law* (Oxford: Oxford University Press, 2012), p. 879.

[17] Ibid., p. 888.

[18] Hannah Arendt, *Imperialism* (part II of *The Origins of Totalitarianism*) (New York: Harcourt, Brace & World, 1951, 1968), pp. vii–viii.

[19] Ibid., p. x.

[20] Ibid., p. 182.

It is indisputable that most African states were colonies of Western European states until the middle of the twentieth century. What is often hard to understand is the continuing impact of the European colonial projects on political violence on the continent today. The first African wars for independence took place after World War II. The Organization for African Unity was launched in 1963 by thirty-two newly independent African states, with the express goals of promoting solidarity and cooperation in pursuit of establishing peace and security while avoiding neocolonialism.[21] Independent African states successfully pushed for human rights in their early years of involvement with the UN, calling for the end of racial discrimination and the vestiges of colonialism.[22]

But the Cold War and its associated arms trade then began to fuel conflict zones in Africa, where rebel groups were vying for regional power and control over resources.[23] During the Cold War, "the expectation of violence and the massive military build-up by each side generated a general sense of anxiety," while the African states were largely relegated to sites of proxy wars and national liberation wars.[24] Ultimately, the Cold War undermined everything. Participation in the international legal system should have been afforded for newly independent African states. Yet, African leaders, once champions of independence and individual rights and freedoms, "turned authoritarian and completely demolished all the institutions of governance that had upheld democratic and human rights values. "[25] Multiparty politics was squashed and its proponents and leaders were killed or otherwise silenced.[26] African leaders then took to using international law to back their political legitimacy, rather than as a source of human rights values, and this dependence on international support gave rise to neocolonialism.[27] The Cold War completely disrupted "the trajectory of the shift from politics to law" that began after World War II

21 Organization of African Unity (OAU), Charter of the Organization of African Unity, 25 May 1963.

22 Juma, "Unclogging the Wheels," pp. 317–318; see also David A. Kay, "The Impact of African States on the United Nations," *International Organizations, vol.* 23 (1969), 20, 26.

23 See Kamari Maxine Clarke, *Fictions of Justice: The International Criminal Court and the Challenge of Legal Pluralism in Sub-Saharan Africa* (Cambridge: Cambridge University Press, 2009), p. 45.

24 Juma, "Unclogging the Wheels," pp. 318–319.

25 Ibid., p. 319; see also Richard L. Sklar, "Democracy in Africa," *African Studies Review*, vol. 26 (1983), 11.

26 Juma, "Unclogging the Wheels," p. 319.

27 See, e.g., Mark Robinson, "Aid, Democracy and Political Conditionality in Sub-Saharan Africa," *European Journal of Development Research*, vol. 5 (1993), p. 85; see also Bruce J. Berman, "Clientelism and Neocolonialism: Center-Periphery Relations and Political Development in African States," *Studies in Comparative International Development*, 9 (1974), p. 3.

and had been fortified by the entry of newly independent African states into the international system in the 1960s.[28]

The regional and internal conflicts that followed the end of the Cold War are thus intimately related to the global economy but are also related to "struggles over the management of Africa's violence through a complex moral sphere to protect the 'victim' but is driven by the quest for justice made possible through donor capitalism."[29] The neocolonialism of today involves the relationship between Europe's "declining colonial power" and the competition between American and Asian states for capitalist control over African resources.[30]

Thus we cannot draw a line separating independent African states from the influence of European colonial powers, or from the influence of capitalism and the global economy today. The same infrastructures that allowed for colonial appropriation of resources on the African continent persist in ensuring that inequality plagues current struggles against authoritarian leaders for control over resources.[31]

We can now turn to the political criticism facing the international criminal courts and tribunals and their handling of African conflicts with an understanding of the political vacuum that still exists in parts of Africa today, and the global events that have persisted in supporting the legitimacy of authoritarian political regimes. We will return to this discussion in Section IV.

III INTERNATIONAL CRIMINAL PROSECUTIONS IN AFRICA

Most ideological criticisms of the international criminal courts have been related to the fact that nearly all of the prosecutions and investigations have been of African individuals. Some have argued that the skewed nature of the courts is evidence that the United Nations and the ICC Prosecutor have inappropriately targeted Africa in determining which individuals should be the focus of investigation and prosecution. In this section, we provide some background on the source of these criticisms, and then offer two responses to the claim that international criminal prosecutions have unfairly targeted Africans.

There have been international criminal tribunals or special courts established by or with the assistance of the United Nations to handle criminal prosecutions related to conflicts in Cambodia, East Timor, Lebanon, Rwanda, Sierra Leone, and Yugoslavia. This list seems, on its face, unobjectionable.

28 Juma, "Unclogging the Wheels," p. 320.

29 Clarke, *Fictions of Justice*, p. 46.

30 Ibid.

31 Ibid., p. 47.

Only two of the six ad hoc tribunals or special courts are in Africa. But when we turn to the ICC, the statistics are quite different.

At one time, and notably at a time when many legal commentators were reflecting on the initial success or failure of the ICC, all of the situations and cases under investigation or prosecution by the ICC were in Africa. As of this writing, it remains the case that only African nationals have been prosecuted by the ICC. Currently, the ICC Office of the Prosecutor has brought twenty-two cases from situations in the following areas: the Central African Republic, the Democratic Republic of the Congo, Darfur/Sudan, Ivory Coast, Kenya, Libya, Mali, and Uganda.[32] Given that the ICC's mandate gives it "jurisdiction over the most serious crimes of concern to the international community *as a whole*,"[33] it makes sense that we ask why the ICC has only prosecuted serious crimes that have occurred in Africa. Many critics have gone further, arguing that this focus on Africa is both intentional and inappropriate. We will consider the normative arguments later in the chapter; in this section we will stick to the available data.

The first response to this argument is empirical. It is true that in the early years of the ICC's operation, it seemed that only situations in African states were appropriate subjects of investigation by the Office of the Prosecutor. And it remains true that the ICC has yet to prosecute any non-Africans. Yet the Office of the Prosecutor is currently conducting preliminary examinations in many other parts of the world, including in Afghanistan, Colombia, Georgia, Guinea, Honduras, Korea, and Nigeria.[34] The Office of the Prosecutor also investigated a situation in Cambodia in 2013 but determined that it did not meet the legal criteria for ICC prosecution.[35] Additionally, the Gambian lawyer Fatou Bensouda took over as Chief Prosecutor for the ICC in 2012. While we do not argue that the nationality of a chief prosecutor should make any difference in his or her decision making, it seems that the birthplace of a chief prosecutor should, at minimum, force us to provide more evidence than the list of prosecutions to claim that her office is biased against African nations. So it appears we have less evidence than we might have had even a few years ago to suggest that the focus of the ICC or other international criminal tribunals is and will be on Africa and Africa alone.

Moreover, now turning to our second (normative) response, the empirical evidence alone cannot support an argument that the international criminal

[32] See ICC Web site, "Situations and Cases," accessed 1 April 2016, www.icc-cpi.int/en_menus/icc/situations%20and%20cases/Pages/situations%20and%20cases.aspx.

[33] Rome Statute, preamble. Italics added.

[34] ICC Web site, "Situations and Cases."

[35] Ibid.

courts and tribunals have inappropriately targeted Africa. There are several reasons why the initial cases were heavily drawn from Africa, and it should be noted that most prosecutions were not initiated by the Office of the Prosecutor. First, the ICC's jurisdiction is limited, both temporally and geographically. The ICC cannot prosecute crimes committed before July 2002.[36] This takes many conflicts in our recent memory off the table for prosecution. Additionally, the ICC can establish jurisdiction over a situation in one of only three ways: (1) referral by a state party, (2) referral by the Security Council using its chapter VII powers,[37] or (3) a *proprio motu* investigation by the Prosecutor.[38] This means that the ICC can only prosecute individuals who have been accused of committing crimes as nationals of a state party, or in the territory of a state party, or where the situation has been referred by the Security Council, *and* where national investigations or prosecutions are not taking place. Finally, the gravity of the crimes (i.e., number of victims) could play into the fact that the situations in Africa have been prosecuted and not others.

As for the ICC's initial prosecutions, four were initiated by self-referrals. The Central African Republic, the Democratic Republic of the Congo, Mali, and Uganda all referred cases to the ICC on the basis that they were unable to prosecute the individuals accused of international crimes. This is not the whole story of each prosecution, as Uganda eventually wanted to reassume the responsibility of prosecuting the leaders of the LRA, but it does show that these cases were not initially sought out by the Office of the Prosecutor at the ICC. Two other situations, those in Libya and Darfur, were the result of referrals from the UN Security Council. These situations could have been referred for political reasons of members of the UN Security Council, but they were not discretionary investigations once they reached the Office of the Prosecutor. The final two situations in the initial group of prosecutions, those in the Ivory Coast and Kenya, were the result of *proprio motu* investigation by the Office of the Prosecutor. However, each of these two cases had features of self-referral cases: the Ivory Coast recognized the jurisdiction of the ICC during the outbreak of civil war, while Kenya failed in implementing domestic accountability mechanisms for election-related violence. Thus not one of the initial prosecutions appears, on its face, to be the result of political bias on the part of the Office of the Prosecutor at the ICC.

36 Rome Statute.

37 See UN Charter, chapter VII.

38 Rome Statute, art. 13(c).

The list of investigations now under way suggests a move toward investigating conflicts outside Africa. This is not due to a change in the structure of the ICC Office of the Prosecutor. The Rome Statute remains the same. It may reflect new policies, or it may be the result of a targeted public relations campaign to demonstrate the global focus of the ICC, or it may simply reflect the situations worthy of investigation in terms of the information the ICC has received in recent months and years. We cannot know without accessing information beyond a mere list of countries and individuals.

The ideological critique needs to be disconnected from the fairness critique, which we take up in Chapter 8. It is true that as a factual matter the ICC sits in the Hague and has mainly drawn its cases from Africa so far. This may indeed be unfair, but more is needed to show that the unfairness is related to an ideological bias. Those who argue that there is a deep ideological bias in the ICC have not made their case and are unlikely to do so in the near future given how few cases have been prosecuted. So the most important point to make here is that no matter what the docket looks like in terms of the nationality of its members, the numbers alone cannot prove a discriminatory or unfair structure or policy of the ICC. An argument that the international criminal courts and tribunals are inappropriately politically motivated will require something more. We can now turn to some of the arguments that the international criminal courts are inappropriately targeting Africans, but that do not rely solely on statistics.

IV EFFECTS OF COLONIALISM TODAY

The first hurdle to overcome in responding to compelling criticisms related to the proportion of international criminal cases and investigations in Africa is to identify why we think the international community should be involved in criminal justice in Africa at all. It is no secret that the number of armed conflicts in Africa is high and appears to be on the rise.[39] It is also no secret that the West played a large role, through colonialism, in creating the conditions that fostered the current conditions of conflict. Some critics have argued that the West's complicity in generating these conflicts should cause us to rethink

[39] Ifeonu Eberechi, "Armed Conflicts in Africa and Western Complicity: A Disincentive for African Union's Cooperation with the ICC," *African Journal of Legal Studies, vol.* 3, no. 1 (2009), 53–76. He notes that "according to the United Nations, since 1970, well over 30 wars have been fought in Africa, most of which have been internal, as opposed to between states." See *Report of the Secretary-General to the UN Security Council: The causes of conflict and the promotion of durable peace and sustainable development in Africa*, UN doc. A/52/871-S/1998/318, April 1998, at para. 4.

the focus on individual criminal accountability in international criminal law. Accordingly, these critics claim, any attempt to enforce international justice in Africa must also look at the role played by the West in generating and aggravating conflict.[40]

Ifeonu Eberechi claims that "it is almost impossible to come across an armed conflict in Africa without a colonial component, as most wars have highlighted the ethnic composition of the African societies – a socio-political mess that white colonialism created."[41] He notes that there were very few intraethnic conflicts prior to colonialism, but once different ethnic groups were forced to join together in a political unit constructed by the colonialists, and ethnic tensions were stoked by the colonialists, the political systems that eventually gained their independence were precarious at best.[42] Even the United States has contributed to the instability on the continent by encouraging African leaders and governments to participate in its "war on terror," by requesting military and legislative actions that have led to increased tensions between Muslims and Christians and political instability.[43] As Eberechi sums up the situation:

> Armed conflicts in Africa are fundamentally unique and complex, especially in relation to their causes. They represent an expression of frustration by a people against their colonial history, corrupt and despotic leaders, as well as the struggle for resource control, boundary adjustments and good governance.[44]

Eberechi argues that the international community's insistence on ensuring that individual leaders are subject to international criminal justice does not make any sense, given the complex nature of the armed conflicts and the positions of the leaders.[45] Rather, it is "a manifestation of the schizophrenic attitude with which it has always approached issues concerning Africa, including peace and security."[46] Eberechi concludes that responsibility for grave crimes in Africa should also fall on the shoulders of the international actors who contributed to the conditions of conflict, and the ICC model of individual responsibility fails to apportion responsibility in this way.[47]

[40] Ibid., p. 54.
[41] Ibid., pp. 56–57.
[42] Ibid., pp. 57–58.
[43] Ibid., p. 72.
[44] Ibid., p. 75
[45] Ibid., p. 76.
[46] Ibid., p. 76.
[47] Ibid., p. 76.

The complicity of the West in causing the overwhelming conflict in parts of Africa cannot be denied; nor should it be ignored. Yet it does not absolve the individuals who are committing atrocities from individual responsibility for their actions, and it should not prevent the individuals from being held accountable for their crimes. Again, the ideological criticisms must be separated from fairness criticisms. That one is rightly held legally accountable for her actions, while another is not, does not change the fact that one has been rightly held legally accountable for her actions. Because its mandate only concerns events that have taken place since 2002, the ICC does not have jurisdiction over colonialists; nor does it have jurisdiction over crimes such as creating ethnic tensions, since these crimes are outside the scope of its mandate. The ICC cannot prosecute colonialists for creating ethnic tensions. But it can prosecute individuals who have overseen mass killing in their own nations. Because that is what the ICC can rightly do, that is what it should do. This does not mean that we should not use other methods to recognize the bad acts of the West. But it does not mean that their contribution to violent situations in African nations should release individuals from their own responsibility for creating violence.

We will now turn to a related, but likely stronger criticism, that the West is now engaging in neocolonialist practices through the international criminal courts and tribunals.

V NEOCOLONIALISM

While the West's participation in colonizing African countries is probably not sufficient to justify leaving individual members of African nations out of international criminal prosecutions, the international criminal structures have also been accused of having a Western bias and of supporting hegemony and neocolonialism. The international criminal courts and tribunals, critics claim, are using more modern tools to control and oppress African peoples. In this section, we will present this argument about neocolonialism and attempt to show that this charge does not succeed.

International courts and tribunals are seen as part of a politically motivated attempt to hold up the practices of northern states and condemn the practices of southern states. Globalization is a key factor in this critique. The system of international law generally, and international criminal law in particular, is said to be aimed at furthering the forcible westernization of all the other states of the world.[48] One way the critique of forcible westernization is run is through criticism of the rhetoric of human rights. Koskenniemi says that human rights

48 See Tor Krever, "International Law: An Ideology Critique,"*Leiden Journal of International Law*, vol. 26, no. 3 (2013), pp. 701–723.

rhetoric "has historically had a positive and liberating effect on societies," but these rights "lose their transformative effect" once they have been institutionalized.[49] The Rawlsian principle of the "priority of the right over the good"[50] can colonize a political culture and prevent space for a community to articulate its own conception of the good.[51] Western principles and values, claim the critics, should not be exported at will.

With respect to this criticism, we concede that the method of forcing individuals and states to be free[52] is objectionable. Of course, all states and even local communities should be in a position to construct their own view of what makes a life good. Yet we do believe there are certain universal principles that establish basic human rights for all individuals across the globe. As Koskenniemi puts it:

> Although international law, too, in this way is a hegemonic politics, "it is nonetheless a form of politics that has some particular virtues" … It is possible to see the expanding practice of making political claims in legal language by an increasing number of international actors in the human rights field, in trade and environment bodies, in regional and universal tribunals and organizations and, not least, in the struggles over the meaning and direction of globalization, as parts of a process of construction of a universal political community.[53]

And there is no reason to think that the independent African states in question would not agree with those principles, particularly in light of the actions taken immediately after their independence and prior to the negative influence of the Cold War. Any attempts to globalize human rights should be limited in scope, and global values should in general not be imposed upon sovereign states.

The charge of neocolonialism against the ICC has been made with respect to several African conflicts. We will start with Darfur and the ICC's case against Omar al-Bashir. In 2008, the ICC Office of the Prosecutor applied for an arrest warrant for al-Bashir, the sitting president of Sudan, on charges of genocide, crimes against humanity, and war crimes.[54] The Pre-Trial Chamber authorized the issuance of arrest warrants for al-Bashir in 2009 and 2010 on the

49 Koskenniemi, *Politics of International Law*, p. 133.
50 John Rawls, *A Theory of Justice* (Oxford: Clarendon Press, 1971), p. 31.
51 Koskenniemi, *Politics of International Law*, p. 133.
52 See Jean-Jacques Rousseau, *The Social Contract, or, Principles of Political Right* (Sydney: George Allen & Unwin, 1895).
53 Koskenniemi, *Politics of International Law*, p. 239.
54 Mahmood Mamdani, "Darfur, ICC and the New Humanitarian Order." *Zeleza Post, vol.* 25 (2008).

charges of crimes against humanity and genocide, respectively.[55] These arrest warrants give rise to an obligation on the part of states to "comply with requests for arrest and surrender."[56]

Critics have argued that this attempt to prosecute al-Bashir (which has failed, thus far, as he is still at large) "sheds light on the politics of the 'new humanitarian order,'" as critics have dubbed the practice of deciding who needs saving and when.[57] It has been claimed that the ICC Prosecutor supported one side of a conflict that began as a civil war without fully understanding the conflict.[58] The African Union (AU) took the step of requesting a delay in the ICC charges based on its assessment that "attempts to arrest Mr. Bashir could further destabilize the situation in Darfur."[59] Thus a dilemma arises for African states as to whether to abide by the obligations set forth by the ICC and arrest al-Bashir, or to avoid appearing to betray the AU and its members.

In line with the African Union's opinion, several African states have failed to comply with their duty to arrest and surrender al-Bashir to the ICC, including Chad, the Democratic Republic of the Congo, Djibouti, Kenya, and Malawi.[60] Most notable, however, was South Africa's failure to arrest al-Bashir. In June 2015, al-Bashir traveled to South Africa, a signatory of the Rome Statute, for an AU summit. An agreement between the AU and South Africa regarding the AU summit provided that the South African government must accord "immunity from personal arrest or detention" to all representatives of AU Member States.[61] The North Gauteng High Court ruled that the ICC obligations must be fulfilled nonetheless and ordered the South African government to "take all reasonable steps to arrest President Al-Bashir."[62] The South African government, however, stood by the agreement with the AU and permitted al-Bashir to leave the country rather than arresting and detaining him. In March 2016, South Africa's Supreme Court of Appeal ruled that South Africa's failure to

55 See Warrant of Arrest for Omar Hassan Ahmad Al-Bashir, Al Bashir (ICC-02/05-01/09), Pre-Trial Chamber I, 4 March 2009; see also Second Warrant of Arrest for Omar Hassan Ahmad Al-Bashir, Al Bashir (ICC-02/05-01/09), Pre-Trial Chamber I, 12 July 2010.

56 Rome Statute, art. 89(1).

57 Mamdani, "Darfur, ICC and the New Humanitarian Order."

58 Ibid.

59 "Mbeki Named to Heal Bashir Rift," *BBC News*, March 6, 2009.

60 Dire Tladi, "The Duty on South Africa to Arrest and Surrender President Al-Bashir under South African and International Law: A Perspective from International Law," *Journal of International Criminal Justice*, vol. 13 (2015), pp. 1027, 1028–1029.

61 See ibid., pp. 1031–1032; see also General Convention on the Privileges and Immunities of the Organisation of African Unity (OAU), sect. C, art. V(1).

62 *Southern African Litigation Centre v. Minister of Justice and Constitutional Development and Others* (27740/2015), High Court of South Africa, Gauteng Division, Pretoria, 24 June 2015, § 2.

arrest and detain al-Bashir in 2015 violated both domestic and international law.[63] So while it seems to the Western world (and many in Africa) that al-Bashir is worthy of prosecution, which may in fact be true, it bears noting that the ICC should be in the practice of investigating the complex political dimensions of conflicts, rather than just obtaining evidence of atrocities.

The ICC case against Kenyan government officials has been subjected to similar criticism. Following postelection violence in 2007, the Kenyan government told the ICC that it would set up a tribunal to prevent impunity for those guilty of participating in the violence. When no such tribunal manifested, the ICC authorized the Office of the Prosecutor to begin an investigation in Kenya, with the intent that the ICC would eventually bring charges against those individuals who were most responsible for the crimes contributing to the postelection violence. While ICC charges were pending against one of the defendants, Uhuru Kenyatta, he was elected as the president of Kenya. The Kenyan government proceeded to refuse to cooperate with the ICC and has tried to assert its sovereignty and jurisdiction over the cases. This has resulted, ultimately, in the dismissal of all four cases.

Kenya and other African states have argued that the ICC has usurped its mandate under the complementarity regime, and that the ICC's persistence in pursuing a head of state reflected disregard for Kenya's political sovereignty. At least in the case of Kenyatta, evidence of his involvement is spotty, and this may or may not be due to his political influence rather than his actual innocence. Regardless, here is another situation in which the ICC should have fully investigated the situation before deciding to assert jurisdiction and proceed with a weak case. In Sections VI and VII, we will focus on the ICC and explore what critics see as two major sources of political involvement in the court.

VI COMPLEMENTARITY

The principle of complementarity has been hailed as a crucial feature of the Rome Statute that forces the international criminal justice system to respect the sovereign authority of states and defer to domestic prosecutions of criminals. However, some critics have argued that the ICC's principle of complementarity actually makes it harder for the court to avoid political decisions as well as political influence over its decision making. We will consider these arguments before arguing that while the ICC must use subjective criteria to

[63] See *The Minister of Justice and Constitutional Development v. The Southern African Litigation Centre* (867/15) [2016] ZASCA 17 (15 March 2016).

make decisions related to complementarity, these decisions are not impermissibly political in nature.

The preamble and article 17 of the Rome Statute confirm the status of the ICC as a court of last resort. The preamble specifically identifies the complementary nature of the ICC with respect to national criminal jurisdictions.[64] Under article 17 a case "being investigated or prosecuted by a State which has jurisdiction over it" is inadmissible "unless the State is unwilling or unable genuinely to carry out the investigation or prosecution."[65] If a state has already investigated a case and has decided not to prosecute an individual, the result must stand "unless the decision resulted from the unwillingness or inability of the State genuinely to prosecute."[66] Finally, where a "person concerned has already been tried for conduct which is the subject of [a] complaint," the case is not permissible unless the proceedings in the other court aimed to shield the individual from criminal responsibility, or "otherwise were not conducted independently or impartially in accordance with the norms of due process recognized by international law and were conducted in a manner which, in the circumstances, was inconsistent with an intent to bring the person concerned to justice."[67] Admissibility may be challenged by the accused or any state with jurisdiction before a Pre-Trial Chamber, or the Pre-Trial Chamber may also challenge the admissibility of the case before the ICC.[68]

Alexander Greenawalt and others argue that the ICC's complementarity principle does not lead to a balance between international justice and domestic sovereignty, but that it puts the ICC in the position of having to make political decisions.[69] He addresses two problems that arise in light of the lack of guidance as to how the principle of complementarity should be applied. Greenawalt claims that the Rome Statute fails to define important terms, namely, what constitutes a trial or an investigation, and that there are "tensions between the collective and individual nature of the determination."[70] The unavoidable result of these problems is that the ICC must answer difficult political questions with respect to complementarity issues.

64 Rome Statute.

65 Rome Statute, art. 17(1)(a).

66 Rome Statute, art. 17(1)(b).

67 Rome Statute, arts. 17(1)(c), 20(3).

68 Rome Statute, arts. 18–19.

69 Alexander K. A. Greenawalt, "Complementarity in Crisis: Uganda, Alternative Justice, and the International Criminal Court," *Virginia Journal of International Law*, vol. 50 (2009), pp. 108–162. Also see Daniel Nsereko, "The ICC and Complementarity in Principle," *Leiden Journal of International Law*, vol. 26, no. 2 (2013), pp. 426–447; and Thomas Obel Hansen, "A Critical Review of the ICC's Practice Concerning Admissibility Challenges and Complementarity," *Melbourne Journal of International Law*, vol. 13 (June 2012), pp. 217–234.

70 Greenawalt, "Complementarity in Crisis," pp. 124–125.

In the case of Uganda, the ICC needed to decide whether to allow complementarity to include a noncriminal traditional dispute resolution model to substitute for the ICC's own trial of leaders of the Lord's Resistance Army, as well as many small fry who were often child soldiers. Greenawalt argues that this critical decision and others were "not guided by legal criteria" and hence asks whether "the Rome Statute delegated authority to the wrong actors" for these critical decisions. Complementarity takes these decisions out of the hands of a state like Uganda, but places the decision into hands that are not qualified to assess what is best for the peace process in a war-torn state.[71]

We argue that this is not an impermissible interaction between the legal and the political. As discussed in other chapters, prosecutorial discretion rests on the principle that decisions should be made according to the interests of justice. There is no reason why the interests of justice are or should be limited to purely legal concerns. In fact, it would be difficult to make a clean cut as to whether certain considerations were even classifiable as purely political or purely legal in nature. The ICC's assessment of a noncriminal traditional dispute resolution mechanism cannot be based on purely legal questions, as the political situation must be understood in order to approach such an assessment. We see complementarity as a realm in which there are legal questions, but also political questions, to be asked in making an assessment.

VII POLITICAL DISCRETION

The most difficult challenge is that the ICC is simply incapable of not considering politics in the decision about whom to prosecute. The ICC was formed by a large group of states that generally (with France and the United Kingdom being notable exceptions) do not have much political power in the world, opposed by powerful states (led by the United States, Russia, and China) that have not ratified the Rome Statute and are very unlikely to do so in the near future. To survive, the ICC must to a certain extent deal with its current precarious political position. Critics have argued that as a result, the ICC is driven by political concerns to such an extent that its vaunted impartiality is doubtful. We concede that there are aspects of the way the ICC has functioned in the past that look far too political for a judicial body, but we maintain that there is no reason why the ICC must function as a political body.

Some critics have alleged that both large and small states are able to manipulate the ICC in order to gain political advantage. Mark Osiel has

[71] Ibid.

recently made a strong case for this claim.[72] Most if not all of the most powerful states in the world have not ratified the Rome Statute and hence remain outside the jurisdiction of the court. The majority of states of the world, those that have ratified the Rome Statute, often trade "self-referrals" for understanding that those who are currently ruling will not be prosecuted, or they use the investigation of insurgent groups in their states as a public relations event that supposedly shows that the world has sided against these insurgents.

Reliance on the neutrality of the Security Council to ensure that appropriate referrals are made may be precarious. The ICC may be in a position of assessing whether political reasons have influenced referrals. As a political organ of the UN, the Security Council has mechanisms in place to prevent that "a merely political referral triggered a criminal investigation,"[73] but the reverse is not the case. There have been and will likely continue to be instances in which cases should be referred to the ICC but are not, as a result of the political makeup of the Security Council. For instance, in 2014, Russia and China blocked the Security Council from adopting a draft resolution that would have referred the conflict in Syria to the ICC for investigation.[74] This could be viewed as a permissible influence of politics on the Security Council, ensuring that it reaches the correct decision, but it is more likely that the two permanent Security Council members voted no on the basis of their relationships with the Syrian president, Bashar al-Assad. And yet, we must remember that this political influence arises outside the ICC, although it did play a role in the ICC's decision making.

As mentioned earlier, Nouwen and Werner have argued that despite its best efforts, the ICC cannot claim that it is not a political entity.[75] They are especially critical of the way the ICC has utilized such categories as "enemies of mankind" to set up a dichotomy between the ICC and its enemies and critics, which they argue is clearly political (or ideological) in a way that undermines the objective status of the ICC. In its starkest terms, critics claim the ICC acts politically by choosing its cases with a view to who it sees as the side of a

[72] Mark Osiel, "The Demise of International Criminal Law," *Humanity*, 16 November 2013, accessded 22 October 2016, http://humanity journal.org/blog/2013/11/demise-international-criminal-court.

[73] Roberto Bellelli, ed. *International Criminal Justice: Law and Practice from the Rome Statute to Its Review* (Burlington, VT: Ashgate, 2013), p. 381.

[74] Press Release, Security Council, Referral of Syria to International Criminal Court Fails as Negative Votes Prevent Security Council from Adopting Draft Resolution, U.N. Doc. SC/11407 (May 22, 2014).

[75] See Nouwen and Werner, "Doing Justice to the Political."

controversy that is its friend. The ICC, they argue, needs to stop picking sides in various internal political matters in states that are in crisis such as Uganda and Sudan.

In another high-profile case before an ad hoc international tribunal, the Special Court for Sierra Leone, Darren Hawkins and Chad Loseee have argued that in decisions about whether to prosecute state leaders, such as Charles Taylor, who was prosecuted, as well as Muammar Qaddafi and Blaise Compaore, who were not prosecuted, political factors played an outsized role. Hawkins and Losee allege that the United States, especially, played a disproportionate role in these investigation and prosecution decisions.[76]

In response, we can only say that these cases are, in fact, likely examples of impermissible political influence. But there is nothing in the structure of the international criminal courts that required them to be. These are instances of failure by the international criminal justice regime, but they are not indicative of systematic failure.

We should also remember, when appealing to individual cases of possible political influence, that we are still in the infancy of the ICC's exercise of jurisdiction. Unfortunately, armed conflicts will likely continue to pop up all over the globe, and it will be easier to assess the actions of the ICC once there is more data to consider. This is one reason for our normative defense: we cannot easily make empirical generalizations, but we can defend the structure of the ICC and its potential.

The aim of this chapter has been to show that the relationship between politics and international criminal law is both inevitable and not necessarily insidious. However, there are political influences and ideologies that must be avoided by the international criminal courts and tribunals in their exercise of jurisdiction and admissibility. The criticisms of the ICC as neocolonialist should give the Office of the Prosecutor pause and cause the Prosecutor to ensure that she adequately investigates political circumstances in addition to collecting evidence. The structure of the ICC and other international criminal tribunals may involve political questions, but they do not necessarily involve undue political influence. In Chapter 8 we take up the fairness issues that have already been mentioned, but now with much greater detail to the arguments that the critics have made that do not relate to colonialism or other global political concerns.

[76] Darren Hawkins and Chad Losee, "States and International Courts: The Politics of Prosecution in Sierra Leone,"*Journal of Human Rights*, vol. 13, no. 1 (January–March 2014), pp. 48–68.

7

Evidence

The next set of objections we consider are the growing concerns about whether international tribunals can operate effectively given the problems with investigating and assessing evidence that needs to be accumulated from war zones[1] and from areas of the world where the very idea of certain forms of truth-telling is problematic. These evidence issues are closely related to the issues of fairness addressed in Chapter 8 of this book, and the aims of international criminal tribunals to balance finite resources with justice for defendants and victims. From the beginning, there have been questions about how very different domestic criminal law traditions can be merged into a fair and effective system of justice. The melding of Anglo-American and Continental systems of jurisprudence has allowed for some creativity, but also for a large number of criticisms that we will deal with in this part of the book.

In Chapter 7, we explore the most commonly cited concerns related to the presentation and use of evidence in international courts and tribunals. In Section I we explain the importance of evidence in criminal trials and provide some background on its historical development. We then look at the nature of international criminal trials and certain aspects of the trial procedures in Section II. Section III turns to specific criticisms that have been leveled against international criminal tribunals, beginning with the investigation procedures. Next, in Section IV we consider the issues related to evidence presented through witnesses. Section V turns to several other issues related to evidence and its use, including in the issuance of an arrest warrant, judgment, and sentencing aspects of a trial. Finally, we assess the overall impact of the problems we have presented and argue that because these problems can be

1 See T. A. Doherty, "Evidence in International Criminal Tribunals: Contrast between Domestic and International Trials," *Leiden Journal of International Law*, vol. 26, no. 4 (2013), pp. 937–945.

addressed (or mitigated) with adequate resources and oversight, the international criminal tribunals and courts remain normatively defensible.

I EVIDENCE AND ITS ROLE IN CRIMINAL TRIALS

In a courtroom, the main activity is determining past facts. Thus, one of the main differences between legal systems involves the practices surrounding fact-finding. In Section I, we will briefly consider the normative foundations of evidence law generally and in both the Anglo-American and Continental systems. This will set our scene for analyzing the hybrid approach to fact-finding taken by most international criminal courts and tribunals.

When we think about how we determine facts about the past, the first distinction we need to make is between evidence and demonstrative proof. In the case of demonstrative proof, the premises of a valid argument provide a "decisive and complete basis for the conclusion."[2] Evidence, on the other hand, goes beyond the content of a given piece of information. An argument based on evidence "constitutes an inductive extension of the range of our information."[3] So while proof is an all-or-nothing concept, evidence admits of degrees.[4] This immediately frustrates courtroom endeavors to "prove" that certain facts about the past are true merely by the presentation of evidence. As Rescher and Joynt note, "human action, in matters of great and of small consequence, is governed by probable evidence, and not by proof."[5] There is a symbiotic relationship between evidence and knowledge, in that we only have access to what we know about facts, rather than the facts per se.[6]

In legal contexts, what constitutes "good" or "probable" evidence must meet a certain standard in order to assign legal responsibility to an individual for a particular action and corresponding state of mind. But we know that this standard does not equate to certainty. It is the best approximation of a historical record, based on the evidence we have access and knowledge. In presenting evidence, the goal is to "convince the judge or jury as to the actual

[2] Nicholas Rescher and Carey B. Joynt, "Evidence in History and in the Law." *The Journal of Philosophy* (1959), pp. 561–578, 561.

[3] Ibid., p. 562.

[4] Ibid., p. 562; see also Joseph Butler, Introduction to *The Analogy of Religion, Natural and Revealed, to the Constitution and Course of Nature* (London: G. Bell and Sons, 1889): "Probable evidence," wrote Bishop Butler, "is essentially distinguished from demonstrative by this, that it admits of degrees; and of all variety of them, from the highest moral certainty, to the very lowest presumption."

[5] Rescher and Joynt, "Evidence in History and in the Law," p. 563.

[6] Ibid., p. 565; see also David Hume, *A Treatise of Human Nature*, vol. 1, edited by David Fate Norton and Mary J. Norton (Oxford: Clarendon Press, 2007).

past occurrence of certain transactions, and to induce them to draw suitable inferences from the overtly presented information to appropriate conclusions with respect to related past events."[7] The objective in any trial is to approach as close to the truth as possible,[8] but again, this is not the truth (or state of affairs) per se. Rather, the trial serves to create a "composition between conflicting claims within the wider social context of a legal system designed to serve the interests of the society as a whole."[9]

In Section II, we will more fully consider some of the differences between the Anglo-American (common law) and Continental (civil law) criminal legal systems. But we will take a brief aside here to provide some historical background and identify some of the most notable differences in terms of fact-finding. While we can look into ancient history for certain aspects grounding criminal law today, we cannot look back more than a few centuries for what grounds modern evidence law.[10] Early juries either were so familiar with the defendants and facts of the cases that they did not require a formal presentation of evidence in order to reach a judgment or were inclined to seek out further information from "informed persons not called into court."[11] It was not until the 1500s that jurors were expected to be ignorant of the facts, rather than familiar, and it was at this point that evidence law began to develop.[12] The European states eventually veered away from the jury-based criminal trial, while the British and other common law jurisdictions continued to develop practices that relied on the need to present evidence to laypersons.

Both the Continental and Anglo-American systems share a commitment to fair treatment of defendants, but they differ in their understanding of how the court can best make a determination of the guilt or innocence of a defendant. Civil law systems place the main responsibility for fact-finding on professional judges, while the lawyers "guide and limit the judicial inquiry in important ways."[13] In common law systems, fact-finding is a shared enterprise, with different roles to be played by the professional judge, the lawyers for the parties, and the jurors.[14] The lawyers in common law systems take on the greatest

[7] Rescher and Joynt, "Evidence in History and in the Law," p. 566.

[8] Edmund M. Morgan, *Some Problems of Proof under the Anglo-American System of Litigation* (New York: Columbia University Press, 1956), p. 128.

[9] Rescher and Joynt, "Evidence in History and in the Law," p. 567.

[10] See generally, John H. Langbein, "Historical Foundations of the Law of Evidence: A View from the Ryder Sources," *Columbia Law Review* (1996): 1168–1202, 1170.

[11] John H. Wigmore, *A Treatise on the Anglo-American System of Evidence in Trials at Common Law* § 1364, 11 (3d ed. 1940); see also Langbein, "Historical Foundations of the Law of Evidence," p. 1170.

[12] Ibid., p. 1171.

[13] Ibid., p. 1168.

[14] Ibid., p. 1168.

burden in "gathering, sifting, and presenting evidence of the facts,"[15] while the judge and jury are tasked with somewhat passive assessment of the evidence presented. These two types of courtroom arrangements are radically different. Yet as we shall see in Section II, each system plays a role in informing the procedures of the international criminal courts and tribunals.

In order most closely to approximate the truth, most courts in both systems have adopted a best evidence principle, which requires fact-finders to "seek the reconstruction of the relevant events by forcing the production of the best evidence available, relying on that evidence alone, and following the epistemologically most effective truth-certifying procedures."[16] When a fact-finder ultimately makes an assertion as to the guilt or innocence of a defendant, it is generally assumed that the fact-finder is claiming to "know" that the defendant is either guilty or innocent.[17] But as we know, the epistemic position of the fact-finder, and thus the justification supporting any assertion based on a knowledge claim, may be stronger or weaker depending on the available evidence. This has led some to argue for a weaker account of what it means to make an assertion, namely, that it is only indicative of a justified belief on the part of the fact-finder.[18] However, it is not important to settle this debate for the purposes of this book, as long as we recognize that any assertion of the guilt or innocence of a defendant made by a fact-finder, however well-supported through the application of the best evidence principle, is necessarily limited by the available evidence and the epistemic position of the fact-finder.

Now that we have recognized the limitations of evidence, we can turn to how courts handle the resultant risks involved in evidence assessment. In both common law and civil law systems, a criminal defendant's guilt must be established by facts that have been established beyond all reasonable doubt.[19] Thus, in the ICC and the ad hoc tribunals, the courts have also adopted the "beyond a reasonable doubt" standard.[20] This standard presumes innocence unless there is clear evidence to the contrary.[21] So

[15] Ibid., p. 1168.

[16] Alex Stein, *Foundations of Evidence Law* (Oxford: Oxford University Press, 2005), p. 12.

[17] See Hock Lai Ho, *A Philosophy of Evidence Law: Justice in the Search for Truth* (Oxford: Oxford University Press, 2008), p. 87.

[18] See ibid., p. 89.

[19] Kevin M. Clermont and Emily Sherwin, "A Comparative View of Standards of Proof," *The American Journal of Comparative Law* (2002): 243–275.

[20] See, e.g., rule 87 (A) ICTY RPE; rule 87 (A) ICTR RPE; art. 66 of the ICC RPE.

[21] The importance of this presumption in international human rights law is noted here: Human Rights Committee, General Comment No. 32, art. 14: Right to equality before courts and tribunals and to a fair trial, U.N. Doc. CCPR/C/GC/32 (2007).

any "doubts that remain unsubstantiated and, consequently, imperceptible (such doubts can be found in every case) do not pass the threshold of reasonableness."[22] The "beyond a reasonable doubt" standard requires that the fact-finder eliminate, on the basis of the evidence, all scenarios in which the defendant could be innocent.[23] Because an instance of doubt is only considered reasonable when it hooks up to credible evidence, this principle aims to control for the errors of human judgment based on emotions, impressions, or bias.

Another realm of evidence law that seeks to control for erroneous convictions includes limitations on the introduction of certain kinds of evidence. One type of evidence that is sometimes excluded from criminal trials is evidence of a defendant's bad character or other bad acts, particularly when they are introduced for the purpose of (erroneously) establishing a "causal connection between the defendant's personality and his or her actions."[24] This is distinguishable from evidence that could be used to establish a defendant's specific mens rea with respect to a particular act or acts, which is permissible.

Anglo-American courts recognize the hearsay rule, which limits the admission of out-of-court statements as "evidence of the truth of their contents."[25] In this vein, and in light of the best evidence principle, in-person witness testimony is preferred (across legal systems) to out-of-court statements of the same witness.[26] However, while civil law systems prefer more direct evidence, they are historically more inclined to permit the introduction of hearsay and opinion evidence.[27] The international criminal courts and tribunals also tend to be more flexible on the admission of hearsay evidence, and will admit hearsay evidence when it is deemed relevant.[28]

Now that we have identified some of the general principles governing evidence in criminal trials, in Section II we will look more closely at the nature of international criminal trials.

[22] Stein, *Foundations of Evidence Law*, p. 173.

[23] Ibid.

[24] Ibid., p. 183, see also Ronald Dworkin, *Taking Rights Seriously* (Cambridge, MA: Harvard University Press, 1978), p. 13.

[25] See, e.g., Federal Rules of Evidence, 801–807.

[26] See Stein, *Foundations of Evidence Law*, p. 198; see also Dale Nance, "The Best Evidence Principle," *Iowa Law Review*, vol. 73 (1998), p. 227.

[27] See Mirjan Damaska, "Of Hearsay and Its Analogues," *Minnesota Law Review*, vol. 76 (1992), pp. 425, 444–449.

[28] See, e.g., *Prosecutor v. Brima, Kamara and Kanu (AFRC Case)*, Case No. SCSL-04-16-PT, Decision on joint defence motion to exclude all evidence from Witness TF1-277 pursuant to Rule 89(c) and/or Rule 95, 24 May 2005, para. 12.

II NATURE OF THE TRIALS

The procedural rules governing the international tribunals and courts differ in certain instances, but they share many fundamental rules and features. In Section II, we will look at the nature of the procedural rules generally before turning to the specific issue of combining ideas from different criminal justice systems around the world.

A *Procedure*

Drawing on the fairness considerations discussed in Chapter 8, we think that international defendants should receive certain procedural protections and assurances. International criminal defendants cannot be tried and convicted to serve a purely expressive purpose of denouncing horrific crimes. It must be proved, beyond a reasonable doubt, that an individual defendant meets the requirements for having committed a particular crime. As Mirjan Damaska explained, procedural mechanisms in international criminal law must result in predictable, consistent, and coherent outcomes.[29]

The principle of equality of arms must inform every aspect of an international criminal trial. It is particularly tricky to ensure that the rights of the accused are balanced against the anticipated expressive benefits of a trial (or conviction) for victims and survivors. But there must be procedures in place to ensure that the prosecution and defense are on a level playing field with respect to resources and treatment by the judges. Respect for the principle of equality of arms is necessary for criminal judicial proceedings to be consistent with human rights standards, and international human rights law suggests that this requires procedural guarantees such as

> the right to be cognizant of the nature and cause of the charges brought against him, the right to have adequate time and facilities for the preparation of the defence, the right to counsel of his own choosing and the right of access to assigned legal assistance, the right to examine or have examined witnesses against him and defence witnesses under the same conditions, [and] the right to have the free assistance of an interpreter.[30]

With respect to evidence, the most important implications of the equality of arms principle involve a fair opportunity to access and present evidence,

[29] See Mirjan Damaska, "The Henry Morris Lecture: What Is the Point of International Criminal Justice?" *Chicago-Kent Law Review*, vol. 83 (2008), pp. 331–335.

[30] Stefania Negri, "The Principle of Equality of Arms and the Evolving Law of International Criminal Procedure," *International Criminal Law Review, vol.* 5, no. 4 (2005), pp. 513–571, 517.

particularly witness testimonies. Neither the defense nor the prosecution should be permitted to withhold information from the other side, as there should be no advantage or disadvantage that accrues simply by virtue of the trial procedure.

B Adversarial v. Nonadversarial

As noted in the introduction and Section I, the melding of Anglo-American and Continental systems of jurisprudence has allowed for some creativity in developing international criminal legal systems, but it has also resulted in some uncertainty regarding the respective roles to be played by the judges, prosecutors, and witnesses. The purpose of this chapter is not to present a comprehensive comparative analysis of the two systems, but rather to reveal the relevant differences and opportunities for confusion or ambiguity.

The Anglo-American system of jurisprudence, otherwise known as the common law system, is adversarial in nature. Damaska describes three typical aspects of a common law system of jurisprudence as "the complexity of the common law regulation; a preoccupation with sifting the material for the fact-finder to hear and see; and an aspiration to structure the analysis of evidence."[31] Most importantly for our inquiry here, the adversarial legal model frames the trial as a dispute between two parties, who are supposed to stand on equal footing in accordance with the equality of arms principle.[32] Each party must have the opportunity to cross-examine any witnesses presented by the opposing party, as this allows all evidence to be questioned and all sources to be verified. There is an "intense preliminary screening of evidence" in the adversarial model because the prosecution and the defense determine what evidence is presented to the judge, and then the judge determines whether or not exclusionary rules apply before agreeing to admit the evidence to the record.[33]

The Continental system of jurisprudence, or the inquisitorial system, on the other hand, does not require adherence to the equality of arms principle. Rather, the inquisitorial system is structured so that there is one party with more power than everyone else; that party is the judge, who historically acted as the prosecutor.[34] These systems are "characterized by separate responsibilities

[31] Mirjan Damaska, *Evidence Law Adrift* (New Haven, CT: Yale University Press, 1997), p. 8.

[32] Michele Caianiello, "Law of Evidence at the International Criminal Court: Blending Accusatorial and Inquisitorial Models," *North Carolina Journal of International Law & Commercial Regulation*, vol. 36 (2011), p. 293.

[33] Damaska, *Evidence Law Adrift*, p. 12.

[34] Ibid.; see also Caianiello, "Law of Evidence at the International Criminal Court," p. 293.

for the investigation or pre-trial phase, conducted by the prosecution or *the juge d'instruction* (examining judge), and the actual trial, conducted by a trial judge or court."[35] All evidence is presented to the impartial judge, who determines how the court should proceed, rather than the prosecutor, as in the adversarial system. This system of jurisprudence is more inclined to permit, say, written testimony than the adversarial system, which would want to allow for cross-examination.

At the international criminal courts and tribunals, the systems are mostly adversarial, but there are some aspects of the trial processes that hearken to a nonadversarial or inquisitorial system (such as the duty of the prosecutor to investigate exculpatory evidence, as discussed in Section II).[36] The courts and tribunals were intended as international bodies, so both Anglo-American and Continental elements were integrated into the procedures. As Mirjan Damaska noted in 1997, just as the ICTY was beginning its operations, it is "no wonder foreign lawyers, when called upon to join their Anglo-American colleagues in a fact-finding enterprise, find it difficult to agree to factual inquiries that incorporate common law doctrines and practices."[37] But it has been argued by some that the international criminal courts and tribunals should adopt a more realistic model of admitted evidence. Kai Ambos claims that "it is no longer important whether a rule is either 'adversarial' or 'inquisitorial' but whether it assists the Tribunals in accomplishing their tasks and whether it complies with fundamental fair trial standards."[38] Others have advocated that international criminal judges utilize managerial powers, maintaining the general adversarial system but permitting judges to insert themselves at times in order to speed up the trial process.[39] The bench can serve many purposes when it takes on a managerial role: "cleaning up the record; clarifying testimony; supplementing, eliciting, and testing testimony, as well as challenging the credibility of witnesses."[40]

We agree with commentators who have suggested that the international courts and tribunals should not be overly concerned with maintaining a

35 Kai Ambos, "International Criminal Procedure: 'Adversarial', 'Inquisitorial' or Mixed?" *International Criminal Law Review*, vol. 3 (2003), pp. 1–37, 3.

36 The ICC in particular employs various aspects of an inquisitorial system, despite its accusatorial structure. See Caianiello, "Law of Evidence at the International Criminal Court."

37 Damaska, *Evidence Law Adrift*.

38 Ambos, "International Criminal Procedure," p. 1.

39 See Maximo Langer and Joseph Doherty, "Managerial Judging Goes International, but Its Promise Remains Unfulfilled: An Empirical Assessment of the ICTY Reforms," *Yale Journal of International Law*, vol. 36 (2011), p. 241.

40 Rosemary Byrne, "Drawing the Missing Map: What Socio-Legal Research Can Offer to International Criminal Trial Practice," *Leiden Journal of International Law*, vol. 26, no. 4 (2013), pp. 991–1007, 1002.

purely adversarial or inquisitorial model. Within the procedural rules of the respective judicial bodies, it is only practical that judges should be able to promote efficient trials by participating in the process of evidence presentation. The inefficiency of the international courts and tribunals may not have been anticipated by those who drafted the procedural rules governing the judicial bodies, but now that we are aware of these problems, we should aim to permit changes to the practices that will allow for more efficient and accurate evidence management during trials. However, allowing for a broader range of practices does not mean that judges will be on equal footing. Judges who have served on the bench in Anglo-American courtrooms may not feel comfortable inserting themselves into the judicial process, while judges who have served on the bench in Continental courtrooms may find it difficult to be merely detached observers.

With these broad issues in mind, let us now turn to specific criticisms of the international criminal courts and tribunals in their handling of evidence. We will start with issues in the realm of investigating possible crimes.

III INVESTIGATION

International criminal courts and tribunals, when presented with accusations of international criminal activity, must obtain evidence of these crimes by sending investigators out into the field. These investigations must be carried out in order to establish whether or not individuals should be served with arrest warrants, as we will explore later in the chapter, but also to establish evidence in a trial once one has commenced. Thus, the investigation is crucial to both the investigation and prosecution phases of international criminal law. Given the centrality of investigations, and the limited resources available to prosecutors, it is no surprise that there have been numerous criticisms leveled at the international courts and tribunals for their handling of field investigations. Let us look at several specific criticisms in turn.

A *Location of Evidence*

International criminal courts and tribunals have had limited access to evidence due to the location and condition of many of the sites requiring investigation, and critics have argued that this arrangement has led to inadequate evidence collection. Critics have raised profound questions about the efficacy or reliability of fact-finding during and after ongoing armed conflicts. The first side of the problem concerns the unreliability of evidence gathered during the fog of war, when people often do not feel able to speak truthfully and crucial evidence may simply be hidden by one party to the conflict or another. The other side of this problem is that if an international prosecutor waits until the armed conflict is over and passions have cooled, there is a risk that the evidence of the crime may have become cold, thereby also impeding the fact-finding process. Indeed, there is unlikely to be any happy medium here.[41]

In some instances, these difficulties are due to a failure on the part of international judicial bodies to allocate sufficient resources and personnel to the investigation process. We believe this is a problem that must be remedied. If international criminal courts and tribunals are to exist, they must expend the resources necessary to gather evidence for trials. Tribunals or special courts should not be created without adequate funding for the process. The ICC must invest adequate funds and personnel in performing investigations, or else they will be seen as lacking the capacity to conduct international criminal trials. Investigation teams must be properly trained and deployed on the ground for sufficient time to conduct investigations, regardless of how far away the site is from the judicial body. Otherwise, the criminal trials will be missing facts that could have been obtained, and this shortcoming does not serve the goals of justice for victims or defendants.

But in many cases, the investigating team will be limited by circumstances that cannot be remedied by allocating more resources. In situations when the conflict is ongoing, investigators may only be able to access certain areas without putting themselves into grave danger. While forensic investigators should try to gather evidence by working cooperatively with the parties to a conflict, they should not be put at undue risk. Even when conflict is not ongoing, there are sometimes logistical difficulties that cannot be overcome by a reasonable influx of resources, such as safety concerns or conditions in which roads are nonexistent, poorly maintained, or impassable.[42] In situations in which the conflict occurred months or years prior to the investigation, or when the conflict is ongoing and evidence collection is dangerous, there is only so much evidence that can be obtained. The circumstances of the investigation must be considered when assessing the value of the evidence, as limited evidence is better than no evidence.

It also seems clear that physical evidence can be tampered with, especially during wartime, and this should make investigators and prosecutors suspicious of evidence that is gathered where it could have been tainted. And here it is clear that there must be new rules for making sure that evidence is not tainted,

41 See Christian DeVos, "Investigating from Afar: The ICC's Evidence Problem," *Leiden Journal of International Law*, vol. 26, no. 4 (2013), pp. 1009–1024.

42 Nancy Combs, *Fact-Finding without Facts: The Uncertain Evidentiary Foundations of International Criminal Convictions* (Cambridge: Cambridge University Press, 2010), p. 147.

such that these rules need to be highly specific to the conditions that are most likely to be present when mass atrocities have taken place. In some cases, it may be that prosecutions simply should not be allowed to proceed if the only available evidence is likely to have been tainted.

This is not to say that tribunals have to be overly cautious as they approach evidence that is gained from the battlefield or long after the events in question. But international tribunals can look to domestic tribunals for guidance here.[43] It may be that not enough evidence can be collected to go forward with a trial, or it may be that the limited evidence collected is sufficient to charge some individuals but not others. These limitations are unfortunate, but they are not so different from the limitations placed on domestic trials. The available evidence is the available evidence. However, some of the issues are endemic to the nature of international crimes, but if we are committed to international criminal prosecution, they should not prevent international criminal tribunals and courts from moving forward.

B Intermediaries

Another limitation on investigatory teams is their access, as outsiders, to witnesses, locations, and general information that might provide fruitful evidence. In many situations, the prosecutors of international criminal courts and tribunals have relied on local information providers known as "intermediaries" to help with investigations. These intermediaries are individuals and organizations who "perform a variety of essential functions," including providing access to evidence and witnesses,[44] as well as information about the social and cultural background of an area. Unfortunately, these intermediaries have not always been properly supervised, and the international criminal tribunals and courts have sometimes failed to maintain control over the direction of their investigations.[45] They are not employees of the judicial bodies, and therefore it has been argued that the judicial bodies have "inappropriately 'delegated' [their] investigative responsibilities to intermediaries, relying on them, in some cases, not only to contact but also to propose potential witnesses."[46] This charge has been leveled most strongly against the Office of the Prosecutor of the ICC.

[43] See John Jackson and Yassin M'Boge, "Integrating a Socio-Legal Approach to Evidence in International Criminal Tribunals," *Leiden Journal of International Law*, vol. 26, no. 4 (2013), pp. 933–945.

[44] DeVos, "Investigating from Afar: The ICC's Evidence Problem," p. 1012.

[45] Ibid.

[46] Ibid., p. 1022.

After the ICC's trial of the Congolese businessman Thomas Lubanga, who was convicted of war crimes in 2012, claims were made that intermediaries coached some of the witnesses presented by the Office of the Prosecutor. In Lubanga's appeal, his lawyers noted that "the Trial Chamber [had] concluded that there was a risk that [three intermediaries] may have persuaded, encouraged or assisted witnesses to give false testimony and thereby committed violations under Article 70."[47] The Office of the Prosecutor decided not to "pursue further investigations or prosecutions against any of the three named intermediaries"[48] because it claimed any action would "have no effect on the conviction rendered by the Trial Chamber against Mr. Lubanga."[49] The Office of the Prosecutor concluded that the Trial Chamber had not relied "on evidence given by witnesses who had been contacted by the three intermediaries" and thus any further action was unnecessary.[50]

We disagree with the Office of the Prosecutor's stance on the issue of corrupt intermediaries, as demonstrated in the Lubanga appeal. That the outcome of the case may not have been influenced by corruption does not indicate that there is not a reason to pursue investigation or prosecution of those accused of wrongdoing. The Office of the Prosecutor must be in the practice of ensuring that the trials not only reach the right result, but do so through fair procedures. This will, at times, require investigation or prosecution of those who have been accused of interfering with the judicial process.

The international criminal courts and tribunals must maintain control over investigations and should not be in position where a local actor can make decisions regarding the scope or direction of an investigation. Prosecutors must be able to develop and maintain good relationships with local actors because of their access, but they must do this through an on-the-ground presence. Intermediaries are a presence in domestic trials as well; investigators work with sources and community members when they are investigating a crime. A lack of awareness of cultural and social information may be greater in international criminal prosecutions than in domestic prosecutions. But this does not change the role an intermediary should play in an investigation; nor does it change the need for multiple intermediaries to ensure that the prosecution receives the widest range of possible information. When they are relied upon solely and too heavily, both domestic and international sources

47 *Prosecutor v. Lubanga*, Prosecution Response to "Requête de la Défense de M. Lubanga aux fins de communication d'éléments de preuve recueillis par le Procureur dans le cadre des enquêtes conduites en vertu de l'Article 70," ICC-01/04-01/06-3069, March 25, 2014, para. 6.

48 Ibid., para. 9.

49 Ibid., para. 18.

50 Ibid., para. 18.

can provide biased information. As noted previously, good investigations will require prosecutors to expend a sufficient amount of money, time, and personnel power in order to obtain the best information.

C *Duty to Investigate Incriminating and Exonerating Evidence*

The final criticism we will consider in this section on investigation is the prosecutor's duty to investigate incriminating and exonerating evidence. Critics have alleged that the Office of the Prosecutor of the ICC has not disclosed exculpatory evidence that it finds, or is aware of, to the defendant, in violation of the ICC statute as well as long-established principle of ethics governing criminal prosecutors.[51] Article 54(1)(a) of the Rome Statute requires that the Office of the Prosecutor disclose all exculpatory evidence that it obtains during the course of its investigation, but also that it actually "investigate incriminating and exonerating circumstances equally."[52] Thus the Rome Statute identifies the role of the prosecutor as "an independent and neutral truth-finder" rather than just as one of two opposing parties.[53] This is at least partly due to the fact that the Office of the Prosecutor has more access to resources, both financial and institutional, with which to carry out an investigation. The Office of the Prosecutor consistently claims that it has looked for potentially exonerating evidence.[54]

However, critics and defense teams alike have argued that the Office of the Prosecutor has generally failed to make sufficient attempts to uncover exonerating evidence.[55] Especially in situations when the resources are limited and the evidence is difficult to obtain, prosecutors have been more focused on obtaining incriminating evidence. In fact, in the Lubanga case the Office of the Prosecutor at the ICC relied on evidence gathered from related cases, which the Pre-Trial Chamber noted as evidence of "the reckless investigative techniques during the first two years of the investigation into DRC."[56]

Similar charges have been leveled against the Office of the Prosecutor at the ad hoc tribunals. Rule 68 of the Rules of Evidence requires disclosure of exculpatory material by the Office of the Prosecutor to the defense. Augustin Ndindiliyimana was one of many defendants to claim that the Office of the

[51] See Caroline Buisman, "The Prosecutor's Obligation to Investigate Incriminating and Exonerating Circumstances Equally: Illusion or Reality," *Leiden Journal of International Law*, vol. 27, no. 1 (2014), pp. 205–226.

[52] Rome Statute, art. 54(1)(a).

[53] Buisman, "The Prosecutor's Obligation to Investigate Incriminating and Exonerating Circumstances Equally," p. 205.

[54] Ibid., p. 211.

[55] Ibid.

[56] Prosecution Response to "Requête de la Défense de M. Lubanga," para. 195.

Prosecutor at the ICTR violated his right to a fair trial by failing to "review documents in its possession and give to the Defence all exculpatory material subject to disclosure pursuant to Rule 68 of the Rules."[57] This is framed as a disclosure obligation, but it largely amounts to a failure to investigate based on the quantity of evidence and lack of resources of the Office of the Prosecutor. The rule that the Office of the Prosecutor should disclose the bulk of potentially exonerating evidence prior to the trial may not be sufficient, in practice.

Article 54(1)(a) here places a duty on the Office of the Prosecutor that is not a duty under the Anglo-American common law system of jurisprudence. While the common law system requires a prosecutor to *disclose* exculpatory or exonerating evidence, it does not place a positive duty to *investigate* with the aim of discovering such evidence. This positive duty reflects the aforementioned attempt to integrate aspects of different domestic legal systems and create a level playing field within the ICC and the ad hoc tribunals. This hybrid role, we think, is both appropriate and necessary to safeguard the right to a fair trial for the defendant. But it does mean that the Office of the Prosecutor's hybrid role is one without a direct domestic counterpart.

However, the problem of balancing efficiency with fairness and justice is one that is seen in all courtrooms, both international and domestic. The Office of the Prosecutor must continue to work to investigate all evidence, as it is necessary for the specific goal of fulfilling the duty established by article 54(1)(a), and also for ensuring that the ICC is seen as a legitimate and fair institution.

In this section, we have considered some of the issues related to investigating alleged crimes and obtaining evidence. In Section IV, we will look at the actual introduction of evidence into the trial record.

IV WITNESSES

We now turn to the trial itself, and begin by looking at the numerous criticisms that have been raised regarding witness testimony. Especially in situations where the crimes were not well-documented, witness testimony is the most crucial aspect of obtaining evidence. But critics have argued that there are many reasons why this testimony lacks evidential weight or presents other problems for international criminal tribunals and courts. We will briefly

57 *Ndindiliyimana et al.*, Judgement, ICTR-00-56-A, 11 February 2014, Appeals Chamber, para. 15. Fyfe, as an intern for the Office of the Prosecutor on the Military II Trial, assisted in drafting responses to rule 68 requests on the part of Ndindiliyimana. She can attest to the huge number of the documents in possession of the Office of the Prosecutor and the paucity of resources of the OTP.

consider a number of these specific criticisms in order to show the breadth of these criticisms, but also the ways in which they might be straightforwardly handled.

A Written v. Live Testimony

As discussed in Section II, the adversarial nature of the international criminal courts and tribunals has meant that there is a general preference for live testimony by witnesses rather than written statements. Article 69(2) of the Rome Statute "provides for the testimony of witnesses to be given in person at the seat of the Court, which is imperative for the examination and cross examination of witnesses."[58] Especially at first, the ad hoc tribunals all expressed a preference for live testimony where possible.[59] Such testimony is preferable for several reasons. First, it allows for the accused person to face her accuser. Cross-examination can immediately follow the testimony in the same location. It is also much easier to assess the credibility of a witness who has testified in person, where the individual can be seen (or at least heard) and questioned. The judges can assess the attitude and demeanor of the witness if they are face to face.[60]

But there is a recognition that live witness testimony may not always be ideal. There may be situations in which the personal safety and security of the witness, or other costs to the tribunal or the witness, may outweigh the right of the accused to cross-examine the witness in person. The ICTY has adopted a system through the introduction of rules 92 *bis* and 92 *ter* to the Rules of Evidence, which allows for the admission of written witness statements in lieu of live witness testimony when the evidence in question goes to the "proof of a matter other than the acts and conduct of the accused as charged in the indictment," and when "other witnesses will give or have given oral testimony of similar facts."[61]

58 Sylvia Ntube Ngane, "Witnesses before the International Criminal Court" *The Law & Practice of International Courts and Tribunals, vol.* 8, no. 3 (2009), pp. 431–457, 433.

59 ECCC internal rule 26 provides that the testimony of a witness or expert during a judicial investigation or at trial shall be given in person, whenever possible. in *Kupreškić et al.* the ICTY appeals Chamber described as a "fundamental principle" that "witnesses shall as a general rule be heard directly by the Judges of the trial Chambers"; see also Mark Klamberg, *Evidence in International Criminal Trials: Confronting Legal Gaps and the Reconstruction of Disputed Events* (Leiden: Martinus Nijhoff Publishers, 2013), p. 365.

60 Ngane, "Witnesses before the international criminal court," p. 433, citing *Prosecutor v. Zejnil Delalic and others*, Decision on the Motion to Allow Witnesses K, L, and M to give their testimony by Means of Video-Link Conference, Case No. IT-96-21, T. Ch. II, 28 May 1997, para. 15; *Prosecutor v. Tadic*, Decision on the Defence Motions to Summon and Protect Defence Witnesses, and on the Giving of Evidence by Video-Link, Case No. IT-94-1-T, T. Ch. II, 25 June 1996, para. 19.

61 ICTY rule 92 *bis*.

We agree with the reasons international criminal courts and tribunals have held up to justify more permissive practices with respect to written witness testimony. The rights of the accused must be balanced against other considerations, and live witness testimony at any cost cannot be required. We would suggest that the ICC and tribunals adopt more explicit guidance to govern the use of written witness testimony, to ensure that the best available evidence is presented to the judges. There are also ways in which defense counsel can be permitted to question witnesses who do not want to testify in open court separately, which would protect the safety of a witness while allowing the accused the chance to cross-examine his accuser. The ICC and tribunals should also continue to develop better and more cost-effective witness protection mechanisms, which we will discuss in more detail later. As is the case in domestic courts, the safety of the witnesses must always be balanced with the desire to obtain as much evidence as possible and treat the defendant as fairly as possible.

B Language and Cultural Barriers

Critics have argued that language barriers, translation problems, and cultural differences have resulted in trial records that could not possibly purport to establish facts.[62] Most trials at the ICC and the tribunals proceed in several languages simultaneously, including at least one local language and at least one UN language (English, French, or both). If there is a judge sitting on the bench who is most comfortable in a different language, there may be yet another translator. This means every statement made by anyone in the room, be it witness, defendant, judge, or attorney, must be simultaneously translated into the other languages. Each person in the courtroom wears headphones in order to receive the translation. This results in an extremely slow trial process, due to the time delay between an original statement and its full translation into one or more languages. For instance, at the ICTR, each statement must be made available in French, Kinyarwanda, and English. However, there are almost no Kinyarwanda-to-English interpreters, so a statement made in Kinyarwanda must first be translated into French, and then translated from French to English, rather than directly from Kinyarwanda to English.[63]

As might be expected, this can result in in-person confusion or transcript discrepancies in accounts of the trial in different languages. In presenting evidence, one word might make a big difference in the meaning of a sentence,

62 See generally, Combs, *Fact-Finding without Facts*.
63 Combs, *Fact-Finding without Facts*, pp. 276–277.

and if it is not translated consistently, individuals who speak different languages may have very different understandings of a piece of evidence or even a court interaction. As Nancy Combs notes, the translation of Kinyarwanda to French is already prone to creating distortions, and these are multiplied when proceedings are translated again into English.[64] These misunderstandings can also occur where parties speak the same language but are from different cultures and have a different interpretation of the same incident involving a sensitive subject. And even when the official transcripts reflect an agreed-upon translation of proceedings, the time required to generate the official transcripts can delay the work of the defense and prosecution teams.

As with many of the other problems facing international criminal courts, some of these issues can be found in domestic courts, especially in multilingual or pluralist societies. Almost no one lives in a completely homogeneous community, and people will always be prone to understanding the same set of facts through their own eyes and with their own interpretation. But the magnitude of these issues is certainly much higher in international criminal courts and tribunals. The opportunities for mistakes or confusion are manifold. Trying to speed up translation is likely to increase these mistakes or confusions, while attempts to slow down to ensure consistency will result in even longer trials, compromising the fairness to the defendants.

These problems are serious. They lead to inefficiency, confusion, and, at times, even errors. As noted in the preceding discussion regarding investigation barriers, the international criminal courts and tribunals must invest in hiring experienced translators and cultural experts to help prevent translation mistakes and hiccups, as well as ongoing training and assessment. Any technological advancements that can aid the translators or the courts in achieving consistent records should be utilized. A defendant who can pay for the best criminal defense attorney in the world will still fail to receive a fair trial if the translators are ill-equipped to provide an accurate account of what has already happened. There is no way to rid international criminal courts and tribunals of cultural and language barriers, but with adequate training and resources, they should not be a barrier to the courts' and tribunals' justice objectives.

C Education and Time Passage Barriers

Also, there are very serious problems with corroboration of testimony in societies that do not have a precise sense of time. Even that a particular event took place on one day versus another can be a matter of cultural variation

64 Combs, *Fact-Finding without Facts*, pp. 277.

that could undermine the attempt to determine whether a corroborating witness is talking about the same event as the original testifying witness. Combs has done terrific work in documenting these problems, which call into question the assumptions that would normally hold about the veracity of testimonial evidence.[65] She claims that in Western countries, except in the case of children, "it is taken for granted that witnesses have the education and skills necessary to convey what they witnessed in a reasonably clear and coherent way."[66] Combs then argues that any expectation that an international witness will have some familiarity with courtroom procedure or of being questioned by a lawyer can constitute a serious obstacle for "the uneducated, the illiterate, and those lacking in certain life experiences."[67]

The problems in answering questions are manifold, and this is even when the witness is able to remember the event in question. In the following passage, Combs identifies some examples of issues that may result in unhelpful witness testimony before an international court or tribunal:

> A witness who has never learned to read or write probably will not know how to read a map. And many international witnesses not only lack the formal education by which they would learn how to measure or tell time, they also lack the kinds of life experiences for which that sort of knowledge would be useful. Witnesses who spend their lives engaged in subsistence farming need to keep track of the rainy and dry seasons but have far less need to know specific months and days. Witnesses who virtually never leave their villages have little reason to look at a map and have even less need to know that it is 6.5 miles to the nearest village. The witness may rarely go there anyway, and when he does, he knows it will take about an hour and a half to walk, and that is all the information he needs. And it should come as no surprise that a witness who has only rarely ever seen an automobile would be unable to describe the automobile that she witnessed by means of the specific terms that Westerners would use.[68]

Some of the problems Combs identifies are also found in domestic scenarios. Not all witnesses in Western societies are well educated. And the issues caused in witness testimony by the passage of time due to delays in trial or other circumstances are sometimes unavoidable. But the unique nature of the international courts and tribunals means that prosecutors and defense attorneys must continue to develop novel and innovative methods of reframing questions and recalling old memories. Some witnesses will require more

65 Ibid.
66 Ibid., p. 63.
67 Ibid., p. 64.
68 Ibid., p. 66.

preparation by the legal team than others. Some interrogation preparation may benefit from the assistance of country or cultural experts. This will, of course, be limited by resources, but in some cases these will be necessary to preserve the ability to obtain testimony from certain witnesses and will increase the efficiency of the witness testimony overall.

D Witness Lying or Tampering

One of the most serious problems is that the various international criminal tribunals and courts have not been able to change a culture that has allowed, even encouraged, the bribing of witnesses and other forms of witness tampering.[69] There are conceptual as well as normative worries about the status of the evidence, especially testimonial evidence, when the society where the alleged crimes occurred does not have a strong prohibition on lying or at least on not exaggerating.[70] The adversarial system is based on the idea that aggressive cross examination of witnesses is a realistic way to determine whether the witnesses are telling the truth. But in some non-Western societies the response to aggressiveness is to try to placate rather than to hold one's ground about the truth of one's story.

Witnesses may lie or otherwise distort the truth for many reasons. A witness may think that the lawyer asking questions is looking for a particular answer, and the witness may be inclined to try to provide that answer to appease the lawyer or to make the interview end sooner. A witness may have revised the narrative of certain events in her head over a long period of time, so that by the time she testifies she does not even know that she is lying. A witness may lie to protect a family member or his own reputation. But a major concern with lying in the international courts and tribunals is the presence of incentives. Combs identifies group-based loyalties and financial incentives as two of the most common incentives for international witnesses.[71]

A group-based loyalty may develop in a witness over time because of the nature of international crimes, since they almost always target people on the basis of their membership in a group.[72] So a witness who is initially cooperative and honest may become biased over time just because she is a member of "the group that was targeted while the defendant is a member

[69] See Robert Cryer, "Witness Tampering and International Criminal Tribunals," *Leiden Journal of International Law*, vol. 27, no. 1 (2014), pp. 191–203.

[70] See Combs, *Fact-Finding without Facts*.

[71] See generally, Combs, *Fact-Finding without Facts*, chapter 5.

[72] Ibid., p. 136.

of the offenders' group."[73] Identification with a group could also generate animosity toward the offenders group or result in fear for one's own life if one testifies honestly.[74]

Financial incentives provide another reason for a witness to lie before an international criminal court or tribunal. These institutions "provide witnesses stipends and services that enable the witnesses to travel to the tribunal and to maintain themselves and their families while the witnesses are away from home."[75] For an unemployed witness, the stipend money may be a windfall of sorts, as may be the other benefits that witnesses receive, and this may encourage the production of false or embellished testimony. Combs concedes, as do we, that the tribunals "must provide witnesses with sufficient financial support to enable them to travel to the tribunals and sustain themselves and their families while they are there."[76] But the tribunals should maintain some oversight with respect to the reimbursement and payment of witnesses. Perhaps an all-inclusive witness package would be more appropriate, where the witnesses' meals and boarding and health care are taken care of, but no money changes hands. Perhaps the amount of the stipend should be monitored closely to ensure that it is not excessive (or insufficient, for that matter). There are ways the tribunals can at least attempt to prevent the practice of providing witness testimony from becoming a business decision, but this problem does appear to be somewhat intractable.

E Witness Protection

The importance of obtaining evidence from certain witnesses must be weighed against the risk that the witness is taking in testifying before the international tribunal or court. The international criminal courts and tribunals provide for various types of witness protection, including nondisclosure of identity, protection from the public and the media, protection from confrontation with the accused, and anonymity, as well as special protections for victims of sexual violence.[77] The ICC and the ad hoc tribunals are structured differently with respect to witness protection. The Rome Statute contains detailed provisions for protecting witnesses and distributes responsibility for the various

[73] Ibid., p. 136.
[74] See generally, ibid., chapter 5.
[75] Ibid., p. 138.
[76] Ibid., p. 138.
[77] See generally Colin T. McLaughlin, "Victim and Witness Measures of the International Criminal Court: A Comparative Analysis," *The Law & Practice of International Courts and Tribunals*, vol. 6, no. 1 (2007), pp. 189–220.

obligations among different organs of the ICC.[78] The ICTR, ICTY, and SCSL are less well organized with respect to witness protection and rely more on the witnesses' home country to coordinate protection.

Domestic jurisdictions are often tasked with providing protection to witnesses. They may be protected via courtroom measures, or they may be provided with the protection of law enforcement on a temporary or ongoing basis, or they may be relocated. These issues are not unique to international criminal courts and tribunals. But when every crime involves atrocities, as is the case at the international criminal courts and tribunals, the danger a witness faces may be significantly more likely. It is unrealistic, although unfortunate, to think that witnesses can be protected at any cost. Not every witness and her entire family can be relocated to another country. This would be logistically and economically impossible. Therefore, the prosecution teams must work with witnesses and witness organization to assess the danger that may exist for any given witness and balance this with the probative (and perhaps personal) value of the testimony.

The problems raised by witness testimony in international criminal courts and tribunals should not be taken lightly. Some of the problems are similar to those faced by domestic courts, but most are at least of greater severity on the international criminal front. We have tried to identify some specific areas where the international criminal courts and tribunals need to be willing to invest adequate resources to maximize the effectiveness of witness testimony, but we recognize that some of these prioritizations will take time and others will be inconsistently implemented as a result of lack of resources, financial or otherwise. We therefore partially adopt something like the more modest view Combs explains in her book, in which she pushes for a flexible standard of reasonable doubt given the relatively poor access to solid evidence.[79] This is in line with the system already in place at the ICC, and with the general deference to judicial discretion at other international criminal tribunals. The international criminal courts and tribunals must, however, constantly assess the probative value of certain pieces of testimony against the requirements for a fair trial.

V OTHER EVIDENCE ISSUES

Finally, we will consider some of the issues related to the use of evidence by prosecutors and defense teams.

[78] Rome Statute, arts. 43, 54, 56, 57, 64, 68, 69.

[79] See Combs, *Fact-Finding without Facts*, chapter 10.

A "Reasonable Basis to Proceed" Standard

The first use of evidence obtained through investigation will be to determine whether or not there is a "reasonable basis to proceed" with the issuance of arrest warrants . Article 15 of the Rome Statute provides that if the Office of the Prosecutor seeks to open an investigation *proprio motu* on the basis of information received and "concludes that there is a reasonable basis to proceed with an investigation," then "he or she shall submit to the Pre-Trial Chamber a request for authorization of an investigation, together with any supporting material collected."[80] This lower standard can be distinguished from standards applied later in the criminal process, as in article 58(1)(a), which details the standard under which an arrest warrant may be issued. The prosecutor may only issue an arrest warrant after the initiation of an investigation if there are "reasonable grounds to believe that the person has committed a crime within the jurisdiction of the Court."[81] However, article 53 appears to construe the standard at the earlier stage of investigation initiation similarly, directing the Prosecutor to consider whether

> the information available to the Prosecutor provides a reasonable basis to believe that a crime within the jurisdiction of the Court has been or is being committed; (b) The case is or would be admissible under article 17; and (c) Taking into account the gravity of the crime and the interests of victims, there are nonetheless substantial reasons to believe that an investigation would not serve the interests of justice.[82]

And yet, because article 53 applies to the conflict generally, rather than the identification that a particular individual committed a crime, it does not serve to limit significantly what could constitute sufficient evidence to meet the "reasonable basis to proceed" standard.

The possible weakness of the article 15, article 53, and article 58 standard was already evident even after the ICC's very first *proprio motu* investigation. The Office of the Prosecutor obtained information regarding crimes against humanity committed in 2007 during postelection violence in Kenya. When it began to analyze the information, the Office of the Prosecutor determined, and the Pre-Trial Chamber concurred, that there was sufficient evidence to constitute a reasonable basis to proceed with an investigation.[83] However, the

80 Rome Statute, art. 15(3).
81 Rome Statute, art. 58(1)(a).
82 Rome Statute, art. 53(1)(a–c).
83 See Request for Authorization of an Investigation Pursuant to Art. 15, Situation in the Republic of Kenya (ICC-01/09-3), Office of the Prosecutor, 26 November 2009.

evidence did not contain any witness statements and was mostly NGO, UN, and media reports.[84] Four defendants were initially charged with participating in the postelection violence in Kenya, including Uhuru Kenyatta, who was elected as the president of Kenya while the charges were pending. All four of the trials were delayed, before the Office of the Prosecutor was eventually forced to withdraw charges against each of the defendants, including Kenyatta, as a result of recanted testimony and the lack of cooperation of other witnesses.

The ICC and the Kenyan government disagree about the Kenyan government's cooperation with the trials. But at least with respect to Kenyatta, there are questions as to whether there was enough evidence initially to pursue a criminal case. There were many new witnesses obtained and a large volume of new evidence was gathered by the Office of the Prosecutor after the charges were confirmed, and while the Office of the Prosecutor was permitted to continue investigation after the confirmation hearing, at least one judge was troubled by the volume of new information.[85] Judge Van den Wyngaert noted that "there are serious questions as to whether the Prosecution conducted a full and thorough investigation of the case against the accused prior to confirmation."[86]

It looks questionable as to whether the Office of Prosecutor met the article 15 and article 53 "reasonable basis to proceed" standard, given the reliance on secondhand accounts in the request for authorization of an investigation. It also looks questionable as to whether the Office of the Prosecutor met the article 58 "reasonable basis to believe" standard with respect to Kenyatta's arrest, given the breadth of information collected after the confirmation hearing. But the evidence was not overwhelming. And Kenyatta's role as sitting president of Kenya certainly calls into question the cooperation of the Kenyan government and provides an explanation as to why other witnesses may have refused to cooperate. That we have some evidence that the standards were applied with broad strokes does not mean that those standards are faulty. The Kenyan cases were complicated, and they were part of the Office of the Prosecutor's first *proprio motu* investigation. We agree that the Kenyatta case was a failure. But we should not dismiss the Office of the Prosecutor's option to initiate investigations and the standards governing the practice, without more empirical data suggesting that it has been abused or cannot work.

84 Ibid.

85 *Prosecutor v. Uhuru Muigai Kenyatta*, Case No. ICC-01/09-02/11–728, Decision on Defense Application Pursuant to Article 64(4) and Related Requests (April 26, 2013), www.icccpi.int/iccdocs/doc/ doc1585619.pdf.

86 Ibid. Anx 2, para. 1 (Van den Wyngaert, J., concurring).

B Obtaining Evidence from States

Another issue related to the use of evidence is the problem of obtaining crucial evidence from states that claim, truthfully or not, that they cannot give evidence to a court or tribunal because of a claimed state need for secrecy. International courts have long struggled to obtain classified documents from states and have been forced to rely instead on circumstantial evidence. This is not ideal, and it is one reason why the Rome Statute and the governing documents of other international courts and tribunals attempt to impose obligations on states to cooperate with requests to supply evidence.

An early instance of this problem appeared during the Blaskic case at the ICTY. A judge in the case issued a *subpoena duces tecum* to the Republic of Croatia and the Federation of Bosnia-Herzegovina, as well as other high-ranking officials.[87] Croatia challenged the requests to provide evidence and argued that "the ICTY had no authority to issue coercive orders to states and high government officials and that, even if the ICTY had such powers, a state still had the right to limit its compliance in order to protect its national security interests."[88] Ultimately, the ICTY Appeals Chamber ruled that it did not, in fact, have the authority to issue subpoenas to states.[89] Because the ICTY did not have enforcement powers, as is the case with all international criminal courts and tribunals, it could not force states to cooperate.

Governments are difficult to convince that they should fulfill their obligations to produce evidence no matter the venue, be it domestic courts or hearings or commissions. However, the problem of state cooperation in international criminal courts and tribunals is not limited to the production of evidence, and it is a reason to continue to develop international respect for the international criminal courts and tribunals. States will likely continue to balk at the production of evidence when it is their own citizens in the dock. But if states see themselves as part of a community, with reciprocal obligations to

87 Subpoena Duces Tecum to the Republic of Croatia, *Prosecutor v. Blaskic*,, IT-95-14-T, Judge McDonald (ICTY 15 Jan. 1997) (Registry Page no. (RP) D488–93); see also Jacob Katz Cogan, "The Problem of Obtaining Evidence for International Criminal Courts," *Human Rights Quarterly*, vol. 22, no. 2 (2000), pp. 404–427, 409.

88 Cogan, "The problem of obtaining evidence for international criminal courts," p. 409, citing Brief of the Republic of Croatia on Subpoenae Duces Tecum, *Prosecutor v. Blaskic*, T. Ch. II, Case No. IT-95-14-PT, 1 (ICTY 1 Apr. 1997) (RP D3682-84); Republic of Croatia, Reply to Subpoena Duces Tecum, *Prosecutor v. Blaskic*.

89 Judgement on the Request of the Republic of Croatia for Review of the Decision of Trial Chamber II of 18 July 1997, *Prosecutor v. Blaskic*, Case IT-95-14-AR108bis, App. Ch., 25–26 (ICTY 29 Oct. 1997), available at www.un.org/icty/blaskic/appeal/ decision-e/71029JT3.html.

other members of the community, they will be more likely to provide material assistance to criminal trials.

C Creating a Historical Narrative

The question of the purpose of international criminal tribunals and courts arises when we consider the analogous purpose of the domestic trial and consider the value of creating a historical narrative of the events surrounding atrocities. Some international courts and tribunals exist alongside alternative justice mechanisms, such as the ICTR (which is housed in Tanzania) and the *gacaca* courts (which are in local communities in Rwanda). But regardless of other justice mechanisms, one purpose of the transcripts of international criminal courts and tribunals can be to create a particular historical narrative.

International criminal courts and tribunals can play an important role in reconciliation generally, and specifically with generating a narrative of the events surrounding atrocities. The introduction of massive amounts of evidence into an official record will provide future generations with the ability to learn through the words of those who actually experienced the atrocities. Witness testimony of those who survived the Rwanda genocide contributes not only to the conviction of those who committed atrocities, but also to the creation of a shared history for the country and its people. As Leo Nwoye notes, "The judicial records and ICTR archives are perhaps the best historical narrative of the genocide and should serve as an authentic public historical record against revisionism."[90]

This desire can exist on either side of the courtroom. During Augustin Ndindiliyimana's defense in 2008, his attorneys persisted in challenging the scope of the ICTR's prosecutions and the very existence of a genocide. Each day, Christopher Black took issue with the characterization of the violence in Rwanda in 1994 as a genocide, insisting on the record that the events should instead be characterized as a civil war.[91] The rhetorical purpose was clear. Black was well aware that the ICTR was not going to recharacterize the conflict. But he is on the record denouncing the ICTR for failing to prosecute members of the Rwandan Patriotic Front (RPF) for the atrocities they are said to have committed in 1994 as well.

We think that courts should recognize the aim of narrative-creation through the trial process, but the courts and judges should not be in a position of

[90] Leo C. Nwoye, "Partners or Rivals in Reconciliation: The ICTR and Rwanda's Gacaca Courts," *San Diego International Law Journal*, vol. 16 (2014), p. 177.

[91] Fyfe appeared in the ICTR Chamber for the Military II Trial May–August 2008, as an intern for the Office of the Prosecutor.

trying to control the direction of the narrative. Because of the various (and sometimes competing) narratives, as well as the other punishment-based goals of international criminal courts and tribunals, handling the overall historical narrative is tricky. There is only so much control that courts can have over what goes into the record, and all sides of the story should be allowed to participate in the construction of the narrative, whether or not it approximates the objective truth.

D *Scope of Evidence*

Moving toward the end of a trial, we consider the problem of having too much evidence and how judges deal with the overwhelming nature of the information presented at trial. In collecting evidence, both the prosecution and defense teams tend to err on the side of gathering and presenting too much evidence rather than not enough, given that they cannot know what the judges will find probative or even admissible.[92] This results in an unwieldy amount of evidence for the trial teams to present efficiently and for judges to sift through in trying to reach a determination as to the guilt or innocence of a defendant. The problem becomes even more serious during joint trials, which were constructed in order to increase efficiency, but may well have decreased trial efficiency (and corresponding fairness to the individual defendants).

These problems have been faced by domestic courts also. International criminal courts and tribunals should take note of the relative value of the joint trials before considering whether they should continue. While we think neither side should be limited in terms of evidence collection or presentation, in service of trial efficiency and accurate fact-finding, we would encourage trial teams to expend resources at the beginning to assess the value of evidence. There must be adequate resources and personnel available to handle case management, or the process will not be worthwhile. Judges should be specific in their requests for evidence organization from both the defense and the prosecution. Reducing the number of documents a clerk or judge has to sift through will help every individual who plays a role in the trial process.

We recognize that the problems the ICC and other international tribunals face with respect to evidence collection, presentation, and utilization are numerous. We have argued, however, that many of these issues can be addressed or moderated through the establishment of consistent policies and

[92] Albin Eser, "The 'Adversarial' Procedure: A Model Superior to Other Trial Systems in International Criminal Justice?" in T. Kruessmann (ed.), *ICTY: Towards a Fair Trial?* (Wien: Intersentia, 2008), pp. 207, 212–213, 215.

procedures, and with commitment of adequate financial and institutional resources. As we have already discussed, the international criminal courts and tribunals have already proved to be expensive endeavors, but they simply cannot conduct the complicated criminal trials they were created to conduct without these resources. Because many of these concerns can be addressed with the (albeit demanding) outlay of time and financial resources, evidence problems do not constitute a normative challenge to international criminal courts and tribunals.

8

Fairness

We conclude with one of the strongest criticisms of international criminal courts and tribunals, and one that encompasses aspects of each of the previous seven chapters: fairness. While there are some aspects of this chapter that address unique problems of fairness in international criminal cases, many of the issues we discuss relate to normative concerns we have already addressed. We see fairness as a concept that runs throughout most of the criticism of the international criminal courts and tribunals, whether with respect to due process accorded to individuals or the standing of certain states in the global community. The main site of these fairness concerns, with respect to both individuals and states, lies in the discretion afforded to prosecutors.

The criticism is most obviously manifested in the claim that a vastly disproportionate number of cases have concerned Africa, and that prosecutors have not pursued equally serious cases in Europe and other parts of the world. Until very recently, the Offices of the Prosecutor were staffed primarily with international law experts from Europe and North America. And it appears that they regarded cases from Africa as politically safer to pursue than cases that occurred in Europe or that implicated European and North American states. Because of this disparity it is also claimed that there has sometimes been prosecutorial overreach and at other times prosecutorial misconduct.

Fairness in international case selection is a difficult issue when there are so many potential cases to take up and relatively few resources available to support international prosecutions. But when the caseload of the ICC during its first decade is skewed so dramatically toward one part of the world, questions will inevitably arise. Even as the criticism grows louder, the ICC Office of the Prosecutor seems unlikely to focus attention anywhere other than Africa. In several instances, the way these cases have been pursued raises fairness issues as well.[1]

In this chapter, we wrap up our defense of international criminal courts and tribunals with a focus on the major criticisms that have been leveled against the fairness of prosecution at international criminal courts and tribunals. In Section I, we give a normative account of fairness and the rule of law as it applies to prosecutors in general. We then consider three primary locations for possible unfairness in international criminal tribunals. Section II looks at a tribunal's mandate and the composition of a prosecutor's office. In Section III, we consider prosecutorial discretion in choosing whom to prosecute from within a tribunal's mandate. In this section, we consider the specific charge that too many Africans are the subjects of prosecutions and that this is evidence of prosecutorial overreach. Section IV looks at another aspect of prosecutorial discretion that can result in claims of unfairness: discretion in determining what actions to prosecute a particular defendant for or what charges to bring against a defendant. Finally, we look at these criticisms as a whole and argue that nearly every charge of unfairness can be met with the response that the problem is no different from those found in domestic criminal law or with suggestions for reform.

I RULE OF LAW

In Chapter 1, we argued for the legitimacy of the exercise of international criminal jurisdiction, whereas more commonly criminal jurisdiction is exercised by domestic governments. In this section, we will connect the legitimacy of international criminal courts and tribunals and concerns about the rule of law to the specific mandate of an international criminal prosecutor.

The rule of law is the principle that law should govern a state, an institution, or individuals, as opposed to the arbitrary decisions of officials of that state or institution. In the *Politics*, Aristotle argued that the rule of law was better than the rule of an individual.[2] Under a rule of law framework, everyone is accountable to the same laws, which must be publicly promulgated, equally enforced, and consistently adjudicated by an independent body. Application of the rule of law principle involves constraining the behavior of the government itself, as well as its individual citizens, and thus the principle developed out of a desire for rulers to be equally accountable under the law. In the United States,

[1] See Ademola Abass, "Prosecuting International Crimes in Africa: Rationale, Prospects, and Challenges," *European Journal of International Law*, vol. 24, no. 3 (August 2013), pp. 933–946.

[2] Aristotle, *Politics*: "He who bids the law rule may be deemed to bid God and Reason alone rule, but he who bids man rule adds an element of the beast; for passion perverts," 1287a28.

for instance, respect for the rule of law can be seen in the priority given to the Constitution as a governing document over the rulings or desires of any individual government official. Each of the three branches of the U.S. government serves to place checks on the other branches and ensure that rule of law governs each, rather than allowing one branch to overpower the other branches and make arbitrary or biased decisions.

The rule of law can be understood either procedurally or substantively. We draw on a much more complete account given elsewhere, and we focus on the procedural aspects of international rule of law.[3] The rule of law guarantees that similar cases and situations will be treated in a similarly fair manner. When we look at the rule of law as a global principle, we can see that the possibility for unfairness is greater than in the domestic sphere because there are fewer checks among and between the institutions. We will further flesh out the meaning of the procedural rule of law as it relates to international criminal law shortly.

Some scholars are skeptical of the moral status of seeking a global rule of law.[4] Goldsmith and Posner advocate a purely instrumental view of international law, in which states should only support international legal institutions when doing so will promote national interests or the interests of nationals.[5] They assume that a state will act rationally to maximize its own interests, and any claims about the influences of international law and institutions on individual or state interests are implausible.[6] On this instrumental view, the rule of law serves to bind those who wish to be bound by international law, and who express preferences that involve being bound by international law, but there is no independent value to the existence of international law.

But if laws can be subject to veto by those on whom they are supposed to exert force, then there is little evidence that the rule of law exists. Contrary to Goldsmith and Posner, we see strong moral reasons to promote and support the rule of law at the international level. Historically, the existence of customary international law, international treaties, and *jus cogens* norms suggests that there is at least a loose global understanding of moral obligations between

3 Larry May, *Crimes against Humanity: A Normative Account* (Cambridge: Cambridge University Press, 2005), chapter 11; see also Lon Fuller, *The Morality of Law* (New Haven, CT: Yale University Press, 1964, 1967), chapter 2, and Cass R. Sunstein, *Legal Reasoning and Political Conflict* (Oxford: Oxford University Press, 1996), chapter 4.

4 See, e.g., Jack Goldsmith and Eric Posner, *The Limits of International Law* (Oxford: Oxford University Press, 2005).

5 Ibid.; see also Allen Buchanan, "The Legitimacy of International Law," in Samantha Besson, and John Tasioulas (eds.), *The Philosophy of International Law* (Oxford: Oxford University Press, 2010), p. 88.

6 Goldsmith and Posner, *Limits of International Law*, pp. 8–9.

and among sovereign states. Surely some of these norms, agreements, and understandings exist largely for the purpose of serving the interests of the individual states. But it is less clear that this is the only motivation for international cooperation. In fact, the relative strength of states appears to guarantee that self-interest is not the only reason for international cooperation. If strong states can get what they want through the use of force, they might be less inclined to agree to be bound by the same rules as weaker states.

Allen Buchanan argues that the principles constituting the international rule of law should include at least the following:

> The law should be general (and when there are departures from generality they should be controlled by processes that are informed by general principles); the law should be understandable and publicly proclaimed; there is a presumption against retroactive law, especially retroactive criminal law; and the administration of the law should be impartial. In a wider sense, the commitment to the rule of law is the commitment to resolving or managing conflicts by effectively institutionalizing the impartial application of publicly known general rules that are based on the assumption that there is to be an accommodation of interests.[7]

This noninstrumental view thus recognizes a moral component to the rule of law: that it is necessary not only to ensure cooperation and peace among states, but that there is also a role for justice, "where justice is understood, first and foremost, though not exclusively, as the realization of human rights."[8] Justice first requires a recognition of human rights, and in the face of atrocity, this means that the rights of both the victims and the accused warrant the exercise of legitimate criminal jurisdiction.

Therefore, we argue that supporting an international rule of law is prior to supporting an international criminal legal regime. The principles of fairness guaranteed by a commitment to the rule of law are necessary to justify criminal jurisdiction and to protect criminal defendants. International criminal jurisdiction cannot be exercised on the basis of the rule of a powerful state and its desire for prosecutions based on victors' justice. Rather, there must be procedural restraints in place to reduce possibilities for bias and arbitrariness in the application of international criminal law. Accordingly, "international tribunals should, among other things, only apply laws prospectively, only apply laws in a way that is evenhanded concerning all who committed the offenses, and only mete out punishments that are clearly deserved."[9]

7 Buchanan, "Legitimacy of International Law," p. 89.
8 Ibid.
9 May, *Crimes against Humanity*, p. 201.

Substantive international criminal law, as it exists today, is relatively consistent across a variety of institutions. Certain kinds of crimes, namely, those that constitute crimes of genocide, crimes against humanity, and war crimes, are recognized by international institutions (if not states and individuals as well) as those deserving of prosecution under international law. The substance of international criminal law will continue to develop, perhaps to incorporate crimes of aggression or certain transnational crimes, but that is not the focus of this chapter on fairness. Rather, we will assume the reasonableness of the substantive criminal laws and focus on the procedural aspects that affect the rule of law, as we see procedural justice as a "gap-filling and norm-strengthening basis for the establishment of a robust system of international law."[10]

We believe that one can capture the idea of an international rule of law.[11] It requires a coherent system of rules, which must be fairly administered and fairly interpreted.[12] It is generally agreed that the rules should (1) be general, not specific; (2) be prospective, not retrospective; (3) be public, not secret; (4) be knowable, not obscure; and (5) require behavior that is performable, not impossible to perform.[13] These seem to be obvious restraints on a system of laws that is intended to ensure fair application and the possibility of individuals knowingly following the laws. In order for the laws to be part of a system, we would add three more requirements: that rules should (6) be consistent with each other, not conflicting; (7) cohere, not be unconnected to each other; and (8) not be arbitrarily changed. Again, without these restraints, it would be challenging for individuals to understand and obey laws. In addition, the administration of the laws should (9) not be selectively enforced; (10) be reflected in what the administrators are doing; and (11) ensure that penalties or punishments are proportionate to the offense. Laws could not be enforced fairly if these restraints did not limit the enforcement. Finally, there are restraints on the interpretation of law, which are the most controversial, and yet they are expressable as desiderata, namely, that (12) disputes about the interpretation of rules must be resolved by public hearings; (13) disputes about interpretation must be resolved by the acts of independent judges; and (14) disputes about interpretation must be subject to appellate review. This last set of restraints will be the least important for purposes of the rest of this chapter, so we will not further defend their necessity.

[10] Larry May, *Global Justice and Due Process* (Cambridge: Cambridge University Press, 2010), p. 11.

[11] See May, *Crimes against Humanity*, chapter 11.

[12] Ibid., p. 203.

[13] Ibid.

The first eleven restraints, however, will prove very important for justifying the fairness of the international criminal courts and tribunals. As noted previously, the possibilities for improper application of the law via strong-arm tactics are more numerous in international law. There must be good reasons to justify international criminal prosecutions in lieu of leaving all criminal prosecution in the hands of domestic courts and tribunals. It is not sufficient to argue for international criminal jurisdiction on the basis of the severity and scope of the crimes. The authority to prosecute and punish, lodged in the prosecutor and the legal institutions, must be grounded in procedural fairness. When international institutions are seen as impartial and effective, states recognize their capacity to resolve disputes and acquiesce to their jurisdiction.

The obligation to ensure the rule of law and procedural fairness falls on the prosecutor at any international criminal court or tribunal. Because they are tasked with conducting investigations and selecting cases and charges, international prosecutors are "the driving force of all international criminal tribunals."[14] This involves considerable discretion at every stage. The intent to grant prosecutorial independence was included in article 42 of the Rome Statute, which provides that the Office of the Prosecutor shall act independently as a separate organ of the court.

> It shall be responsible for receiving referrals and any substantiated information on crimes within the jurisdiction of the Court, for examining them and for conducting investigations and prosecutions before the Court. A member of the Office shall not seek or act on instructions from any external source.[15]

The drafters of the Rome Statute believed that the ICC would not be able to accomplish its goals without an impartial prosecutor, free to "pursue cases impartially, based above all on legal merit."[16] There are limited political and judicial oversight mechanisms in place to ensure that the prosecutorial discretion is not abused, but ICC prosecutors are not held accountable in the same way a domestic prosecutor might be subject to certain external mechanisms.[17]

14 Luc Côté, "Independence and Impartiality," in L. Reydams et al. (eds.), *International Prosecutors* (Oxford: Oxford University Press, 2012), pp. 319, 321; see also Jenia Iontcheva Turner, "Accountability of International Prosecutors," in Carsen Stahn (ed.), *The Law and Practice of the International Criminal Court* (Oxford: Oxford University Press, 2015), pp. 384–385.

15 Rome Statute, art. 42.

16 Côté, "Independence and Impartiality," p. 322.

17 See Frederic Mégret, "Accountability and Ethics" in L. Reydams et al. (eds.), *International Prosecutors*, p. 418; see also R. Wright and M. Miller, "The Worldwide Accountability Deficit for Prosecutors," *Washington and Lee Law Review* 67 (2010), pp. 1587, 1600–1609.

As we will explore throughout the rest of this chapter, the statutes and rules governing the international criminal institutions must (and do) contain certain provisions to protect the rights of the accused and the impartial application of the law. But how these rules are followed or implemented is nearly always at the discretion of the prosecutor. We will now turn to the prosecutor's mandate as a main source of fairness or unfairness.

II THE PROSECUTOR AND THE SCOPE OF HER MANDATE

The first place we may find unfairness in international criminal tribunals is in the office of a prosecutor. First, let us consider how to deal with the possibility of unfairness due to the scope of a prosecutor's mandate.

A Victors' Justice?

The ICC can establish jurisdiction over a situation in one of three ways: (1) referral by a state party, (2) referral by the Security Council using its chapter VII powers,[18] or (3) a *proprio motu* investigation by the Prosecutor.[19] Where a matter has been referred, prosecutorial discretion to investigate and prosecute is regulated by article 53 of the Rome Statute. Article 53 provides that the Prosecutor shall consider (1) whether he has sufficient factual evidence to support a reasonable basis for investigation or sufficient basis for an arrest warrant or summons,[20] (2) whether a matter is admissible in terms of article 17,[21] or (3) whether it is in the interests of justice to proceed.[22] But for now, let us focus on the initial establishment of jurisdiction.

A case only comes before the ICC when it has been referred by a state party or the Security Council, or the Office of the Prosecutor decides to investigate on its own initiative. The third option is an important safeguard that would allow the Offices of the Prosecutor to investigate accusations of international crimes made by a nonstate party with little political power. Such a complaint may be ignored by state parties or the Security Council (especially if the accused are citizens or leaders of a member state of the Security Council), but the ICC would still be in a position to investigate and establish jurisdiction. Therefore, it seems that the ICC's establishment of jurisdiction over a

18 See UN Charter, chapter VII.
19 Rome Statute, art. 13(c).
20 Ibid., arts. 53(1)(a), (2)(a).
21 Ibid., arts. 53(1)(b), (2)(b).
22 Ibid., arts. 53(1)(c), (2)(c).

particular situation, at least initially, is an unlikely candidate for a criticism of unfairness.

However, the jurisdictions of the ad hoc tribunals are more limited in scope and more susceptible to criticisms of unfairness. First, ad hoc tribunals are generally established through the authority of the Security Council. This means that in situations when a member of the Security Council is involved or has even indirect interests, the Security Council may fail to approve the creation of an ad hoc tribunal or may influence the scope of the mandate, preventing equal access of victims to justice.

Further, when an ad hoc tribunal is created, it is usually with the recognition, formal or otherwise, that there have been international crimes committed. This means that ad hoc tribunals are generally established with the understanding that certain entities or groups of individuals have broken international criminal laws (or norms). However, this model is not conducive to adjudicating situations that resemble civil wars between two factions of one nation. Rather this model is likely to determine one group to be the aggressor and (at least) one group to be the victim. While the scope of an ad hoc tribunal's mandate is generally broad, not explicitly limited to prosecuting crimes committed by only one side of a conflict, the result is often exactly that.

For example, the ICTR's jurisdiction is limited to acts of genocide and crimes against humanity, as defined in the ICTR Statute, and violations of article 3 common to the Geneva Conventions and of Additional Protocol II committed in Rwanda, or by Rwandan nationals in neighboring states, between January 1, 1994, and December 31, 1994.[23] This tribunal was established pursuant to a Security Council resolution,[24] and it may seem very broad on its face. It does not limit the jurisdiction over persons on the basis of their ethnic identity, although it does not establish jurisdiction over any crimes committed outside Rwanda by non-Rwandan nationals. In terms of the ICTR Statute, any person who has been accused of committing an international crime within these broad time and geographic boundaries should be subject to prosecution by the ICTR. Thus, there should be no formal concern with the fairness of the scope of ad hoc tribunal jurisdiction.

And yet, we know that only certain individuals have been tried before the ad hoc tribunals. In 2006, the Appeals Chamber of the ICTR took judicial

[23] UN Security Council, *Statute of the International Criminal Tribunal for Rwanda (as last amended on 13 October 2006)*, 8 November 1994.

[24] S.C. Res. 955, U.N. Doc. S/RES/955 (Nov. 8, 1994).

notice of the fact that a genocide had occurred in Rwanda during the time and geographic boundaries identified by the ICTR Statute, perpetrated against the Tutsis.[25] Earlier trial cases had already resulted in the same finding, and this finding may help explain the attitude of the Offices of the Prosecutor and the institution itself that only individuals on one side of the conflict in Rwanda should be brought to trial before the ICTR. Judicial notice of the fact that a genocide occurred in Rwanda does not preclude the commission of war crimes or crimes against humanity by Tutsi individuals, but despite evidence of the commission of these crimes, not a single Tutsi has been tried before the ICTR.

This issue is better suited for discussion in Section III on prosecutorial discretion, but it is important to refer to it now in the context of jurisdiction because clearly there are other factors at play in the determination of who should be prosecuted by an ad hoc tribunal. There is very little evidence that the scope of such tribunals has been unfairly limited, in technical terms, but claims about unfairness in the practical application of the jurisdiction may carry some weight.

B Composition of Prosecutor's Office

Another claim that has been made about unfairness in the foundation of the international criminal legal process is that the composition of a prosecutor's office makes the court more prone to bias. We will discuss this bias in more detail when we move on to prosecutorial discretion, but in the broadest terms, it has been argued that the identity of the prosecutor may have some impact on what situations or individuals are subject to prosecution, and the treatment of those individuals by the court.

The prosecutors at Nuremberg were appointed by the states that were the four original signatories of the London Agreement, although the case was largely directed by the American prosecution team.[26] This was unlikely to have been set up in any other way, as it was the first modern tribunal of its kind, but it is certainly subject to claims of at least the appearance of victors' justice.

Since its inception, the ICC Prosecutor was Argentinean and male, and his staff was largely Western, despite the fact that nearly all of the cases pending before the ICC were against African leaders. This has resulted in criticism

[25] See *Prosecutor v. Karemera*, Case No. ICTR 98-44-AR73(C), Decision on Prosecutor's Interlocutory Appeal of Decision on Judicial Notice, ¶¶ 33–38 (June 16, 2006).

[26] Robert Conot, *Justice at Nuremberg* (New York: Carroll & Graf, 1983), p. 59.

from, among others, the African Union, that the composition of the ICC Office of the Prosecutor is resulting in unfair prioritizing of prosecutions in Africa. If the composition of the ICC Office of the Prosecutor is not diverse and does not include very many Africans, this at least gives the appearance of unfairness. However, the new Chief Prosecutor at the ICC is both female and African; therefore, going forward any criticisms of unfairness should be focused on prosecutorial discretion rather than bias based on the identity of the Prosecutor.

The ad hoc tribunals have had a somewhat diverse lineup of lead prosecutors, which are appointed by the Security Council. The current ICTY Prosecutor is Belgian and male, but past prosecutors have included both men and women from Venezuela, South Africa, Canada, Sweden, and Switzerland.[27] The representation here, while somewhat geographically diverse, has admittedly been mostly Western and not racially diverse. The current ICTR Prosecutor is a Gambian male, and the previous ICTR Prosecutor was a Swiss female. The Special Court for Sierra Leone's lead prosecutors were all from the United States, but the post of deputy prosecutor, who was appointed by the Government of Sierra Leone, was filled by a more diverse group of individuals.[28] Two Canadian men have led the Office of the Prosecutor at the Special Tribunal for Lebanon.[29] So it seems that there is more work to be done in ensuring that the Offices of the Prosecutor are led by more diverse individuals in terms of geography, race, and gender. In particular, there should be more African and Asian leadership in the Offices of the Prosecutor. These appointments are made at the discretion of the Security Council, which should make it a priority to increase diversity in the future.

III PROSECUTORIAL DISCRETION IN CHOOSING WHOM TO PROSECUTE

The loudest claims of unfairness at international criminal tribunals are related to decisions made by prosecutors about whom to prosecute from within their mandate. We will begin by looking at this problem generally before turning to the specific criticisms regarding prosecutorial discretion and misconduct in Africa.

27 See ICTY Web site, www.icty.org.
28 See RSCSL Web site, www.rscsl.org.
29 See STL Web site, www.stl-tsl.org.

A Prosecutorial Discretion

The preamble of the Rome Statute states that "the most serious crimes of concern to the international community as a whole must not go unpunished and … their effective prosecution must be ensured by taking measures at the national level and by enhancing international cooperation."[30] It goes on to indicate that the ICC was established "for the sake of present and future generations,"[31] to facilitate jurisdiction over "the most serious crimes of concern to the international community as a whole."[32] Alone, the preamble of the Rome Statute reads as an unwavering commitment to prosecute the most serious international crimes.

But the preamble of the Rome Statute does not conclusively determine which crimes should be prosecuted under international criminal law. As Cécile Aptel argues:

> International criminal prosecutions, concerning only the gravest crimes, are inherently selective. They are based on a sordid paradox: the worse the crimes (genocide, crimes against humanity, war crimes) and higher the number of victims and perpetrators, the more selective international prosecutors must be in choosing the crime scenes and the suspects to investigate and prosecute.[33]

This means that prosecutors must "determine which allegations and suspects to investigate, on the basis of cases' hypothesis, and in the process disregard other serious allegations and suspects against whom there may be credible evidence."[34]

As noted previously, article 53 of the Rome Statute provides the ICC Prosecutor with the discretion to consider (1) whether he has sufficient factual evidence to support a reasonable basis for investigation or sufficient basis for an arrest warrant or summons,[35] (2) whether a matter is admissible in terms of article 17,[36] or (3) whether it is in the interests of justice to proceed.[37] So there are three openings for the ICC Prosecutor to utilize discretion in determining whom to prosecute, and we will consider them in turn.

30 Rome Statute, preamble.
31 Ibid.
32 Ibid.
33 Cécile Aptel. "Prosecutorial Discretion at the ICC and Victims' Right to Remedy Narrowing the Impunity Gap," *Journal of International Criminal Justice* 10, no. 5 (2012): p. 1360.
34 Ibid.
35 Rome Statute, arts. 53(1)(a), (2)(a).
36 Ibid., arts. 53(1)(b), (2)(b).
37 Ibid., arts. 53(1)(c), (2)(c).

The first basis for discretion, lack of evidence, is challenging for the ICC Prosecutor in that he or she must decide when an open investigation should be closed due to lack of information. It is sometimes unclear whether any more evidence will be forthcoming and hence whether a prosecution should even proceed. Further, even in cases when it is clear that there is not enough evidence for a prosecution, the ICC Prosecutor is in the difficult position of foreclosing one possibility for justice for victims, and this may prevent the prosecutor from exercising this discretion when appropriate. We will look more closely at an example of possible prosecutorial misconduct related to lack of evidence in the Section III.B on African prosecutions.

The second basis for prosecutorial discretion is admissibility. Article 17 of the Rome Statute states that a case is inadmissible where

> (a) The case is being investigated or prosecuted by a State which has jurisdiction over it, unless the State is unwilling or unable genuinely to carry out the investigation or prosecution; 13 Rome Statute of the International Criminal Court (b) The case has been investigated by a State which has jurisdiction over it and the State has decided not to prosecute the person concerned, unless the decision resulted from the unwillingness or inability of the State genuinely to prosecute; (c) The person concerned has already been tried for conduct which is the subject of the complaint, and a trial by the Court is not permitted under article 20, paragraph 3; (d) The case is not of sufficient gravity to justify further action by the Court.[38]

Determining the status of a national investigation (or unwillingness to prosecute) is not without ambiguity. The ICC Prosecutor must consider whether any existing domestic proceedings are legitimate or "for the purpose of shielding the person concerned from criminal responsibility for crimes,"[39] as well as the fairness, efficiency, and resources of the domestic proceedings.[40] The limitations set by article 17 are meant to allow for domestic criminal proceedings to take priority over those permitted by the universal jurisdiction of the ICC, but without denying defendants and victims adequate opportunities for justice.

The third and final basis for prosecutorial discretion is broad and allows the ICC Prosecutor to avoid prosecuting when it would be contrary to the interests of justice. In general, this means that the ICC Prosecutor may favor peace and security of a region over strict fairness in prosecuting all crimes that fall under her jurisdiction. Or it may mean that the ICC will not prosecute

38 Ibid., arts. 17(1)(a)–(d).

39 Ibid., art. 17(2)(a).

40 Ibid., arts. 17(2)(b)–(c).

in favor of allowing for local peace processes to go forward (in lieu of official domestic proceedings). The broad language in this part of the Rome Statute leaves the most room for the ICC Prosecutor to decide against prosecuting an individual in light of surrounding circumstances.

Unfortunately, these three bases for prosecutorial discretion also open the door for overreach, misconduct, and injustice. The third basis for prosecutorial discretion is the hardest to reconcile with the preamble of the Rome Statute, which concludes by resolving to "guarantee lasting respect for and the enforcement of international justice."[41] What is the ICC Prosecutor to do in a situation when a nation has developed a truth and reconciliation process to move on after a national crisis with many victims, and all of the accused criminals are guaranteed amnesty in exchange for their participation? Should the ICC Prosecutor step aside on the basis of article 17? On the basis of the interests of justice?

In order to answer these questions and interpret article 53 and article 17 of the Rome Statute properly, we need a better understanding of what constitute appropriate considerations of justice. Errol Mendes argues that the proper balance to be struck between peace and justice involves the mandate of the prosecutor under the Rome Statute and its preamble.[42] Following the determinations of jurisdiction and admissibility, Mendes claims that "there has already been a decision that evidence indicating the gravity of the alleged [crimes] is actually or potentially very high, is admissible under the criteria laid down in the Statute and that there are sufficient grounds to proceed with the investigation or prosecution."[43] For Mendes, this means that the inclusion of "gravity of the crime" as an explicit factor in assessing the interests of justice should "lead to a strong presumption against any extraneous factor, such as potential peace negotiations, being taken into account in determining when it is in the interests of justice NOT to proceed with an investigation or prosecution."[44] While the prosecutor should take into account the circumstances of the accused, the interests and participation of victims, and the gravity of the crimes, Mendes thinks that the high thresholds for jurisdiction and admissibility result in "the strongest of presumptions in favour of seeking accountability for the most serious of crimes."[45]

[41] Ibid, preamble.

[42] Errol Mendes, *Peace and justice at the International Criminal Court: A Court of Last Resort* (Northampton, MA: Edward Elgar, 2010), p. 30.

[43] Ibid., p. 31.

[44] Ibid., p. 31.

[45] Ibid., p. 33.

Margaret deGuzman argues that the questions of justice cannot be adequately answered because the ICC "suffers from low purposive legitimacy" as a result of its lack of articulated goals and values for its work.[46] This, she claims, makes selection decisions "patently inconsistent" and may detract from the ICC's legitimacy rather than upholding it as a partner with domestic institutions in seeking peace and justice.[47] DeGuzman also draws attention to the possibility that the ICC Prosecutor cannot decline to investigate a situation "on the grounds that the national government is addressing crimes through alternatives to prosecution such as truth commissions or traditional reconciliation methods," as Human Rights Watch argues is the case.[48]

We think both deGuzman and Mendes take the interpretation of "the interests of justice" too far to the extreme. The more plausible interpretation is that the ICC Office of the Prosecutor has a moderate level of guidance as to the purpose and goals of the ICC. Under this interpretation, the prosecutor is explicitly charged with seeking justice in the face of atrocities, but retains discretion to permit flexibility in how best to seek justice. This is not an objective determination by any means, but that is because issues of balancing peace and justice simply cannot be based on a list of purely objective criteria.

We view the role of the ICC Prosecutor as the main source of implementing rule of law and fairness considerations, but we also recognize that this role is not without oversight. Ultimately, the ICC Prosecutor's assessment of the interests of justice is subject to being overturned by the judges in the Pre-Trial Chamber, as they can invalidate the ICC Prosecutor's decision not to pursue a case and require her to proceed.[49] Thus, the balance among peace, justice, and ending impunity should remain subject to a moderate degree of interpretation on the part of the ICC Prosecutor.

The issues at the ad hoc tribunals with respect to prosecutorial discretion are slightly different, given the scope of the prosecutor's mandate at each tribunal, but our conclusion is similar. The temporary tribunals must balance goals of peace and justice with concerns of expediency and pragmatism. At the ICTY and the ICTR, for instance, the number of potential suspects who could have been investigated and then prosecuted was massive. As the ICTY Appeals Chamber recognized, the limited resources of international criminal tribunals necessitate "a broad discretion in relation to the initiation

[46] Margaret M. deGuzman, "Choosing to Prosecute: Expressive Selection at the International Criminal Court." *Michigan Journal of International Law* (2012), p. 276

[47] Ibid., p. 296.

[48] Ibid.; Human Rights Watch, "The Meaning of 'The Interests of Justice' in Article 53 of the Rome Statute" (2005), p. 2, http://hrw.org/campaigns/icc/docs/ij070505.pdf.

[49] Rome Statute, art. 53(3)(b).

of investigations and in the preparation of indictments" on the part of the prosecutor.[50]

The choice has already been made to address a specific conflict through a temporary tribunal, so the discretion of the prosecutor is limited to the individuals, not the conflict itself. This generated the need to limit the size of the defendant pool and shifted the international criminal tribunals' mandates from "persons responsible" for atrocities to "those who bear the greatest responsibility" for atrocities.[51] However, this is not necessarily insidious. It means any decision not to prosecute could result in a domestic prosecution, which is much more likely than if the ICC Office of the Prosecutor declines to investigate. What may be more of a problem is the possibility that the temporary tribunals are operating under a mandate influenced by a form of victors' justice. If it can be argued that there were crimes committed on both sides to a conflict, then one side is likely not to be prosecuted by a tribunal because of prosecutorial discretion and the influence of a particular narrative on the creation of the tribunal. But we would argue that even in cases when this is a possibility, such as the ICTR's failure to prosecute any members of the Rwandan Patriotic Front (RPF), the internal conflict caused by such prosecutions may prevent achievement of the tribunal's goals. It is unfortunate that there were no RPF prosecutions, but that does not mean the ICTR would have been the right place for them to occur.

B *Prosecutorial Overreach and Misconduct in Africa*

1 Failure to Exercise Discretion

The ICC's case against Kenyan leaders for postelection violence committed between 2007 and 2008 has been held up as a striking example of the ICC's unwillingness to forgo prosecutions against African leaders, even where the reasons for exercising prosecutorial discretion are strong. Recently, the ICC dropped all charges against the president of Kenya, Uhuru Kenyatta, as well as against three other Kenyan leaders. Although the case against Kenyatta has been dropped, there are still good arguments that the ICC Prosecutor acted impermissibly. Major questions have arisen through the international reaction to the ICC's issuance of an arrest warrant for a person who was the front-runner for president and who eventually was elected president of Kenya.

[50] See *Prosecutor v. Delalić, Mucić, Delić and Landžo*, IT-96-21 Appeals Chamber, ICTY, 20 February 2001, para. 602.

[51] Luc Côté, "International Criminal Justice: Tightening Up the Rules of the Game," *International Review of the Red Cross*, vol. 88, no. 861 (2006): pp. 133–144, 137.

In particular, why did the ICC resist for so long the request to delay the trial until after the election or until the defendant was no longer a current head of state? Regardless of the legal issues, the ICC has at least the appearance of unfairness when it is deaf to reasonable requests for postponement of a very high-profile case concerning a very popular African leader.[52]

Similar concerns have been raised about the attempt by the ICC to prosecute Omar al-Bashir, the sitting head of state in Sudan. One of the main worries here is that the prosecutors have tried to isolate al-Bashir in an attempt to take him to the Hague, but most of these efforts have backfired, with al-Bashir even more powerful and popular than before. And there is some reason to think that al-Bashir has sought to retaliate for the investigation and arrest warrant by making it increasingly dangerous and deadly to be a humanitarian aid worker in the Darfur region of Sudan. This example of overreaching and possible misconduct by the ICC Prosecutor has made attempts to arrest other defendants even more difficult.

The criticism concerning the caseload's primarily coming from Africa seems to us largely accurate as a statement of what the ICC in particular has done so far. It is of course something that can be corrected, and if it is not, and soon, the criticism will stand as an indication that the ICC does not display even the appearance of being fair. But if one were to include all the cases from the ad hoc tribunals over the last two decades, there have been quite a number of cases not from Africa – cases concerning international crimes in the former Yugoslavia, Iraq, Lebanon, Cambodia, and East Timor. So, while the cases from Rwanda and Sierra Leone, when added to the current cases mean that the international courts and tribunals have still taken a majority of cases from Africa, it is not an overwhelming majority, if the other ad hoc tribunals' cases are added to the ICC's cases.

Another response is to point out that if the facts are true as alleged, then al-Bashir certainly deserves to be prosecuted for the mass atrocities committed in Darfur. The crimes alleged in Kenya are not as clear-cut, but if there had been sufficient evidence that there was a massacre in Kenya after an election midway into the last decade, a prosecution should have gone forward. More worrisome is the idea that because these people are sitting heads of state they should be considered beyond the reach of international criminal law. The international rule of law will surely suffer if there are two sets of rules, one for

[52] See Ben Batros, "The Judgment on the Katanga Admissibility Appeal, Judicial Restraint at the ICC," *Leiden Journal of International Law*, vol. 23, no. 2 (2010), pp. 343–362; see also Susana Sacouto and Katherine Cleary, "The Katanga Complementarity Decisions: Sound Law but Flawed Policy," *Leiden Journal of International Law*, vol. 23, no. 2 (2010), pp. 362–374.

the powerful and one for everyone else. And there must be a rationale for why some state leaders who have been charged, such as al-Bashir, have not been arrested and taken to the Hague, as well as why some state leaders have not even been investigated, such as Assad, when it is clear they should have been. If there are no rationales forthcoming, this would be a very serious indictment. But we will argue that there are rationales available.

2 Preventing Alternative Peace Processes

We focus on political issues elsewhere in this book, but we should briefly discuss here some other claims that international criminal tribunals are treating Africans and conflicts in Africa unfairly. Specifically, the imposition of certain legal structures is preventing alternative peace processes or mischaracterizing civil wars.

As noted earlier, it is a challenge to balance the third basis for prosecutorial discretion ("the interests of justice") with the preamble of the Rome Statute (calling for an end to impunity and the punishment of those responsible for "the most serious crimes of concern for the international community"). This is especially the case when the ICC Prosecutor is unfamiliar with traditional peace processes or may be unaware of the impact of international criminal prosecution on these processes.

We see the ICC's role in transitional justice processes as one of negative responsibility. The ICC Office of the Prosecutor should refrain from taking action that will clearly impede truth and reconciliation or other alternative justice mechanisms and should be open to hearing domestic feedback regarding plans for peace processes. But it is not the ICC's role to aid in the development of transitional justice mechanisms. It is the job of the ICC Office of the Prosecutor to work with these mechanisms and provide access to evidence and other resources when possible.

The various legal structures that sought justice after the Rwandan genocide have been relatively successful at coexisting and sharing the peace and justice burdens. The ICTR has prosecuted the big fish, and smaller fish have been subject to domestic prosecution and/or *gacaca* court reconciliation processes. The complementary processes have not functioned or cooperated perfectly by any means, but they have all achieved at least some of their objectives. The construction of the ICTR, therefore, did not necessarily prevent the development and flourishing of traditional peace processes, and this is good evidence that the ICC and other international criminal tribunals would not necessarily prevent traditional peace processes in other conflicts.

The main concern we have as to potential conflict between international criminal justice mechanisms and transitional justice mechanisms is the problem of scarce resources. If there is only a certain amount of money that can be spent pursuing justice, and the creation of complementary processes is not an option, it is difficult to know how to balance peace and justice considerations. As we have said throughout this chapter, this is not an objective assessment. All we can say here is that it will be best to leave these sorts of decisions as much in the hands of the victims as possible. Good faith efforts to use scarce resources on domestic transitional mechanisms should be respected by the ICC.

A final concern is how to proceed in hazy situations that might be better characterized as local issues of civil conflict. Here, too, we would err on the side of respecting domestic determinations as to how peace and justice should be sought. The international community should stand ready to provide resources and judicial support in such situations but should not be in the position of imposing a particular solution on cases of a questionably international nature.

IV PROSECUTORIAL DISCRETION IN CHARGING

A *Unfairness toward Defendants*

Not only does the Prosecutor have discretion in deciding which conflicts to pursue and which individuals to charge, but he or she must also make decisions about the crimes with which to charge a defendant. Even those who support the international criminal courts and tribunals have been critical of prosecutorial decisions to reduce or modify charges on the basis of efficiency, politics, or other considerations.

One reason that has been given by a former ICC prosecutor for selective strategies of charging defendants was "to provide a sample that is reflective of the gravest incidents and the main types of victimization."[53] This allows the Prosecutor to "express condemnation of all the varieties of wrongdoing perpetrated in a situation."[54] The desire to express condemnation is a worthwhile objective for the ICC, and the desire to express condemnation across a wide expanse of victims is also laudable. Yet the ICC Prosecutor must be careful not to treat defendants unfairly. However, it is not necessarily unfair for the Prosecutor to limit the charges against certain defendants and seek all possible charges against others. It

[53] deGuzman, "Choosing to prosecute," citing International Criminal Court, Office of the Prosecutor, Prosecutorial Strategy 2009–2012, p. 7.

[54] Ibid.

would only be unfair to seek more charges than is appropriate or for which there is evidence against a certain defendant. Bias would only occur in the decision about who could receive a reprieve from certain charges. But part of the ICC's role is not even to give the appearance of being unfair or biased, and therefore the Prosecutor should be careful about announcing such strategies so bluntly. The public may have a hard time understanding these sorts of strategies, and the ICC Prosecutor should be careful to explain fully her reasons for not pursuing certain charges against certain defendants.

As an example, the ICC's first defendant, Thomas Lubanga, was only charged with recruiting child soldiers. However, some have argued that there was enough evidence to charge him with crimes of sexual violence and other serious war crimes. In this case, it seems that the investigation against Lubanga was incomplete and there was a chance that he was going to be released from custody, but Prosecutor Moreno-Ocampo may have wanted to make a statement about the norm against the recruitment of child soldiers, so he proceeded with the prosecution of Lubanga for that charge and not the charges of murder and rape.[55] It is not procedurally unfair that Lubanga was not tried for murder or rape, but it may be substantively unjust. The Prosecutor must balance, as always, considerations of justice against considerations of efficiency and efficaciousness.

At the international criminal tribunals, the weight of inconsistent prosecution may be heavier, especially when there may be similar cases with similar defendants accused of committing similar crimes, yet the actual charges against the defendants are markedly different. These instances will certainly give the impression that the tribunal is biased and the treatment of defendants is unfair. In the courts and tribunals set up for a specific conflict, the prosecutor should be more wary of differential prosecution strategies and should aim to treat all defendants equally. As at the ICC, there may be reasons to charge defendants on the basis of a wide range of objectives, but the preference should be for consistency and any strategies resulting in variations should be expressed publicly.

As with the other types of prosecutorial discretion, there is a modicum of oversight from the judicial bench. While a prosecutor makes the decision to charge a defendant with particular crimes, judges can provide a recharacterization of "the facts to convict a defendant of crimes not charged" as long as they do not stray from the facts presented in the charging document.[56] This

[55] *Prosecutor v. Lubanga*, ICC-01/04-01/06, International Criminal Court (ICC), 14 March 2012.

[56] deGuzman, "Choosing to Prosecute," p. 275, citing Regulations of the Court as amended on 14 June and 14 November 2007, ICC-BD/ 01-02-07, Reg. 55 (entered into force Dec. 18, 2007); see also *Prosecutor v. Lubanga*, Case No. ICC-01/04/-01/06 OA 15 OA 16, Judgment on the Appeals of Mr. Lubanga Dyilo and the Prosecutor, PP88-100 (Dec. 8, 2009).

allows judges to disagree with a prosecutor's decision to charge a defendant with particular crimes, depending on whether or not the judge agrees with a particular prosecutorial strategy.

B Unfairness toward Victims

The more insidious issue with inconsistent and selective prosecution is the unfairness toward victims, which is better characterized (as earlier) as unjust rather than procedurally unfair.[57] Even though one of the expressed purposes of the international criminal courts and tribunals is to respond to the retributive aspirations of victims, we have also seen that this is not the only purpose of the judicial institutions. Nor is it the case that this purpose does not have to be balanced against other considerations of fairness, efficiency, and efficacy. But this remains the most unfortunate aspect of prosecutorial charging strategies.

One particular type of crime that has been skipped over or dropped from a list of charges against international criminal defendants are crimes of sexual violence. There are several reasons for this strategy. First, crimes of sexual violence are hard to prove. The evidence of sexual violence is largely circumstantial in nature, and the physical evidence that can be obtained is almost never obtained or preserved in situations of mass atrocity. Longer-lasting physical evidence can present its own problems. Sexually-transmitted diseases cannot be traced to a specific source, even if it can be established that an accused person and a victim both suffer from the same condition. Children who are born as a result of rapes can be DNA tested to prove parentage, but a mother or child may have personal or psychological reasons for not wanting to participate in such testing.

In addition, prosecutors have often made the decision to forgo prosecuting defendants for crimes of sexual violence and instead focus on "more serious crimes" such as murder and genocide. As noted previously, the Lubanga case had to forgo the charge of rape in order to proceed with the trial at all. This is unfortunate. It is unfortunate that resources are so limited at the international criminal courts and tribunals that the prosecutors have to be in a position to forgo one charge in order to prepare adequately to prosecute someone for a different crime. But the missed opportunity of expressive impact is also unfortunate. If a prosecutorial strategy has expressive aims, the expression that sexual violence is an unacceptable practice in conflict is an important one to be made.

57 See Larry May and Paul Morrow (eds.), *Procedural Justice* (Burlington, VT: Ashgate, 2012).

Women and girls were systematically singled out for rape, slavery, and other forms of sexual violence during World War II. Yet the international military tribunal that followed World War II largely ignored sexual violence as a crime.[58] The prosecution of crimes of sexual violence, when it happened, occurred in conjunction with prosecution of other crimes and was not recognized as a distinctive sort of atrocity.[59] The prosecution of gender-based crimes at the ICTY and ICTR reflects a shift in jurisprudence, and while much progress has been made to recognize the nature of gender-based crimes and sexual violence, these crimes have been "investigated and indicted only after concerted pressure by women's rights organizations and feminist scholars to prosecute the crimes."[60] The most important legacy of the ICTR and the ICTY results from the decisions delivered by their Trial and Appeals Chambers defining sexual assault crimes and advancing "the rule of law and the human rights of women."[61] Female victims must be seen as equally deserving of justice as male victims, and the movement toward this recognition is beginning to be apparent in prosecutorial decisions and judicial rulings.

The new ICC Prosecutor has made it clear that "sexual and gender-based crimes are amongst the gravest under the [Rome] Statute."[62] She has indicated that the Office of the Prosecutor will seek to "combine its efforts to prosecute those most responsible with national proceedings for other perpetrators" and pay "particular attention to the commission of sexual and gender-based crimes at all stages of its work: preliminary examination, investigation, and prosecution."[63] We applaud this commitment on the part of the ICC Prosecutor, and

[58] See, e.g., John Murphy, "Crimes against Peace at the Nuremberg Trial," in *The Nuremberg Trial and International Law* (George Ginsburg and V. N. Kudriavtsev eds., 1990), p. 141; see also Kelly Askin, "Prosecuting Wartime Rape and Other Gender-Related Crimes under International Law: Extraordinary Advances, Enduring Obstacles," *Berkeley Journal of International Law*, vol. 21 (2003), pp. 288, 301.

[59] See generally ibid., pp. 301–302.

[60] Ibid., p. 317.

[61] Tamara Francita Lawson, "A Shift toward Gender Equality in Prosecutions: Realizing Legitimate Enforcement of Crimes Committed against Women in Municipal and International Criminal Law," *Southern Illinois University Law Journal*, vol. 33, no. 2 (2009), p. 214; see, e.g., *The Prosecutor v. Delaic*, Case. No. IT-96-21-T, Judgment, Para. 495 (Nov. 16, 1998) (echoing the modern view of rape in both the statutory articulation of the crime and the international tribunal's interpretation of the conduct); see also *Prosecutor v. Kunarac, Kovac, and Vukovic*, Case No. IT-96-23 & IT-96-23/1, 2000 WL 33706075 (ICTY, Nov. 2000); *Prosecutor v. Furundzija*, Case No. IT-95-17/1, 2000 WL 33705648 (ICTY, March 2000); Prosecutor v. Tadic, Case No. IT-94-1-T (ICTY, May 1997).

[62] The Office of the Prosecutor, International Criminal Court, Policy Paper on Sexual and Gender-Based Crimes (June 2014), https://www.icc-cpi.int/iccdocs/otp/otp-Policy-Paper-on-Sexual-and-Gender-Based-Crimes--June-2014.pdf.

[63] Ibid.

we hope to see evidence of the ICC's commitment in future investigative and prosecutorial decisions.

It is clear that prosecutorial overreaching and misconduct are endemic to all legal systems, not merely international ones. There are ways to restrain prosecutors that have been tried in domestic settings and proven successful most of the time and could be tried in international tribunals as well. International criminal law poses an especially difficult challenge in this area because there is no clear popular constituency that can put pressure on wayward prosecutors, as we indicated earlier. But there are oversight bodies nonetheless that can be employed more than they have been in order to counteract some of the worst abuses or appearances of abuse by the ICC Office of the Prosecutor.

It is also a reasonable criticism of some of the practices of the ICC Office of the Prosecutor that there has been resistance to delay that might otherwise be cautioned in light of certain political concerns. This is the flip side of the earlier worries about the politicization of international tribunals. In some cases, it might be good to take political considerations into account. And this is most likely to be true if the delay is asked for so as to aid a fledgling democratic political order in a part of the world where there have not been many democratically elected state leaders. Being sensitive to such political concerns is also prudent if the ICC is to halt its negative popularity spiral. To be sure, the ICC might never be popular; nor should we measure the success of the ICC in popularity terms. But, as we have said, since the ICC has to rely on the cooperation of states across the world to do its work, it should also not be blind to the way it is perceived.

The rule of law must be paramount, and it must appear to be paramount, at the ICC and other international courts and tribunals. The heaviest burden of maintaining the rule of law through procedural fairness will fall on the Office of the Prosecutor at each institution, as a result of the varying instances at which a prosecutor can exercise discretion. The challenge of balancing considerations of fairness, justice, peace, and efficiency will continue to face the Office of the Prosecutor, as the main door through which individuals and states can face unfair treatment, but this challenge is an opportunity to ensure the best outcomes and fit the international criminal justice system to various situations. There are ways in which the prosecutors can continue to improve their practices; we find the judicial structures normatively defensible, and in fact the fairest way to deal with crimes of mass violence.

9

Concluding Remarks

Throughout this book we have examined many of the most influential objections to international criminal tribunals and courts. Our emphasis has been on the normative criticisms that we have grouped around eight concepts. In each case, we have begun, where the critics often do not, with an examination of the philosophical grounds for concepts such as legitimacy and punishment as applied to the international domain. The discussion has been enriched by providing this theoretical framing of the issues. Of course, such philosophical and normative framing has not directly rebutted the critics of international criminal tribunals. But it is our hope that the issues are now much clearer than they were before.

Normatively, we have argued that there are several significant reasons for supporting international criminal tribunals. First, rather than being sources of insurmountable problems, we argued that considerations of legitimacy and sovereignty tell in favor of these tribunals. For international trials to take place to prosecute international crimes, some international body needs to be set up in a way that attains legitimacy and does not infringe on state sovereignty. We argued that the ICC has legitimacy by bootstrapping – that is, by the acceptance of the court by relevant players, especially by many states, in lieu of legitimacy by following procedures to which they have already agreed. Similarly, sovereignty is not abridged largely because of the acceptance of a form of divided sovereignty by the relevant players, again primarily by many states. Many states see their sovereignty enhanced by having international criminal tribunals, as was seen when more than one hundred states signed the Rome Statute establishing the ICC.

Second, considerations involving norms of responsibility and punishment also lead to support for international criminal tribunals. International crimes present the normative problem of how to hold individuals responsible for what are group crimes, such as genocide. And while there are better and worse ways to hold individuals responsible, the ICC has fastened onto a model tracking the control that a given participant had, which seems well supported normatively. Control by a participant is similar to will and intention, which has broad support as the key to criminal responsibility at the domestic level. And once there is a normative ground for ascriptions of responsibility at international criminal tribunals, considerations of punishment, even as difficult as they are, are easier to resolve as well. Concerning punishment we once again employ a bootstrapping method by which appeal is made to retribution, deterrence, and expressivism, all of which are well accepted normative reasons to punish in domestic contexts, now applied to the international context.

Third, economic and political norms can also be cited, again not to undermine but to undergird international criminal tribunals. Economic norms of rationality and reasonableness militate in favor of international criminal tribunals, since there are strong reasons to increase rather than decrease the incentives on individuals and states to minimize harms. Politically, the norms against colonialism and neocolonialism support attempts to bring oppressive leaders to justice. And while there is a worry that the ICC is pursuing too many African leaders and not enough oppressive leaders in other parts of the world, norms calling for ending oppression do not undermine the international prosecutors' actions in Africa.

And, fourth, highly practical considerations involving evidentiary consistency and prosecutorial fairness also can be appealed to for normative support for international criminal tribunals. There is a strong normative consensus that consistency and fairness be afforded to those accused of international crimes. International criminal tribunals have struggled to satisfy these norms, but we have argued that progress was being made and that there were no structural impediments for these normative constraints to be realized in the ICC and the ad hoc tribunals. Once again, the consensus that was reached when the ICC procedures were established shows the normative support such procedures have for many states today.

Nonetheless, the criticisms we have considered when taken all together constitute a formidable condemnation of international criminal law today. If anything, these criticisms have become more influential in recent years, especially since the ICC has begun to prosecute individuals in the name of the international community. Even the idea that there is an international community that can authorize criminal trials has been under assault. It is too easy to dismiss these criticisms as mere ideology or as stemming from a misunderstanding of the history of the rise of international criminal tribunals. We have tried to give these critics their due and to engage them as providing an often heartfelt critique from scholars who are often fundamentally committed to the goals of international justice and peace.

As we have argued, the great hope of international law with such institutions as international criminal tribunals is that human rights abuses, wherever they occur in the world, will be confronted and the perpetrators of such abuses will be brought to justice and punished. We readily admit that this promise has not yet been kept. But despite this fact, and despite the strong pessimism that runs through contemporary critiques, we have provided grounds for optimism. And, in addition, we have argued extensively that the critics have often overstated the case against these tribunals.

By focusing on normative and philosophical issues, we have sought to enlarge the debate about international criminal tribunals in a way that opens the discussion to the kind of issues that have been at the heart of the movement toward a global order that has progressed since the end of World War II and the founding of the United Nations. In part we were motivated by the fact that many critics have not considered the rise of international criminal tribunals in a historical context or in a larger normative frame that has brought legal institutions to bear on a world where globalization has already diminished the importance of state borders.

We have begun to explore the new ways of conceptualizing such matters as responsibility and punishment in the new globalized order. Even more fundamentally, we have also explored the relation of law to politics in the international realm, as well as how to conceive of sovereignty when states are of diminished importance. Even such basic ideas of legitimacy and fairness may need to be reconceptualized in light of the new international order. Yet we have also addressed the challenge to the new international order itself by those who argue normatively that we would be better off with a restoration of strong state borders where criminal matters are all handled domestically rather than internationally. This last issue has not been dealt with in the detail that it requires mainly because that would have required a book-length treatment on its own. Instead, concerning this issue of domestic versus international prosecutions, we have provided many reasons to think that the two can complement each other, rather than seeing domestic criminal law as a competitor of international criminal law.

Another issue we have not given full attention to is whether international law, and especially international criminal law, can continue to progress without international tribunals. We have admitted that in the future the role now played by international tribunals in administering international law could be filled by domestic or regional tribunals administering international law.

Yet, we have stressed that the time for such a change is far enough off in the future to make a defense of international criminal tribunals still a pressing matter today.

International criminal tribunals began life in the dramatic setting of a partially reconstructed Nuremberg, Germany, which had been devastated just months before the trials. And most importantly, at Nuremberg German political and military leaders were prosecuted. The idea that the leaders of one of the most powerful states ever to exist would occur within Germany is a lasting legacy. Of course, in this case the trials could not have occurred in Germany without the defeat of Germany by the Allied States. It is unclear what it would take today, more than six decades after the Nuremberg trials, for the political and military leaders of a sovereign state to be prosecuted by a tribunal in that state where the prosecution would be for violations of international not domestic laws. Perhaps this will occur only after sovereignty is not only reconceived but radically altered functionally.

Our goal in this book has not been to predict the future of domestic prosecutions for international crimes. Instead, our more modest goal has been normatively to defend international prosecutions in international criminal tribunals today. We have not tried to paper over the problems that have vexed, and continue to vex, these prosecutions. In each chapter we have offered responses to the critics of international criminal tribunals along with suggestions about needed reforms of those tribunals.

Among the most pressing problems that we have agreed to be afflicting the ICC is the process of case selection. While all criminal processes involve prosecutorial discretion, the problems at the ICC go further than in most domestic jurisdictions. One revision that would go a long way to diminish the chorus of critics would be for the ICC Office of the Prosecutor to be much more transparent in disclosing how cases are selected. Lack of transparency worries even those who are sympathetic to the working of the court. But for the ICC to become more transparent, only fairly minor changes in the court would have to take place. And so, as in most cases, we have argued that reform rather than disbandment is needed.

Let us end with a bit more historical background that will help us to get a perspective on the importance of the kind of extraordinary proceedings that characterize international criminal tribunals today. We shall focus on trials of two kings, one in the middle of the seventeenth century and the other reigning between World War I and World War II. Both cases show, if nothing else, the extent of the repercussions of trials of political leaders for the current and future actions of heads of state once these rulers recognize that they can be subject to prosecution for atrocities and wrongdoing.

The first case is the trial of Charles I for the mass murder of his own people in England in the middle of the seventeenth century. Here is the statute that established the tribunal:

> The High Court of Justice is to try King Charles I "to the end that no Chief Officer or Magistrate whatsoever may hereinafter presume traitorously and maliciously to contrive the enslaving or destroying of the English nation, and expect impunity for doing so."[1]

Geoffrey Robertson comments, "The thinking behind this court was that heads of state – and not only the heads of the state of England – might be deterred from cruel actions if they knew they might be punished for them, irrespective of sovereign immunity."[2]

The second trial concerns the former German kaiser, Wilhelm II, who was proposed to be prosecuted for crimes committed during World War I. As Kirsten Sellars puts it:

> Their arguments for trying him rested on negative bases. First, if he were not tried for the violation of the principles of international law, then these principles would never be completely vindicated. And second, if he were not tried for breaches of the laws of war, then the case against his subordinates would be weakened.[3]

As it turned out, the ex-kaiser was not prosecuted, but many believe the discussion about trying the kaiser was very important for the subsequent trial of Nazi German political leaders at Nuremberg after World War II.

It has been clear for more than three hundred years that political leaders could and should be prosecuted for their actions that caused massacres or other major crimes. It has also been clear for centuries that there are indeed international crimes, and it is important that they are prosecuted for humanity's sake. In our book we have also defended such trials from the criticisms of those who deny either that there are international crimes or that political leaders are prosecutable for these crimes. Those who remain unconvinced by our arguments need to address the seventeenth-century concern about impunity.

1 See Geoffrey Robertson, "The Tyrannicide Brief," in Morten Bergsmo, Cheah Wui Ling, and YI Ping (eds.), *Historical Origins of International Criminal Law*, Vol. I (Brussels: Torkel Opsahl Academic, 2014), p. 117. Robertson claims that the statute uses the term "impunity" in its international criminal law sense.

2 Ibid.

3 See Kirsten Sellars, "Trying the Kaiser: The Origins of International Criminal Law,"in *Historical Origins of International Criminal Law*, vol. I, p. 198.

Bibliography

Abass, Ademola. "Prosecuting International Crimes in Africa: Rationale, Prospects, and Challenges," *European Journal of International Law*, vol. 24, August 2013, pp. 933–946.

Aeschylus. *Eumenides*, in *Aeschylus' Oresteia*, edited and translated by Alan H. Sommerstein, Cambridge, MA: Harvard University Press/Loeb Classical Library, 2008.

Agreement for the Prosecution and Punishment of the Major War Criminals of the European Axis, and Charter of the International Military Tribunal, London, 8 August 1945.

Akhavan, Payam. "The International Criminal Tribunal for Rwanda: The Politics and Pragmatics of Punishment," *American Journal of International Law*, vol. 90, no. 3, 1996, pp. 501–510.

Amann, Diane Marie. "Group Mentality, Expressivism, and Genocide," *International Criminal Law Review*, vol. 2, no. 2, 2002, pp. 93–143.

Ambos, Kai. "International Criminal Procedure: 'Adversarial,' 'Inquisitorial,' or Mixed?"*International Criminal Law Review*, vol. 3, 2003, pp. 1–37.

Aptel, Cécile. "Prosecutorial Discretion at the ICC and Victims' Right to Remedy Narrowing the Impunity Gap," *Journal of International Criminal Justice*, vol. 10, no. 5, 2012, pp. 1357–1375.

Arendt, Hannah. *Imperialism* (part II of *The Origins of Totalitarianism*), New York: Harcourt, Brace & World, 1951, 1968.

"Organized Guilt and Universal Responsibility," *Jewish Frontier*, 1948, reprinted in Larry May and Stacey Hoffman eds., *Collective Responsibility*, Savage, MD: Rowman & Littlefield, 1991, pp. 273–284

Aristotle, *Politics*, in *Basic Works of Aristotle*, edited by Richard McKeon and translated by Benjamin Jowett, New York: Random House, 1941, pp. 1127–1316.

Askin, Kelly. "Prosecuting Wartime Rape and other Gender-Related Crimes under International Law: Extraordinary Advances, Enduring Obstacles," *Berkeley Journal of International Law*, vol. 21, 2003, pp. 288–349.

Bagaric, Mirko and John Morss, "International Sentencing Law: In Search of a Justification and Coherent Framework," 6 *International Criminal Law Review*, vol. 6, 2006, pp. 191–255.

Barton, John H. and Barry E. Carter, "International Law and Institutions for a New Age,"*Georgetown Law Journal*, 1992–1993, pp. 535–562.
Bassett, Marisa R. "Defending International Sentencing: Past Criticism to the Promise of the ICC," *Human Rights Brief*, vol. 16, 2009, pp. 22–60.
Batros, Ben. "The Judgment on the Katanga Admissibility Appeal, Judicial Restraint at the ICC," *Leiden Journal of International Law*, vol. 23, no. 2, 2010, pp. 343–362.
Beitz, Charles. *Political Theory and International Relations*, Princeton, NJ: Princeton University Press, 1979.
Bellelli, Roberto. ed. *International Criminal Justice: Law and Practice from the Rome Statute to Its Review*, Burlington, VT: Ashgate, 2013.
Bentham, Jeremy. *An Introduction to the Principles of Morals and Legislation*, New York: Macmillan, 1948.
Berman, Bruce J. "Clientelism and NeoColonialism: Center-Periphery Relations and Political Development in African States," 9 *Studies in Comparative International Development*, vol. 3, 1974, pp. 3–25
Bodin, Jean. *Six Livres de la Republique* (1576), translated by Julian H. Franklin as *On Sovereignty: Four Chapters from the Six Books of the Commonwealth*, Cambridge: Cambridge University Press, 1992.
Bolton, John. "Universal Jurisdiction: Too Easily Sweeps Political Differences into Legal Arena," *Legal Times*, January 11, 1999.
Brennan, Geoffrey, Lina Eriksson, Robert E. Goodin, and Nicholas Soutwood, *Explaining Norms*, Oxford: Oxford University Press, 2013
Buchanan, Allen. "The Legitimacy of International Law," in Samantha Besson, and John Tasioulas, eds., *The Philosophy of International Law*, Oxford: Oxford University Press, 2010, pp. 79–96.
Buisman, Caroline. "The Prosecutor's Obligation to Investigate Incriminating and Exonerating Circumstances Equally: Illusion or Reality," *Leiden Journal of International Law*, vol. 27, no. 1, 2014, pp. 205–226.
Burke-White, William W. "Complementarity in Practice: The International Criminal Court as Part of a System of Multi-Level Global Governance in the Democratic Republic of Congo," *Leiden Journal of International Law*, vol. 18, 2005, pp. 557–590.
Butler, Joseph. *The Analogy of Religion, Natural and Revealed, to the Constitution and Course of Nature*, London: G. Bell and Sons, 1889.
Byrne, Rosemary. "Drawing the Missing Map: What Socio-Legal Research Can Offer to International Criminal Trial Practice," *Leiden Journal of International Law*, vol. 26, no. 4, 2013, pp. 991–1007.
Caianiello, Michael. "Law of Evidence at the International Criminal Court: Blending Accusatorial and Inquisitorial Models," *North Carolina Journal of International Law & Commercial Regulation* vol. 36, 2011, pp. 287–297.
Cassese, Antonio. "The Legitimacy of International Criminal Tribunals and the Current Prospects of International Criminal Justice," *Leiden Journal of International Law*, vol. 25, no. 2, 2012, pp. 491–501.
Clarke, Kamari Maxine. *Fictions of Justice: The International Criminal Court and the Challenge of Legal Pluralism in Sub-Saharan Africa*, Cambridge: Cambridge University Press, 2009.
Clark, Phil. *The Gacaca Courts, Post-Genocide Justice and Reconciliation in Rwanda: Justice without Lawyers*, Cambridge: Cambridge University Press, 2010.

Clermont, Kevin M. and Emily Sherwin, "A Comparative View of Standards of Proof," *The American Journal of Comparative Law*, 2002, pp. 243–275.

Cogan, Jacob Katz. "The Problem of Obtaining Evidence for International Criminal Courts." *Human Rights Quarterly*, vol. 22, no. 2, 2000, 404–427.

Combs, Nancy. *Fact-Finding without Facts: The Uncertain Evidentiary Foundations of International Criminal Convictions*, Cambridge: Cambridge University Press, 2010.

Conot, Robert. *Justice at Nuremberg*, New York: Carroll & Graf, 1983.

Côté, Luc. "International Criminal Justice: Tightening Up the Rules of the Game," *International Review of the Red Cross*, vol. 88, no. 861, 2006, pp. 133–144.

"Independence and Impartiality" in L. Reydams et al., eds., *International Prosecutors*, Oxford: Oxford University Press, 2012, pp. 319–415.

Craven, Matthew. "Colonialism and Domination," in Bardo Fassbender and Anne Peters eds., *The Oxford Handbook of the History of International Law*, Oxford: Oxford University Press, 2012, pp. 862–889.

Cryer, Robert. "Witness Tampering and International Criminal Tribunals," *Leiden Journal of International Law*, vol. 27, no. 1, 2014, pp. 191–203.

Damaska, Mirjan. *Evidence Law Adrift*, New Haven, CT: Yale University Press, 1997.

"Of Hearsay and Its Analogues " *Minnesota Law Review*. vol. 76, 1992, pp. 444–449.

"The Henry Morris Lecture: What Is the Point of International Criminal Justice?" *Chicago-Kent Law Review*, vol. 83, 2008, pp. 331–335.

Danner, Alison Marston. "Constructing a Hierarchy of Crimes in International Criminal Law Sentencing," *Virginia Law Review*, vol. 87, no, 3, May 2001, pp. 415–501.

Davidovic, Jovana. "Timor-Leste and Transitional Justice: Should We Pursue International Prosecutions for the Crimes Committed in East Timor in 1999? in Larry May and Andrew Forcehimes eds., *Morality, Jus Post Bellum, and International Law*, Cambridge: Cambridge University Press, 2012, 78–112.

DeGuzman, Margaret M. "Harsh Justice for International Crimes?" *Yale Journal of International Law*, vol. 39, 2013, pp. 1–35.

"Choosing to Prosecute: Expressive Selection at the International Criminal Court," *Michigan Journal of International Law*, 2012, pp. 265–320.

DeVos, Christian. "Investigating from Afar: The ICC's Evidence Problem," *Leiden Journal of International Law*, vol. 26, no. 4, 2013, pp. 1009–1024.

Doherty, T. A. "Evidence in International Criminal Tribunals: Contrast between Domestic and International Trials," *Leiden Journal of International Law*, vol. 26, no. 4, 2013, pp. 937–945.

Drumbl, Mark A. "Child Pirates: Rehabilitation, Reintegration, and Accountability," *Case Western Reserve Journal of International Law*, vol. 46, 2013, pp. 235–244.

Atrocity, Punishment, and International Law, New York: Cambridge University Press, 2007.

Reimagining Child Soldiers in International Law and Policy, Oxford: Oxford University Press, 2012.

Dutton, Yvonne. "Crime and Punishment: Assessing Deterrence Theory in the Context of Somali Piracy," *George Washington International Law Review*, vol. 46, 2014, pp. 607–646.

Dworkin, Ronald. *Taking Rights Seriously*, Cambridge, MA: Harvard University Press, 1978.

Eberechi, Ifeonu. "Armed Conflicts in Africa and Western Complicity: A Disincentive for African Union's Cooperation with the ICC," *African Journal of Legal Studies*, vol. 3, no. 1, 2009, pp. 53–76.
Elster, Jon. *Ulysses and the Sirens*, Cambridge: Cambridge University Press, 1979.
Eser, Albin. "The 'Adversarial' Procedure: A Model Superior to Other Trial Systems in International Criminal Justice? in T. Kruessmann, ed., *ICTY: Towards a Fair Trial?* Wien: Intersentia, 2008, pp. 207–215.
Extraordinary Chambers in the Courts of Cambodia, "Introduction to the ECCC," http:// eccc.gov.kh/en/about-eccc/introduction, accessed 14 June 2015.
Extraordinary Chambers in the Courts of Cambodia. Internal rule 26.
Federal Rules of Evidence 801–807.
Feinberg, Joel. *Doing and Deserving*, Princeton, NJ: Princeton University Press, 1970.
Harm to Others. Vol. I. *The Moral Limits of the Criminal Law*, Oxford: Oxford University Press, 1984.
Fox-Decent, Evan. *Sovereignty's Promise: The State as Fiduciary*, Oxford: Oxford University Press, 2012.
Fox-Decent, Evan and Evan J. Criddle, "The Fiduciary Constitution of Human Rights," *Legal Theory*, vol. 15, 2009, pp. 301–336.
Fuller, Lon L. "Positivism and Fidelity to Law: A Reply to Professor Hart," *Harvard Law Review*, vol. 71, no. 4, 1958.
The Morality of Law, New Haven, CT: Yale University Press, 1963.
Galbraith, Jean. "The Good Deeds of International Criminal Defendants," *Leiden Journal of International Law*, vol. 25, 2012, pp. 799–813.
Gauthier, David. "Three against Justice: The Fool, the Sensible Knave, and the Lydian Shepherd," *Midwest Studies in Philosophy*, vol. 7, no. 1, September 1982, pp. 11–29.
General Convention on the Privileges and Immunities of the Organisation of African Unity (OAU). CAB/LEG/24.2/13 Adopted October 25, 1965, http://www.au.int/en/sites/default/files/treaties/7760-file-general_convention_privileges_immunities_organization_african_unity_0.pdf.
Glasius, Marlies. "Do International Courts Require Democratic Legitimacy?" *European Journal of International Law*, vol. 23, February 2012, pp. 43–66.
Goldsmith, Jack and Eric Posner, *The Limits of International Law*, Oxford: Oxford University Press, 2005.
Greenawalt, Alexander K. A. "International Criminal Law for Retributivists," *University of Pennsylvania Journal of International Law*, vol. 35, no. 4, 2014, pp. 987–988.
"Complementarity in Crisis: Uganda, Alternative Justice, and the International Criminal Court," *Virginia Journal of International Law*, vol. 50, 2009, pp. 107–162.
Grotius, Hugo. *De Jure Belli ac Pacis* (On the Laws of War and Peace) (1625) translated by Francis W. Kelsey, Oxford: Oxford University Press, 1925.
Hansen, Thomas Obel. "A Critical Review of the ICC's Practice Concerning Admissibility Challenges and Complementarity," *Melbourne Journal of International Law*, vol. 13, June 2012, pp. 217–234,
Hamilton, Alexander, James Madison, and John Jay, *The Federalist Papers*, 1787–1788.
Happold, Matthew. "The International Criminal Court and the Lord's Resistance Army," *Melbourne Journal of International Law*, vol. 8, May 2007, pp. 159–184.

Haque, Adil Ahmad. "Retributivism: The Right and the Good," *Law and Philosophy*, vol. 32, no. 1, 2013, pp. 59–82.

Hart, H. L. A. and A. M. Honore, *Causation in the Law*, 2nd ed., Oxford: Oxford University Press, 1985.

Hart, H. L. A. *The Concept of Law*, Oxford: Oxford University Press, 1960.

"Positivism and the Separation of Law and Morals," *Harvard Law Review*, vol. 71, no. 4, 1958, pp. 593–629.

"Prolegomenon to the Principles of Punishment," in *Punishment and Responsibility: Essays in the Philosophy of Law*, Oxford: Oxford University Press, 2008.

Hawkins, Darren and Chad Losee. "States and International Courts: The Politics of Prosecution in Sierra Leone, *Journal of Human Rights*, vol. 13, no. 1, January–March, 2014, pp. 48–68.

Hobbes, Thomas. *Leviathan* (1651), *The English Works of Thomas Hobbes*, vol. III, edited by William Molesworth, London: John Bohn, 1839.

Ho, Hock Lai. A *Philosophy of Evidence Law: Justice in the Search for Truth*, Oxford: Oxford University Press, 2008.

Hola, Barbara, Alette Smeulers and Catrien Bijleveld, "Is ICTY Sentencing Predictable? An Empirical Analysis of ICTY Sentencing Practices," *Leiden Journal of International Law*, vol. 22, 2009, pp. 79–97.

Holmes, Oliver Wendell, Jr., "The Path of the Law," in *Collected Legal Papers*, New York: Harcourt, Brace, 1920, pp. 167–202.

Human Rights Committee, General Comment No. 32, Art. 14: Right to Equality before Courts and Tribunals and to a Fair Trial, U.N. Doc. CCPR/C/GC/32, 2007.

Human Rights Watch, The Meaning of "The Interests of Justice" in Article 53 of the Rome Statute 2 (2005), http://hrw.org/campaigns/icc/docs/ij070505.pdf.

Hume, David. *Enquiry Concerning the Principles of Morals* (1757) in *Enquiries Concerning Human Understanding and the Principles of Morals*, 3rd ed., edited by L. A. Selby-Bigge, Oxford: Oxford University Press, 1975.

A *Treatise of Human Nature*, vol. 1, edited by David Fate Norton and Mary J. Norton, Oxford: Clarendon Press, 2007.

Hyde, Charles C. *International Law, Chiefly as Interpreted and Applied by the United States*, Boston: Little, Brown, 1945.

International Criminal Court Statute. UN General Assembly, *Rome Statute of the International Criminal Court* (last amended 2010), 17 July 1998, ISBN No. 92-9227-227-6

International Criminal Court web site, "Situations and Cases," available at https://icc-pi.int/en_menus/icc/situations%20and%20cases/Pages/situations%20and%20cases.aspx.

International Criminal Tribunal for Rwanda. Rule 87 (A) ICTY RPE; Rule 87 (A) ICTR RPE; Art. 66 of the ICC RPE.

International Criminal Tribunal for Yugoslavia. Judgment on the Request of the Republic of Croatia for Review of the Decision of Trial Chamber II of 18 July 1997, Prosecutor v. Blaskic;, Case IT-95-14-AR108bis, App. Ch., ¶¶ 25–26 (ICTY 29 October 1997).

International Criminal Tribunal for Yugoslavia. Brief of the Republic of Croatia on Subpoenae Duces Tecum, Prosecutor v. Blaskic;, T. Ch. II, Case No. IT-95-14-PT, ¶ 1 (ICTY 1 April 1997) (RP D3682-84).

International Criminal Tribunal for Yugoslavia. Republic of Croatia, Reply to Subpoena Duces Tecum, Prosecutor v. Blaskic.

Jackson, John and Yassin M'Boge. "Integrating a Socio-Legal Approach to Evidence in International Criminal Tribunals," *Leiden Journal of International Law*, vol. 26, no. 4, 2013, pp. 933–945.

Jackson, Robert. Opening Statement in volume II of *Trial of the Major War Criminals Before the International Military Tribunal*, Nuremberg: IMT, 1947.

Janis, Mark. "The Nature of Jus Cogens," *Connecticut Journal of International Law*, vol. 3, 1988, pp. 359–363.

Jokic, Aleksandar, ed., *War Crimes and Collective Wrongdoing*, Oxford: Blackwell, 2001.

Juma, Laurence "Unclogging the Wheels: How the Shift from Politics to Law Affects Africa's Relationship with the International System." *Transnational Law and Contemporary Problems*, vol. 23, 2014, pp. 305–356.

Kant, Immanuel. *Metaphysics of Morals* (1797), translated by Mary McGregor, Cambridge: Cambridge University Press, 1996.

The Philosophy of Law (1796), translated by W. Hastie, Edinburgh: T. and T. Clark, 1887.

Kay, David A. "The Impact of African States on the United Nations," *International Organizations*, vol. 23, 1969, pp. 20–26.

Keenan, Patrick. "The New Deterrence: Crime and Policy in the Age of Globalization," *Iowa Law Review*, vol. 91, 2006, pp. 505–516.

Keller, Andrew N. "Punishment for Violations of International Criminal Law: An Analysis of Sentencing at the ICTY and ICTR," *Indiana International and Comparative Law Review*, vol. 12, 2001, pp. 53–74.

Kendall, Sara. "Donors' Justice: Recasting International Criminal Accountability," *Leiden Journal of International Law*, vol. 24, no. 3, 2011, pp. 585–606.

Klabbers, Jan. "Just Revenge? The Deterrence Argument in International Criminal Law," *Finnish Yearbook of International Law*, vol. 12, 2001, pp. 249–267.

Klamberg, Mark. *Evidence in International Criminal Trials: Confronting Legal Gaps and the Reconstruction of Disputed Events*, Dordrecht: Martinus Nijhoff, 2013.

Koh, Steven Arrigg. "Geography and Justice: Why Prison Location Matters in US and International Theories of Criminal Punishment," *Vanderbilt Journal of Transnational Law*, vol. 46, 2013, pp. 1267–1320.

Koskenniemi, Martti. "Between Impunity and Show Trials," *Max Planck Yearbook of International Law*, vol. 6, 2002, pp. 1–35.

The Gentle Civilizer of Nations: The Rise and Fall of International Law 1870–1960, Cambridge: Cambridge University Press, 2001.

The Politics of International Law, London: Bloomsbury, 2011.

Krever, Tor."International Law: An Ideology Critique," *Leiden Journal of International Law*, vol. 26, no. 3, 2013, pp. 701–723.

Ku, Julian and Jide Nzelibe, "Do International Criminal Tribunals Deter or Exacerbate Humanitarian Atrocities?" *Washington University Law*, vol. 84, no. 4, 2006, pp. 777–833.

Ku, Julian and John Yoo, "Globalization and Sovereignty," *Berkeley Journal of International Law*, vol. 31, 2013, pp. 210–234.

Taming Globalization: International Law, the US Constitution, and the New World Order, Oxford: Oxford University Press, 2012.

Lang, Anthony. "Crime and Punishment: Holding States Accountable," *Ethics & International Affairs*, vol. 21, no. 2, 2007, 239–257.
Langer, Maximo and Joseph Doherty. "Managerial Judging Goes International, but Its Promise Remains Unfulfilled: An Empirical Assessment of the ICTY Reforms," *Yale Journal of International Law*, vol. 36, 2011, pp. 241–305.
Langbein, John H. "Historical Foundations of the Law of Evidence: A View from the Ryder Sources," *Columbia Law Review*, 1996, pp. 1168–1202.
Lauterpacht, Hersch. *The Function of Law in the International Community*, Oxford: Oxford University Press, 1933.
Lawson, Tamara Francita. "A Shift toward Gender Equality in Prosecutions: Realizing Legitimate Enforcement of Crimes Committed against Women in Municipal and International Criminal Law," *Southern Illinois University Law Journal*, vol. 33, no. 2, 2009, pp. 1–35.
Lowe, Vaughan. *International Law*, Oxford: Oxford University Press, 2007.
Luban, David. "A Theory of Crimes against Humanity," *Yale Journal of International Law*, vol. 29, 2004, pp. 85–167.
McAuliffe, Padraig. "Suspended Disbelief? The Curious Endurance of the Deterrence Rationale in International Criminal Law," *New Zealand Journal of Public and International Law*, vol. 10, December 2012, pp. 227–262.
McLaughlin, Colin T. "Victim and Witness Measures of the International Criminal Court: A Comparative Analysis," *The Law & Practice of International Courts and Tribunals*, vol. 6, no. 1, 2007, pp. 189–220.
Mamdani, Mahmood. "Darfur, ICC and the New Humanitarian Order," *The Zeleza Post*, vol. 25, 2008, pp.
May, Larry. *Crimes against Humanity: A Normative Account*, New York: Cambridge University Press, 2005.
Global Justice and Due Process, New York: Cambridge University Press, 2010.
Limiting Leviathan: Hobbes on Law and International Affairs, Oxford: Oxford University Press, 2013.
The Morality of Groups, Notre Dame, IN: University of Notre Dame Press, 1987.
War Crimes and Just War, New York: Cambridge University Press, 2007.
May, Larry and Paul Morrow, eds., *Procedural Justice*. Burlington, VT: Ashgate, 2012.
"Mbeki Named to Heal Bashir Rift," *BBC News*, March 6, 2009.
Mendes, Errol. *Peace and Justice at the International Criminal Court: A Court of Last Resort*. Northampton, MA: Edward Elgar, 2010.
Mill, John Stuart. *On Liberty* (1859), edited by Elizabeth Rapaport, Indianapolis: Hackett, 1978.
The Minister of Justice and Constitutional Development v. The Southern African Litigation Centre (867/15) [2016] ZASCA 17 (15 March 2016).
Morgan, Edward. *Some Problems of Proof under the Anglo-American System of Litigation*, New York: Columbia University Press, 1956.
Moore, M. S. "The Moral Worth of Retribution" in F. Schoeman, ed., *Responsibility, Character, and the Emotions*, Cambridge: Cambridge University Press, 1988.
Morgenthau, Hans. *Die internationale Rechtspflege, ihr Wesen und ihre Grenzen*, Leipzig: Noske, 1929.
Murphy, John. "Crimes against Peace at the Nuremberg Trial," in George Ginsburg and V. N. Kudriavtsev eds., *The Nuremberg Trial and International Law*, Boston, MA: Martinus Nijhoff Publishers, 1990, pp. 141–154.

Nance, Dale. "The Best Evidence Principle," *Iowa Law Review*, vol. 73, 1998, pp. 227–297.
Ndindiliyimana et al., Judgment, ICTR-00-56-A, 11 February 2014, Appeals Chamber.
Judgment, ICTR-00-56-T, 17 May 2011, Trial Chamber.
Negri, Stefania. "The Principle of 'Equality of Arms' and the Evolving Law of International Criminal Procedure," *International Criminal Law Review*, vol. 5, no. 4, 2005, pp. 513–571.
Neuffer, Elizabeth. *The Key to My Neighbor's House: Seeking Justice in Bosnia and Rwanda*, London: Bloomsbury, 2000.
Ngane, Sylvia Ntube. "Witnesses before the International Criminal Court," *The Law and Practice of International Courts and Tribunals*, vol. 8, no. 3, 2009, pp. 431–457.
Nouwen, Sarah M. H. and Wouter G. Werner, "Doing Justice to the Political: The International Criminal Court in Uganda and Sudan," *European Journal of International Law*, vol. 21, November, 2010, pp. 941–965.
Nsereko, Daniel. "The ICC and Complementarity in Principle," *Leiden Journal of International Law*, vol. 26, no. 2, 2013, pp. 426–447.
Nwoye, Leo C. "Partners or Rivals in Reconciliation: The ICTR and Rwanda's Gacaca Courts," *San Diego International Law Journal*, vol. 16, 2014, pp. 119–177.
Office of the Prosecutor, International Criminal Court, Policy Paper on Sexual and Gender-Based Crimes (June 2014), https://icc-cpi.int/iccdocs/otp/OTP-Policy-Paper-on-Sexual-and-Gender-Based-Crimes–June-2014.pdf.
International Criminal Court. Request for Authorization of an Investigation Pursuant to Art. 15, Situation in the Republic of Kenya (ICC-01/09-3), Office of the Prosecutor, 26 November 2009.
Ohlin, Jens David. "Proportional Sentences at the ICTY," in Bert Swart, Alexander Zahar, and Göran Sluiter eds., *The Legacy of the International Criminal Tribunal for the Former Yugoslavia*, New York: Oxford University Press, 2011.
"Second Order Linking Principles: Combining Vertical and Horizontal Modes of Liability," *Leiden Journal of International Law*, vol. 25, no. 3, 2012, pp. 771–797.
"Towards a Unique Theory of International Criminal Sentencing," in George Ginsburg and V. N. Kudriavtsev eds., *The Nuremberg Trial and International Law*, Boston, MA: Martinus Nijhoff Publishers, 1990, pp. 373–404.
The Assault on International Law, New York: Oxford University Press, 2015.
Organization of African Unity (OAU), Charter of the Organization of African Unity, 25 May 1963.
Osiel, Mark. *Making Sense of Mass Atrocity*, New York: Cambridge University Press, 2009.
Obeying Orders, New York: Transaction, 1999.
"The Demise of International Criminal Law," *Humanity*, November 16, 2013, http://humanity journal.org/blog/2013/11/demise-international-criminal-court.
Peskin, Victor. *International Justice in Rwanda and the Balkans: Virtual Trials and the Struggle for State Cooperation*, New York: Cambridge University Press, 2008.
Plato, *Republic*, Book II, 359c–360b, translated by G. M. A. Grube and revised by C. D. C. Reeve, in *Plato: Complete Works*, edited by John M. Cooper, Indianapolis: Hackett, 1997.
Posner, Eric. "Assad and the Death of the International Criminal Court," *Slate*, September 19, 2013.

Posner, Eric and Alan Sykes. *Economic Foundations of International Law*, Cambridge, MA: Harvard University Press, 2013.

Posner, Richard. *The Problems of Jurisprudence*, Cambridge, MA: Harvard University Press, 1990.

Pruitt, William R. "Aggravating and Mitigating Sentencing Factors at the ICTR: An Exploratory Analysis," *International Criminal Law Review*, vol. 14, no. 1, 2014, pp. 148–176.

Prosecutor v. Brima, Kamara and Kanu (AFRC Case), Case No. SCSL-04-16-PT, Decision on joint Defence motion to exclude all evidence from Witness TF1-277 pursuant to Rule 89 and/or Rule 95, 24 May 2005.

Prosecutor v. Delaic, Case. No. IT-96-21-T, Judgment, Nov. 16, 1998.

Prosecutor v. Delalic´, Mucic´, Delic´ and Landzˇo, IT-96-21 Appeals Chamber, ICTY, 20 February 2001.

Prosecutor v. Furundzija, Case No. IT-95-17/1, 2000 WL 33705648, ICTY, March 2000.

Prosecutor v. *Gatete*, Judgment, Case no. ICTR-2000-61-T Tr. Ch. III, 31 March 2011.

Prosecutor v. Karemera, Case No. ICTR 98-44-AR73(C), Decision on Prosecutor's Interlocutory Appeal of Decision on Judicial Notice, June 16, 2006.

Prosecutor v. Kunarac, Kovac, and Vukovic, Case No. IT-96-23 & IT-96-23/1, 2000 WL 33706075, ICTY, Nov. 2000.

Prosecutor v. Lubanga, ICC-01/04-01/06, International Criminal Court, 14 March 2012.

Case No. ICC-01/04/-01/06 OA 15 OA 16, Judgment on the Appeals of Mr. Lubanga Dyilo and the Prosecutor, PP88-100, December 8, 2009.

Prosecution Response to "Requête de la Défense de M. Lubanga aux fins de communication d'éléments de preuve recueillis par le Procureur dans le cadre des enquêtes conduites en vertu de l'Article 70," ICC-01/04-01/06-3069, March 25, 2014.

Prosecutor v. Tadic, Case No. IT-94-1-T (ICTY, May 1997), http:// icty.org/x/cases/tadic/tjug/en/tad-tsj70507JT2-e.pdf.

Decision on the Defence Motions to Summon and Protect Defence Witnesses, and on the Giving of Evidence by Video-Link, Case No. IT-94-1-T, T. Ch. II, June 25, 1996.

Prosecutor v. Uhuru Muigai Kenyatta, Case No. ICC-01/09-02/11–728, Decision on Defense Application Pursuant to Article 64(4) and Related Requests, April 26, 2013, http://icccpi.int/iccdocs/doc/ doc1585619.pdf.

Prosecutor v. Zejnil Delalic and others, Decision on the Motion to Allow Witnesses K, L, and M to give their testimony by Means of Video-Link Conference, Case No. IT-96-21, T. Ch. II, May 28, 1997, para. 15.

Rabkin, Jeremy. *Law without Nations*, Princeton, NJ: Princeton University Press, 2005.

"Recalling the Case for Sovereignty," *Chicago Journal of International Law*, vol. 5, 2005, pp. 435–460.

Radbruch, Gustav. "Gesetzliches Unrecht und ¨ubergesetzliches Recht [Statutory Lawlessness and Supra-Statutory Law]," 1 *Suddeutsche Juristen-Zeitung* [SJZ], vol. 105, 1946, pp. 105–108 (Ger.), translated in 26 *Oxford J. Legal Studies*. Translated by Bonnie Litschewski Paulson and Stanley L. Paulson, 2006.

Rawls, John. *A Theory of Justice*, Oxford: Clarendon Press, 1971.

Raz, Joseph. *The Morality of Freedom*, Oxford: Oxford University Press, 1984.

"Human Rights without Foundations," in Samantha Beeson and John Tasioulis, eds., *The Philosophy of International Law*, Oxford: Oxford University Press, 2010, pp. 321–337.

Raz, Joseph and Avishai Margalit, "National Self-Determination," *The Journal of Philosophy*, vol. 87, no. 9, September 1990, pp. 439–461.

Rescher, Nicholas and Carey B. Joynt, "Evidence in History and in the Law." *The Journal of Philosophy*, 1959, pp. 561–578.

Robertson, Geoffrey. "The Tyrannicide Brief," in Morten Bergsmo, Cheah Wui Ling, and Yi Ping, eds., *Historical Origins of International Criminal Law, Vol. I*, Brussels: Torkel Opsahl Academic, 2014, pp. 115–140.

Robinson, Darryl. "A Cosmopolitan Liberal Account of International Criminal Law," *Leiden Journal of International Law*, vol. 26, no. 1, 2013, pp. 127–153.

Robinson, Mark. "Aid, Democracy and Political Conditionality in Sub-Saharan Africa," 5 *European Journal of Development Research*, vol. 85, 1993, pp. 85–99.

Robinson, Paul H. "Competing Conceptions of Modern Desert: Vengeful, Deontological, and Empirical," *Cambridge Law Journal*, vol. 67, 2008, pp. 145–175.

Robinson, Paul H. and John M. Darley, "The Role of Deterrence in the Formulation of Criminal Law Rules: At Its Worst When Doing Its Best," *Georgetown Law Review*, vol. 91, 2002, pp. 949–1002.

Rotberg, Robert and Dennis Thompson, eds., *Truth v. Justice: The Morality of Truth Commissions*, Princeton, NJ: Princeton University Press, 2000.

Rousseau, Jean-Jacques. *The Social Contract, or, Principles of Political Right*, London: George Allen & Unwin, 1895.

Sacouto, Susana and Katherine Cleary, "The Katanga Complementarity Decisions: Sound Law but Flawed Policy," *Leiden Journal of International Law*, vol. 23, no. 2, 2010, pp. 362–374.

Schabas, William. *The Abolition of the Death Penalty in International Law*, Cambridge: Cambridge University Press, 2002.

Scharf, Michael. *Balkan Justice*, Raleigh, NC: Carolina Academic Press, 1997.

Schmitt, Carl. *The Concept of the Political: Expanded Edition*, Chicago: University of Chicago Press, 2008.

Schotel, Bas. "Doing Justice to the Political: The International Criminal Court in Uganda and Sudan: A Reply to Sarah Nouwen and Wouter Werner, *European Journal of International Law*, vol. 22, 2011, pp. 1153–1160.

Second Warrant of Arrest for Omar Hassan Ahmad Al-Bashir, Al Bashir (ICC-02/05-01/09), Pre-Trial Chamber I, July, 12 2010.

Sellars, Kirsten. "Trying the Kaiser: The Origins of International Criminal Law," in Morten Bergsmo, Cheah Wui Ling, and Yi Ping, eds., *Historical Origins of International Criminal Law, Vol. I*, Brussels: Torkel Opsahl Academic Publishers, 2014, pp. 195–212.

Simmons, A. John. "Justification and Legitimacy," *Ethics*, vol. 109, no. 4, July 1999, pp. 739–771.

Sklar, Roger L. "Democracy in Africa," *African Studies Review*, vol. 26, 1983, pp. 11–24.

Sloane, Robert D. "The Expressive Capacity of International Punishment: The Limits of the National Law Analogy and the Potential of International Criminal Law," *Stanford Journal of International Law*, vol. 43, 2007, pp. 39–94.

Sluiter, Goran and Sergey Vasiliev. *International Criminal Procedure: Towards a Coherent Body of Law*, London: Cameron, 2009.

Southern African Litigation Centre v. Minister of Justice and Constitutional Development and Others (27740/2015), High Court of South Africa, Gauteng Division, Pretoria, June 24, 2015.

Special Court for Sierra Leone, http://rscsl.org/.
Special Tribunal for Lebanon, "About the STL," http://stl-tsl.org/en/about-the-stl/511-about-the-stl, modified 18 November 2011.
Stewart, James. "The End of 'Modes of Liability' for International Crimes," *Leiden Journal of International Law*, vol. 25, no. 1, 2012, pp. 165–219.
Strawson, Peter F. "Freedom and Resentment," *Proceeding of the British Academy*, vol. 48, 1962, pp. 1–25.
Stein, Alex. *Foundations of Evidence Law*, Oxford: Oxford University Press, 2005.
Stewart, James G. "Overdetermined Atrocities," *Journal of International Criminal Law*, vol. 10, 2012, pp. 1189–1218.
Sunstein, Cass R. *Legal Reasoning and Political Conflict*, Oxford: Oxford University Press, 1996.
"On the Expressive Function of Law," *University of Pennsylvania Law Review*, 1996, pp. 2021–2056.
Thoreau, Henry David. *Walden or Life in the Woods*, Boston: Ticknor & Fields, 1854.
Tladi, Dire. "The Duty on South Africa to Arrest and Surrender President Al-Bashir under South African and International Law: A Perspective from International Law," *Journal of International Criminal Justice*, vol. 13, 2015.
Turner, Jenia Iontcheva. "Accountability of International Prosecutors," in Carsen Stahn, ed., *The Law and Practice of the International Criminal Court*, Oxford: Oxford University Press, 2015, pp. 384–95.
United Nations Charter, Chapter VII, 24 October 1945, 1 UNTS XVI, www.un.org/en/documents/charter/.
United Nations Secretary-General, "Report of the Secretary-General, In Larger Freedom – Towards Development, Human Rights, and Security for All," UN Doc. A/59/2005, ¶ 138, March 21, 2005.
Report of the Secretary-General to the UN Security Council: The causes of conflict and the promotion of durable peace and sustainable development in Africa, UN doc. A/52/871-S/1998/318, April 1998.
United Nations Security Council, Referral of Syria to International Criminal Court Fails as Negative Votes Prevent Security Council from Adopting Draft Resolution, U.N. Doc. SC/11407, May 22, 2014.
Referral of Syria to International Criminal Court Fails as Negative Votes Prevent Security Council from Adopting Draft Resolution, U.N. Doc. SC/11407, May 22, 2014.
S.C. Res. 977, U.N. Doc. S/RES/977, February 22, 1995.
S.C. Res. 955, U.N. Doc. S/RES/955, November 8, 1994.
UN Security Council, *Statute of the International Criminal Tribunal for Rwanda* (as last amended on 13 October 2006), November 8, 1994.
US v. Park, 421 U.S. 658, 95 S. Ct. 1903, 1975.
Vattel, Emer de. *The Law of Nations or the Principles of Natural Law* (1758), translated by Charles G. Fenwick, Washington, DC: Carnegie Institute of Washington, 1916.
van Sliedregt, Elies. *Individual Criminal Responsibility in International Law*, Oxford: Oxford University Press, 2012.
Verwoerd, Wilhelm and Villa-Vilencia, eds., *Looking Back, Reaching Forward: Reflections on the Truth and Reconciliation Commission in South Africa*, Cape Town: University of Cape Town Press, 2000.

Walzer, Michael. *Just and Unjust Wars*, New York: Basic Books, 1977.
Warrant of Arrest for Omar Hassan Ahmad Al-Bashir, Al Bashir (ICC-02/05-01/09), Pre-Trial Chamber I, March 4, 2009.
Wellman, Christopher Heath. "Liberalism, Samaritanism, and Political Legitimacy," *Philosophy and Public Affairs*, vol. 25, no. 3, Summer 1996, pp. 211–237.
Wigmore, John H. A *Treatise on the Anglo-American System of Evidence in Trials at Common Law*, 3d ed., Boston: Little, Brown. 1940.
Woods, Andrew K. "Moral Judgments & International Crimes: The Disutility of Desert," *Virginia Journal of International Law*, vol. 52, no. 3, Spring 2012, pp. 633–681.
Wright, R. and M. Miller, "The Worldwide Accountability Deficit for Prosecutors," *Washington and Lee Law Review*, vol. 67, 2010, 1587–1609.

Index

Lightning Source UK Ltd.
Milton Keynes UK
UKOW05n0730050517
300558UK00004B/40/P

9 781107 128200